LANGUAGE AND LITERACY SERIES

Dorothy S. Strickland, Founding Editor
Celia Genishi and Donna E. Alvermann, Series Editors

ADVISORY BOARD: *Richard Allington, Kathryn Au, Bernice Cullinan, Colette Daiute,*
Anne Haas Dyson, Carole Edelsky, Mary Juzwik, Susan Lytle, Django Paris, Timothy Shanahan

continued

For volumes in the NCRLL Collection (edited by JoBeth Allen and Donna E. Alvermann) and the Practitioners Bookshelf Series (edited by Celia Genishi and Donna E. Alvermann), as well as other titles in this series, please visit www.tcpress.com.

Language and Literacy Series, *continued*

Race, Justice, and Activism in Literacy Instruction

EDITED BY

Valerie Kinloch
Tanja Burkhard
Carlotta Penn

Foreword by Yolanda Sealey-Ruiz

TEACHERS COLLEGE PRESS

TEACHERS COLLEGE | COLUMBIA UNIVERSITY
NEW YORK AND LONDON

Published by Teachers College Press, 1234 Amsterdam Avenue, New York, NY 10027

Copyright © 2020 by Teachers College, Columbia University

Cover design by adam b. bohannon. Cover photo by Anna Om / Adobe Stock.

Library of Congress Cataloging-in-Publication Data is available at loc.gov

ISBN 978-0-8077-6321-6 (paper)
ISBN 978-0-8077-6322-3 (hardcover)
ISBN 978-0-8077-7816-6 (ebook)

Printed on acid-free paper
Manufactured in the United States of America

Always with unwavering love and a commitment to equity, justice, and freedom, we dedicate this book to:

The memory and courage of
Mr. Louis Kinloch, Jr.,
who lived life as if he owned it because he did;

Nia Sheronne Burkhard-Smith,
who inspires hope for the future in her family and friends; and

Frances Penn,
a treasured Black woman teacher who leads with love.

Contents

From the Present
to the Past and Back Again

The Fight for Literacy Attainment
Against the Odds

In Season 2, Episode 9, of *She's Gotta Have It*, an original Netflix series created and directed by Spike and Tonya Lee, protagonist Nola Darling unveils her self-portrait, *I Am Your Mirror*, set behind a velvet curtain. Guests who attend Nola's solo exhibition emerge from the veil angry, upset, and appalled that Nola created art that they described as disturbing, controversial, and "bringing Black people down" by exhibiting their pain and not promoting their healing. *I Am Your Mirror* depicts Nola's body painted with red, white, and blue stripes and white stars (symbolizing the American flag) as she hangs midair, lynched by her own braids. If one were to watch the entire Netflix series (including episodes from Season 1), one may view the painting as a representation of Nola's growth (political, emotional, and artistic) as much as a depiction of a dark period in America's history—a time when Black people were enslaved and terrorized, and Black women in particular were dehumanized and discarded as worthless property. Nola is mostly unbothered by the reactions of her exhibition guests, and she firmly defends her artistic choices. For Nola, American history confirms that *I Am Your Mirror* is an accurate representation of vicious moments that happened and should not be forgotten—the lynching of Black people, the abuse of the Black female body, and the strangling of Black people's dreams, their possibilities, and their potential. Nola's truth in her art is *America's truth*.

From its very inception, America was created on the idea that Black and Indigenous people should only exist for the purpose of serving white people toward the advancement of white domination (Kendi, 2016). Vestiges of America's treatment of Black people and others who have been dehumanized and marginalized through white domination ideology and upheld by America's institutions are still with us today and are seen most vividly in the field of education. Frameworks like critical race theory, for example, provide scholars and educational activists with a lens to interrogate and resist white domination through the use of counterstories—stories that stand against the single-sided, stereotypical ones told to keep Black people and other communities in subjugated positions.

Counterstories, including the ones that exist throughout history (for example, Frederick Douglass's fight for literacy and freedom), offer true-life examples of how Black people have historically survived white domination and found a way to thrive in spite of it.

This book, *Race, Justice, and Activism in Literacy Instruction*, edited by Valerie Kinloch, Tanja Burkhard, and Carlotta Penn, curates powerful stories told through research by literacy scholars who have taken up the battle for social justice in literacy education. Their research is in the tradition of truth telling and resistance against the devaluing of those who are indigenous, with migrant experiences, and otherwise marginalized based on the social constructions of race, class, gender, and other intersectional and interlocking identities (Crenshaw, 1991). The chapters in this book, as well as the poetry that appears between some of the chapters, remind us why literacy education remains a modern-day battlefield for justice. It invites us to remember a time when it was illegal for enslaved Africans and free Black people to read and write, and frames the struggle that continues for literacy in classrooms for Children of Color, although we are far removed from slavery, a quarter of the way into the 21st century and deep into the digital age.

Case in point: In 1831 and 1832, statutes were passed in the state of Virginia prohibiting meetings to teach free Black people to read or write. Those found violating the law had to pay a fine between $10 and $100. The Alabama Slave Code of 1833 included the following law:

> [S31] Any person who shall attempt to teach any free person of color, or slave, to spell, read or write, shall upon conviction thereof by indictment, be fined in a sum of not less than two hundred fifty dollars, nor more than five hundred dollars. (Smithsonian American Art Museum, 2014)

The Alabama Slave Code of 1833 and other codes like it restricted aspects of enslaved people's lives to varying degrees, depending on the state. These codes controlled slave travel, marriage, education, and employment. From the beginning of the white domination project that began with their enslavement, Black people were forbidden to read and write. There was fear that slaves who were literate could forge travel passes and escape. There was also fear that writing could be a means of communication that would make way for insurrections and mass escapes. This history involving literacy is important to understand. Frederick Douglass (2003), American statesman and former slave, made a compelling argument for the power of literacy in his autobiography. Many teachers are not familiar with Douglass's struggle to become literate, nor do they understand that there are many other stories and successful battles for literacy that come from the ancestral history of the children they serve.

Often, what is etched in the minds of teachers is the image and idea that Black, Brown, and other marginalized children are perpetually "struggling" readers and writers, or, more pernicious, nonreaders and nonwriters. Thus, it is crucial to understand how past literacy struggles for Black people and others are present in educators' minds today. As a result, the literacy classroom is a contested area—a site to fight for freedom of language, representation, and expression of culture, and the telling of stories that matter to Black, or "dark," children (Love, 2019, p. 2). *Race, Justice, and Activism in Literacy Instruction* powerfully and convincingly centers arguments on the significance of anti-racist teacher preparation, culturally responsive pedagogy, the power of engaging youth in their own learning, and the necessity of community activism. It speaks to educators during a time where mindsets and sentiments about dark children harken back to stereotypes created about them during enslavement and America's Jim Crow era (1877–1955).

This volume provides contemporary research and a critical understanding of why the fight for literacy is of great importance. These scholars offer essential questions and provide ideas and approaches for those educators who push for social justice in literacy instruction. Collectively, the scholarship presented in this volume asks (and answers) the question: If literacy education isn't for liberation, then what is it for?

—Yolanda Sealey-Ruiz

REFERENCES

Crenshaw, W. K. (1991). Mapping the margins: Intersectionality, identity politics, and violence against women of color. *Stanford Law Review, 43*(6), 1241–1299.

Douglass, F. (2003). *Narrative of the life of Frederick Douglass, an American slave.* Boston, MA: Bedford/St. Martin's Press. (Originally published 1845)

Kendi, I. X. (2016) *Stamped from the beginning: The definitive history of racist ideas in America.* New York, NY: Bold Type Books.

Love, B. L. (2019). *We want to do more than survive: Abolitionist teaching and the pursuit of educational freedom.* Boston, MA: Beacon Press.

Smithsonian American Art Museum. (2014). Literacy as freedom. Retrieved from americanexperience.si.edu/wp-content/uploads/2014/09/Literacy-as-Freedom.pdf

Acknowledgments

We open our acknowledgments by remembering the life and legacy of Shirley Anita St. Hill Chisholm, who was born on November 30, 1924, and whose life was one committed to educational equity, racial and gender equality, and human rights. Chisholm was a founding member of the Congressional Black Caucus (1969) as well as the first Black congresswoman (1968) and first Black person to campaign with a major political party for the U.S. presidency (1972). Our acknowledgment of Chisholm represents not only our recognition of and respect for her life, but also our unwavering belief that Black women have always been and will always be extraordinary leaders, trailblazers, warriors, activists, and visionaries. Black women have always paved the way for economic, educational, political, and social progress. As with Chisholm, we believe that women, generally, and Black women, specifically, "in this country must become revolutionaries" and "must refuse to accept the old, the traditional roles and stereotypes" (1970, pp. xvi–xvii). Without question, we (Valerie, Tanja, and Carlotta) are able to walk, write, act, think, exist, love, and survive in this world because of Shirley Chisholm and so many other Black women who have shown us what it means to be, always, "unbought and unbossed" (Chisholm, 1970).

The idea for this book came into existence because of intimate conversations shared among a group of Black women who were brought together on a predominantly white college campus. We thank our Sista-Friends and Homegirls Ryann Randall and Halima Alhassan for engaging in these conversations with us and for giving us the motivation to think deeply about race, equity, and activism. We will keep on pushing with and because of you.

To our partners, children, grandchildren, parents, aunts, uncles, cousins, and other family members and friends, we say thank you for always supporting and encouraging the individual and collective work we do. We are because you are, and we love you dearly and deeply.

We also thank Emily Spangler and Teachers College Press for taking a chance on this project and shepherding it to completion. Thanks, Emily, for all of your expert editorial advice, responses to our inquiries, and for your encouragement throughout the process.

And to the contributors to and readers of this book, thank you in advance for your commitment to thinking with us about race, equity, and activism in literacy instruction. We hope this work represents but one indication of our dedication to build on, extend, and contribute new work to literacy studies, to education, and to our interactions one with another as we stand "unbought and unbossed" (Chisholm, 1970).

With love, because of equity, and for justice,
Valerie, Tanja, and Carlotta

REFERENCE

Chisholm, S. (1970). *Unbought and unbossed*. Boston, MA: Houghton Mifflin.

Race, Justice, and Activism in Literacy Instruction

An Introduction

Valerie Kinloch, Tanja Burkhard, and Carlotta Penn

I LEAVE YOU FINALLY A RESPONSIBILITY TO OUR YOUNG PEOPLE. The world around us really belongs to youth, for youth will take over its future management. Our children must never lose their zeal for building a better world. They must not be discouraged from aspiring toward greatness, for they are to be the leaders of tomorrow. Nor must they forget that the masses of our people are still underprivileged, ill-housed, impoverished and victimized by discrimination. We have a powerful potential in our youth, and we must have the courage to change old ideas and practices so that we may direct their power toward good ends. (Mary Jane McLeod Bethune, 1999, p. 62)

As though our lives have no meaning and no depth without the white gaze. I've spent my entire writing life trying to make sure that the white gaze was not the dominant one in any of my books. (Toni Morrison, 1998)

. . . the idea of mattering is essential in that you must matter enough to yourself, to your students, and to your students' community to fight. But for dark people, the very basic idea of mattering is sometimes hard to conceptualize when your country finds you disposable. How do you matter to a country that is at once obsessed with and dismissive about how it kills you? How do you matter to a country that would rather incarcerate you than educate you? How do you matter to a country that poisoned your child's drinking water? (Bettina Love, 2019, p. 2)

1

WE MATTER

In her essay "My Last Will and Testament," educator and civil rights leader Mary Jane McLeod Bethune writes, "Faith, courage, brotherhood, dignity, ambition, responsibility—these are needed today as never before" (McCluskey & Smith, 1999). She asks that those who truly care about, believe in, and love Black people understand the work that lies ahead in "completing the establishment of equality for the Negro." In large part, this work requires us to have "A RESPONSIBILITY TO OUR YOUNG PEOPLE," to encourage them to live in their greatness, and to ensure that their "powerful potential" is nurtured and sustained. Bethune's "My Last Will and Testament" was published in the August 1955 issue of *Ebony Magazine* 3 months after her death and during a political time in the United States when full equality for People of Color, and especially for Black women, was still highly contentious. Bethune remained relentless in her efforts to advocate for and secure the rights of Black women when it came to education, employment, business ownership, and voting.

Almost 65 years after the publication of Bethune's "My Last Will and Testament," equality for People of Color in this country remains elusive. One need only turn on the news, go on social media, spend time with young people in many of our urban public schools, and be in community with poor and working-class families to know that Black and Brown lives are in danger and under constant attack. One need only do an online search for "voting rights" to know that across the nation, states are passing voter suppression laws (such as new voter ID laws, elimination of early voting, limited voting times and locations), making it nearly impossible for Black and Brown people, including LGBTQIA folx, elderly people, those with disabilities, and college students to cast their ballots. Along with attacks on voting rights, our government has increased its attempts to defund public education; detained and separated migrant children from their families; contaminated the drinking water in many Black, Brown, and Indigenous communities; debased African countries; and reinforced a politics of exclusion that disempowers countless Black and Brown folx. These attacks represent "the explicit workings and intersections of misogyny, capitalism, systemic violence, racism, and other forms of state- and nation-sanctioned oppressions [that] have always been a part of the fabric of Black life in the United States" (Kinloch, 2019, pp. 51–52).

There is no question that voting suppression, the detainment of children, the contamination of drinking water, and the defunding of public education, among other horrific occurrences, are not only intolerable, but also strategic racist events meant to systematically sustain human oppression. What is equally painful is that these events are symptoms of a larger, more pervasive problem: In this country, Black and Brown lives remain disposable to the white imaginary, and Black and Brown lives are always in danger within a white supremacist, patriarchal, capitalist nation. To prove this point, one need only look up the names Tanisha Anderson, Sandra Bland, Rekia Boyd, Michael

Brown, Miriam Carey, Terence Crutcher, Jordan Davis, Eric Garner, Freddie Gray, Kimani Gray, Trayvon Benjamin Martin, and among others, Antwon Rose. It is no accident that "the lives of Black queer and trans folks, disabled folks, **undocumented folks**, folks with **records, women,** and **all Black lives** along the gender spectrum" (blacklivesmatter.com/about/) have always been in harm's way, always being seen as marginal, dispensable, without meaning, with no value, having no matter, and not even mattering at all.

In her powerful book, *We Want to Do More Than Survive: Abolitionist Teaching and the Pursuit of Educational Freedom*, Bettina Love (2019) moves us to consider the many oppressive, racist tactics that get enacted onto, and are used against, "dark people" (p. 2). Such tactics would have us believe that "dark people" do not matter. She asserts, "The very basic idea of mattering is sometimes hard to conceptualize when your country finds you disposable" (p. 2). The reality that entire communities are considered disposable becomes painfully clear when one further considers the enactment of state-sanctioned violence—through policing, the enforcement of violent immigration practices, border walls, and incarceration practices—against Communities of Color both historically and presently.

For us (Valerie, Tanja, and Carlotta), such realities and our knowingness that "dark people" do matter (Love, 2019, p. 2) have shaped our individual and collective commitments to Black life, freedom, and excellence within the United States and throughout the Black diaspora. These realities came to a head for us in 2015, the year we began talking about editing a book on race, justice, and activism in literacy instruction. We were visibly shaken by the ongoing threats against People of Color in this nation and around the globe. Daily, we gathered in the space of a "diversity and inclusion" office on the campus of a predominantly white institution in the U.S. Midwest, lamenting over the centuries-long injustices inflicted on Black and Brown children, youth, and adults. Aloud, we wondered how injustices (such as systemic racism, sexual violence, linguistic persecution, educational inequities, social and economic inequalities) continue to materialize, get enacted, and go unpunished within a nation that constitutionalized the phrase "Life, Liberty and the pursuit of Happiness." We wondered, to borrow the words of Toni Morrison (1998), why so many people continue to believe that "our [Black] lives have no meaning and no depth without the white gaze," especially in a nation, to return to Bettina Love's (2019) point, "that would rather incarcerate you than educate you" (p. 2).

And we arrived at 2015, a year, like many others, that continued to bubble over with hashtags (including #abolishice, #AntwonRose, #BlackLivesMatter, #Ferguson, #NiaWilson), justice movements (#SayHerName, #FightFor15, #LoveWins, March for Our Lives, Black Youth Project 100), and social media campaigns (America in Transition and their MyTransStory online campaign, #BlackOnCampus, #StudentBlackOut, #Health4All). These and other justice-committed events were all concerned with the civil and human rights of Black and Brown people. In 2015, we were also upset about the plight of children in U.S. schools and neighborhoods, curious about the futures of educational praxis and institutions with respect to creating and sustaining truly equitable, humanizing learning contexts and conditions for Students of Color and, by extension, their families, friends, community advocates, and teachers. We remain highly encouraged by the important activist work occurring within schools and communities across this nation and around the world, work that has at its core equity, justice, and social equality.

It goes without question that the plight of too many Black and Brown folx, especially during the 21st century, has been structurally, politically, economically, and educationally marked by racial disparities, racism, oppression, and violence. From the school-to-prison pipeline, increasing drop-out and push-out rates, and unfair schooling policies and disciplinary practices, to the overrepresentation in special education classes, and encounters with teachers' implicit and explicit biases, it is clear that Black and Brown students do not fare well within the U.S. educational system. It is a devastating reality that too many Black and Brown students do not feel safe, loved, and protected in schools, and that many do not see schools as intellectually stimulating environments that nurture their minds, souls, and spirits. As we write this, we are keenly aware of the importance of remaining committed to, and working for, justice and liberation for "dark people" inside schools and within literacy teaching and teacher education, specifically, and throughout society and the world, generally. We do this work because Black and Brown lives have always mattered and must continue to matter.

TOWARD JUSTICE

In working toward a framework that enables us to move toward justice, we turn to the United Nations Convention on the Rights of the Child. The convention recognizes education, literacy, and liberty as essential human rights that children all across the world are entitled to and deserve. It also calls for children's access to an education that nurtures their personalities, intellects, and interests, and ensures their universal human freedom. We turn to the Rights of the Child statement because of its demand that children—and their cultural identities, families, and ways of being—are not only honored, but also protected. There are many examples of how this philosophy is taken up within and beyond the United States, especially when it comes to grassroots organizing online and on the ground.

For instance, in April 2018, high school student Allan Monga sued the National Endowment for the Arts (NEA) for the right to compete in the organization's national poetry contest. He felt that he had no choice but to take legal action after NEA had disqualified him because of his status as an asylum seeker from Zambia, who fled to the United States only 8 months prior to the competition. After winning his case and becoming a finalist, Monga recited passages from published writings by W.E.B. Du Bois (Walsh, 2018).

Another example is Marley Dias who, at 11 years old, decided she was tired of being assigned books that were primarily about "white boys and their dogs" (quoted in McGrath, 2017). However, when she went looking for books with Black girl main characters—people who looked like her—she became frustrated that there were not many from which to choose. That inspired her to start a campaign called 1000 Black Girl Books (#1000BlackGirlBooks). According to Marley, she chose to effect change by collecting and donating books to communities, working with educators and politicians to change the literary landscape as it relates to racial diversity, and writing her own Black girl book (McGrath, 2017; see also grassrootscommunityfoundation.org).

These and many other examples reflect creative and courageous ways young people are asserting themselves and insisting, to return to the United Nations Convention on the Rights of the Child, that their lives and literacies matter and are valued. Marley Dias and Allan Monga are not only demanding that their voices be heard, but also that their lives and literacies be understood as mattering. Young people across the nation and the world are making space to center their histories, cultures, lives, and literacies. For literacy teaching and teacher education, they demonstrate the need for critical, activist-oriented spaces, in schools and in communities, where students are supported to create, reimagine, and produce literacy narratives grounded in justice, and where they are also encouraged to interrogate inequities and inequalities that limit freedom. This is important work if we are to move toward (and ensure) justice.

There are many students, teachers, researchers, and community folx who are engaging in the activist work of moving toward justice. In this book, we present some of their literacy stories, artifacts, and engagements as we situate race, justice, and activism in literacy instruction. It is our hope that by doing so, we will contribute to ongoing efforts that centralize and emphasize (and that do not marginalize and oppress) Black and Brown lives. Providing us inspiration for this work, Feigenbaum (2014) contends that the discrepancy within legislation that appears equitable yet works to further disadvantage marginalized communities produces a type of *rigged citizenship* for People of Color, thus historically and presently disallowing them full citizenship. In order to expose, analyze, and operationalize literacy instruction against the outgrowths of rigged citizenship, students, educators, community members, and everyone must seriously take up this work. We must commit to moving toward and sustaining justice in literacy instruction, teacher education, and community engagements.

Framing of Terms

To frame this work through a lens that is both coherent and fluid, we offer the following considerations for the concepts of race, justice, and activism in literacy instruction, which are central to this book. Lalik and Hinchman (2001) and Banks (1993) define *race* as a "human construction having social, historical, and political dimensions" that in U.S. society has been operationalized to categorize, subjugate, and empower people and "to produce and sustain inequitable power relations and concomitant resource distribution patterns" (Lalik & Hinchman, 2001, p. 531). Considering race and racism in literacy research and instruction not only enables us to better understand the social, historical, and political dimensions at play, but also to explore more deeply how young people negotiate their identities, positioning, and knowledges through multiple literacies. Relying on Jones's (2018) scholarship helps us further frame this work around the idea that we must pursue social justice through literacy instruction and research. McInerney (2012) argues that "the nature and causes of injustice have cultural, social and political dimensions that demand new responses from governments, policymakers and education institutions" (p. 32). For us, this means that the pursuit of social justice requires us to attend to all three of these dimensions if we are truly committed to justice and equity in schools and throughout society. This is our effort *toward justice*.

STORYING RACE, JUSTICE, AND ACTIVISM IN LITERACY INSTRUCTION: OVERVIEW OF CHAPTERS

We open with Carlotta's section overview before turning our attention to Chapter 1 by Leigh Patel, titled "Generations of Fugitive Literacy Teacher Education and Activism." Her chapter opens up an important conversation about how "the history of literacy for social change provides . . . much more fruitful questions, which have to do somewhat with the place of teacher education, specifically, literacy teacher education, but also practices that are grounded in a political economic analysis of domination and freedom." As you read her chapter, we ask that you contemplate *what* you know about literacy, *how* you know what you know about literacy, and *in what ways* literacy teachers and researchers are, or should become, activists.

In, Chapter 2, "'What Happens Here Can Change the World': Preparing Literacy Teachers in the Digital Age," Detra Price-Dennis examines how the emerging digital literacy practices and pedagogies of two Preservice Teachers of Color (PTC) impacted how they worked with 5th-grade students to focus their learning on race, culture, and language. As you read her chapter, we ask that you consider her closing reflection questions about the types of rich conversations teacher educators and researchers should have "with preservice teachers about data, privacy, and digital citizenship."

We place Price-Dennis's chapter in conversation with Chapter 3 by Ijeoma E. Ononuju, BernNadette T. Best-Green, and Danny C. Martinez titled "Students Developing Critical Language and Literacy Perspectives." They are honest about their concerns regarding the multiple, shifting justice commitments of preservice literacy teacher education students, some of whom are comfortable while others are uncomfortable openly talking about white privilege and racism. As you read their chapter, we hope you are drawn to their reflective questions about the importance of students examining their own privileges as a way to foster their critical literacy practices and commitments.

Limarys Caraballo and Lindsey Lichtenberger's Chapter 4, "Rethinking Curriculum and Pedagogy in Schools: Critical Literacies and Epistemologies in Theory and Practice," extends conversations about research, praxis, and action in literacy instruction. They highlight how engagements within an after-school program can positively impact one's classroom teaching experiences. As you read their chapter, we hope you are drawn to their reflective questions about reframing literacy instruction by centering activism, equity, and justice in literacy teaching.

Chapter 5, "Arlene's Actionist Work: A Case Study of Writing and Self-Activism," by Maneka D. Brooks and Arlene M. Alvarado speaks to the importance of understanding how silence can be transformed into action and activism. They examine how one's literacy experiences, interactions with educators, and relationships with family can lead to forms of self-activism. As you read their chapter, we ask you to imagine how literacy teaching can become a site of activism for young people.

In Chapter 6, "Pardon This Disruption: Cultivating Revolutionary Civics Through World Humanities," Tamara Butler, Jenell Igeleke Penn, and Johnny Merry demonstrate nuanced ways high school students think about writing, humanity, and justice through "actionist work." They emphasize connections among texts, art, relationships, and community-engaged initiatives. As you read their chapter, we ask you to consider how classroom teaching can foster equitable learning that supports students' creativities and justice engagements.

To reflect on lessons learned from the first six chapters, we offer a poetic reflection titled "Poetic Musings: Remembering Our Black Youth/Our Black Lives." Here we remember and honor the lives of Black youth violently taken from us. Along with our musings and Tanja's section overview, we hope to encourage readers to continue writing, fighting, and pushing for liberating literacies and social justice in the world.

Donja Thomas's Chapter 7, "One Love, One Heart," focuses on the role of Blackness and Black Studies in literacy instruction with high school students, and argues that teachers need to make visible Black cultural, historical, and intellectual knowledge. As you read her chapter, we ask you to imagine specific ways love, humanity, and justice can be center stage in literacy teaching and learning.

Chapter 8 by Jamila Lyiscott, "The Politics of Ratchetness: Exploring Race, Literacies, and Social Justice with Black Youth," explores how youth in an out-of-school youth participatory action research (YPAR) program incorporated hip-hop, spoken word, and critical digital literacies as liberating tools to mediate their social realities and pursue justice during the peak of the Black Lives Matter movement (BLM). As you read her chapter, we ask that you turn your attention to how Black youth leverage their critical literacies to advance an activist agenda of love and liberation.

In Chapter 9, "A Black Lives Matter and Critical Race Theory–Informed Critique of Code-Switching Pedagogy," Sina Saeedi and Elaine Richardson problematize the field's accommodation of anti-Black racism by juxtaposing code-switching concepts to current movements for justice to demonstrate a commitment to eradicating anti-Blackness. As you read their chapter, we encourage you to focus on how language and literacy teaching should better attend to Black lives mattering.

Vaughn W. M. Watson, Matthew Deroo, and Erik Skogsberg's Chapter 10, "Multiliteracies Toward Justice in Literacy Teaching and Research," examines meanings of youth enacting community-engaged multiliteracies in research and practice. As you read their chapter, we ask you to focus on how Youth of Color are extending meanings of teaching, literacy, and justice beyond classroom spaces.

The final chapter, Chapter 11, "Building Stories Toward a Common Cause: Coalitional Inquiry as Activism," by María Paula Ghiso, Gerald Campano, Grace Player, Brenda Krishanwongso, and Frianna Gultom, explores how storytelling and the arts can forge coalition across difference and in support of educational equity and immigrant rights. As you read their chapter, we ask you to think about how community–university partnerships can serve as rich sites for strengthening what we know about teaching, justice, equity, communities, and transnational knowledge.

In closing, we (Tanja Burkhard, Carlotta Penn, and Valerie Kinloch) offer another poetic reflection, "Poetic Musings: Where Do We Go from Here?" We draw inspiration from the last six chapters as we wonder aloud about the direction we must take and how a focus on race, justice, and activism in literacy instruction will move us toward our larger goal of liberating literacies for Black and Brown people. Our poetic reflection leads into Valerie's "Not a Conclusion: Keeping Focused on Race, Justice, and Activism," which brings the arguments shared in this book together and leaves us contemplating the role of literacy instruction in larger conversations about race, justice, and activism.

REFERENCES

Banks, J. (1993). The canon debate, knowledge construction, and multicultural education. *Educational Researcher, 22*(5), 4–14

Bethune, M. M. (1999). My last will and testament. In A. T. McCluskey & E.M. Smith (Eds), *Mary McLeod Bethune: Building a better world: Essays and selected documents* (pp.55–64). Bloomington, IN: Indiana University Press.

Feigenbaum, P. (2014). *Collaborative imagination: Earning activism through literacy education.* Retrieved from hdl.handle.net/2027/spo.3239521.0022.206

Jones, S. (2018). *Portraits of everyday literacy for social justice: Reframing the debate for families and communities.* New York, NY: Palgrave Macmillan.

Kinloch, V. (2019). "Unbought and unbossed": On being Black, woman and transgressive in the fight for justice. In Y. Lincoln and G. Cannella, G. (Eds.), *Employing critical qualitative inquiry to mount nonviolent resistance* (pp. 43–57). Gorham, ME: Myers Education Press.

Lalik, R., & Hinchman, K. A. (2001). Critical issues: Examining constructions of race in literacy research: Beyond silence and other oppressions of white liberalism. *Journal of Literacy Research, 33*(3), 529–561. doi:10.1080/10862960109548122

Love, B. L. (2019). *We want to do more than survive: Abolitionist teaching and the pursuit of educational freedom.* Boston, MA: Beacon Press.

McGrath, M. (2017, June 13). From activist to author: How 12-year-old Marley Dias is changing the face of children's literature. *Forbes Magazine.* Retrieved from forbes.com/sites/maggiemcgrath/2017/06/13/from-activist-to-author-how-12-year-old-marley-dias-is-changing-the-face-of-childrens-literature/#409224e14ce0

McInerney, P. (2012). Rediscovering Discourses of Social Justice: Making Hope Practical. In Down, B., & Smyth, J. (Eds). *Critical voices in teacher education: Teaching for social justice in conservative times* (1st edition.). New York: Springer. doi:10.1007/978-94-007-3974-1

Morrison, T. (1998, March). Interview on *Charlie Rose.* Public Broadcasting Service. Retrieved from youtube.com/watch?v=F4vIGvKpT1c

Walsh, J. (2018, April 19). NEA tries to boot refugee student from National Poetry competition. *New York Magazine.* Retrieved from nymag.com/daily/intelligencer/2018/04/nea-tries-to-boot-refugee-student-from-poetry-competition.html

PART I OVERVIEW

Carlotta Penn

In her 1974 graduation speech, Deborah Williams honors the strong student–teacher relationships at the Black Panther Party's Oakland Community School as central to her positive experience there. She states, "Here, the teachers care more about us. However, our teachers are not just our teachers . . . they are our comrades. . . . In the last year, I have worked really close with them" (Williams, 1974). Williams concludes that understanding the value and meaning of freedom was her most important lesson, and she expresses gratitude to her teachers that she knows how to solve problems she may confront in the world. In classifying her teachers as comrades who care about and work closely with students while challenging them to think critically, Williams highlights the Panther Party's commitment to "education as the practice of freedom" (Freire, 1970/2000; hooks, 1994). She also reminds us of the vast troves of information, of language and laughter, of growing, questioning, and learning, that children acquire under the direction of teachers. The student–teacher relationships Williams cherished are as important now for Black students and other Youth of Color as they were for those young people in the 1970s and 1980s, fighting for an "education for our people that exposes the true nature of this decadent American society [and] teaches us our true history and our role in the present-day society" (Newton, 2002, p. 55).

Literacy teachers in particular have enormous impact on children, and because of this gargantuan responsibility, we must support teachers by encouraging them to go beyond standardized English language and literacy instruction. Literacy teacher praxis must aspire to the highest callings: to love the children in their schools, to prepare them to "read the word and the world," as they realize dreams in a society where freedom—"the indispensable condition for the quest for human completion" (Freire, 1970/2000, p. 47)—is universal. It is not hyperbole to state that literacy instruction changes lives—Patel reminds us in Chapter 1 that "fugitive literacy" has deep roots and that preservice teachers need to know "the history of how literacy has been used as acts of defiance and survivance." In the chapters of this section, the authors demonstrate that the conversations, commitments, and "actionist work" taken up by literacy teachers have real-life consequences for the children who come under their care—and for the teachers themselves.

In Chapter 2, Price-Dennis, for example, argues that preservice teachers need to understand the value of teaching with digital literacies that center a social justice stance within literacy instruction. Relatedly, Ononuju, Best-Green, and Martinez's Chapter 3 asks us to recognize the toll it takes for Teachers of Color to disrupt colonizing practices within traditional classrooms. This is the point throughout all the chapters in this first section: to work against colonization and move toward transformation.

Indeed, literacy instruction changes lives, especially if it centers justice and activism in theory and practice. Caraballo and Lichtenberger's Chapter 4 demonstrates this point by highlighting connections among literacy research, praxis, and action, and Chapter 5 by Brooks and Alvarado extends this discussion by showing how literacy can support students to move beyond forced silence and into activism. The power of this type of literacy work, as Butler, Penn, and Merry document in Chapter 6, can have positive implications for how young people see themselves in classrooms and communities and how they come to embrace an equity stance.

Taken together, the chapters and reflections in this first section offer some needed direction for literacy teacher educators, preservice teachers, and practicing teachers who believe, as we do, that teaching is fundamentally an "act of love," and therefore a commitment to "the cause of liberation" (Freire, 1970/2000, p. 89). They demonstrate, to return to Deborah Williams's (1974) graduation speech, that "teachers are not just our teachers . . . they are our comrades."

REFERENCES

Freire, P. (1970/2000). *Pedagogy of the oppressed*. New York, NY: Continuum.

hooks, b. (1994). *Teaching to transgress: Education as the practice of freedom.* New York, NY: Routledge.

Newton, H. P. *The Huey P. Newton reader* (D. Hilliard & D. Weise, Eds.). New York, NY: Seven Stories Press, 2002.

Williams, D. (1974, June 22). Address of Deborah Williams. *Black Panther Newspaper, 11* (26). Retrieved from itsabouttimebpp.com/Oakland_Community_School/pdf/YI.pdf

CHAPTER 1

Generations of Fugitive Literacy Teacher Education and Activism

Leigh Patel

Schools of education, especially in the United States, reside in peculiar and particular places and spaces on college campuses. Many schools of education had their start as training schools for teachers who, over the years, have remained largely a population of white women. As schools of education came to also engage in research, questions have remained about their grounding and place within larger university structures. For decades, scholars (Lagemann, 2002) have debated whether education is a field of study unto itself, and, consequentially, if there are research methods and, more recently, stances toward justice that apply to education differently from other fields. Yet the history of literacy for social change provides much more fruitful questions about the place of teacher education—specifically, literacy teacher education—and also practices that are grounded in a political economic analysis of domination and freedom.

I aver that in order to understand literacy teacher education, both in universities and community-based settings, we must also explore what it has meant and can mean relative to the purposes of freedom, to a better and more just society, and to imagine into existence those better versions. But I propose that one of the most powerful knowledges that preservice teachers need is the history of how literacy has been used as an act of defiance and survivance (Baird, 2016; Vizenor, 2008). This knowledge is crucial to prepare our teachers not as agents who deliver and perpetuate inequity (Bowles & Gintis, 2011), but as cultural workers striving to enact equity, justice, and collectivity.

FROM "NORMAL SCHOOLS FOR TEACHER PREPARATION" TO RESEARCH AND PRAXIS

Many schools of education, particularly those that were created by state and federal governments in the 1800s, were not started as places for research but as "normal" schools, with the word *normal* implying that these schools would help high school graduates develop the competencies to deliver and teach curriculum in K–12 settings that established and maintained normed and normalized curricula for a nation that was only about 200 years old. As many noted scholars have documented, the earliest orthodoxy of schools aimed to extinguish Indigenous knowledge systems (Battiste, 2017) through boarding schools, and simply made it illegal for enslaved Black peoples and their descendants to be literate. Furthermore, schools of education, as they progressed from normal schools to university entities, are largely known as "cash cows," particularly their master's certification programs; certification programs bring in tuition fees and rely on faculty and practicing teachers to guide preservice teachers through practicum experiences, in order to eventually be certified as teachers. Undercited and yet directly relevant to a political, economic, and feminist analysis of teacher education is Madeleine Grumet's (1988) book *Bitter Milk*. Grumet spells out the ways schools of education, founded first as a holding place for nonqueer white women before they married, still hold vestiges of this demographic and politic. Following this inauspicious but grounded history, it becomes more comprehensible why the field of teacher education, including literacy teacher education, is more feminized than feminist. Grumet (1988) details the ways that schooling, and by proxy, myriad teacher education programs, are more likely to pronounce a love of children without an analysis of power that makes well-being a simple fact for some children, while others experience population-level suffering and acceleration to death (Gilmore, 2007).

LITERACY AS POWER

Literacy and literacy education hold great power, so much so that this settler nation has attempted to use literacy as a tool for cultural genocide and has sequestered it from enslaved peoples and expendable migrant labor forces. Although this indictment reads as if it might be a thing of the past, this cultural genocide, or at least its attempt, continues into the 21st century. Teacher preparation programs abound with methods courses for decontextualized teaching of English language learners but rarely teach about the sociopolitical history that has made migration both a fraught material reality and a conduit for racialization (Flores & Rosa, 2015; Oliveira, 2018). Teacher preparation programs are now interested in diversity to keep pace with an era in which racism continues to thrive, but the image of racism is no longer acceptable (Bonilla-Silva, 2006; Weems, 2012). The interest in diversity and inclusion is largely articulated through who is admitted and hired and those who are appointed to "diversity work" (Ahmed, 2012). Yet teacher preparation programs still typically start foundations courses with Eurocentric theory, such as the progressive views of John Dewey, who contrasted a democratic civic education with the lesser exercises that the "uncivilized" taught in family and informal settings. Or foundations courses include writings by a few of the visible and senior education researchers of color for 1 week out of a 15-week course. The veneer is apparent. At best, these inclusions are launching pads, but more frequently, at worst, they are cosmetic, doing little to disrupt who can write, read, and be read.

Because I spent virtually every Saturday of my K–12 years in public libraries, it is even more poignant to me that this past decade has seen the literal removal of texts addressing liberation from public high schools (Acosta, 2014), challenges to books that tell the reality of both Black enslavement and freedom (ALA, 2018), and challenges to books such as *To Kill a Mockingbird* (Lee, 2010) for their profanity. But there is no objection to the perpetuation of the white savior trope in Lee's book and myriad other books that are taught as part of the canon. Books are not removed from libraries or schools because of problematic tropes of white people saving the other. Neither do teacher education programs, largely staffed by white professors, consider what is being implicitly taught when a mostly white professoriate teaches courses about literacy and, perhaps, justice (Haddix, 2015).

In addition to these concerning trends of what is objectionable and what is not, ahistorical curriculum in schooling persists, and through the reading of those texts, a young person might be bamboozled into thinking that Black history began at the point of European capture. Or they might learn, through omission of accurate history, that the founding fathers of the nation did not willfully participate in the creation of a republic in which only land- and chattel-owning white men were entitled to formal education. Liberty for all? No. Yet these narratives create and justify structures, literal buildings, curricula, and standards that teachers and students must parrot.

FROM FALSE NARRATIVE TO DISRUPTION

So, then, what should literacy teacher education do and demand to reckon with and intervene in these structures of colonialism and racist capitalism? What disruption is right and righteous in the name of literacy as a fundamentally human and humanizing practice (Kinloch, 2018)? First and foremost, literacy must be taught along with the histories of how literacy was withheld from populations under the heel of settler colonialism. Literacy education must include the lessons about marronage that can only be learned by studying the fugitive acts (Patel, 2016) of literacy used by enslaved peoples on Turtle Island, in the Caribbean, on the African continent, and even in slave ships and then fields planted and sowed by unpaid labor. From the "Door of No Return" in the slave castles in Cape Coast, Ghana, the fugitive practices of enslaved peoples developing, sharing, and teaching one another common languages provide one of the most indelible and profound realities of the power of literacy. Literacy has always been present and at great risk for some. And those peoples who were banished from literacy pursued it by secreting away texts, by a parent or elder tracing the alphabet on the palm of a young child. These histories are a very different start for literacy courses from debates about whole language versus phonics. These histories also disrupt the national narratives of liberty for all.

We must also contend with the fact that hundreds of Black teachers of various gender identities took it upon themselves to engage in literacy when it was illegal for them to be literate. Literacy is intimately tied to humanity, and more than that, it is collective. For decades and centuries, it was also Black educators in Southern states who, before, during, and after Reconstruction, created networks of support, curricula, leadership, and furtive passageways all in the interest of forwarding literacy and language fluency as a profound humanizing and empowering act for individuals and collectives (Walker, 2018). The amount and texture of organizing, collective knowledge building, strategizing, and strategically keeping this hidden from a white supremacist nation is a deeply important part of knowing how literacy education and freedom have always had a history with each other.

WHAT DOES THIS MEAN FOR LITERACY METHODS COURSES?

The first university course I taught was a literacy theory and methods course in the 1990s. I had the great fortune of teaching this course to new and experienced teachers, many of whom would later be impacted by the rumbling engine of high-stakes assessment and questionable psychometrics justifying adequate yearly progress. We read works by bell hooks, Paulo Freire, James Baldwin, June Jordan, and Lucy Calkins, and we wrote regularly, because teaching literacy means one must also read and write.

In the spring of 2018, I again taught a master's course in literacy education. By this point, I had been teaching literacy methods courses for roughly 15 years, but the political context of education had changed significantly. When I attended to the business of planning this course, I paused. I thought about the fact that this generation of preservice students (most of whom were in their early 20s) had not only been born after 9/11 but also had been almost entirely educated in formal schools under the heel of high-stakes assessment. Most of them were first-generation college students, and in keeping with how racism and classism have been intertwined, many came from working-class families. In fact, they were brilliant and overextended, and yet they showed up to class every week, as best they could.

In planning and teaching the course, I considered what might be important questions for students who had been educated almost exclusively under the shadow and threat of America Reads, No Child Left Behind, and Race to the Top. Few of them had ever had the chance to participate in reading and writing workshops, but they had all been tested, again and again. How could I engage these preservice teachers in the intoxicating history and always-present promise of literacy as revolutionary, as catalytic, as deeply personal, and always political? My fear was that they had been overly impacted by federal policies that were based on questionable psychometrics (Cabrera, 2011), looming threats and realities of school shutdowns (Ewing, 2018), the school–prison nexus (Meiners, 2010), and a centuries-old conflation between task completion and learning (Patel, 2015). And yet, I had also been working with youth, over those same years, who have embodied and actualized what I consider a deep concept of civic engagement. From the Dreamers movement, including Undocuqueer, to the many young people who had been moved to action after Michael Brown's murder in 2015, there was also a sense of public citation and activism pulsing beyond the walls of formal education.

With all of this in mind, I chose not to start this particular literacy methods course with the classical theories of literacy education. I turned away from the rather well-worn curricula for this kind of upside down. The valuable contributions of many scholars who had been the foundation of my literacy methods courses, including scholars of various racialized and gendered categories and class backgrounds, took a back seat to first and foremost reminding ourselves what it felt like and meant to read a text that touched our souls. We read and viewed texts that seemed like they had been beckoning us to remind ourselves that we are all literate, in many ways. Our core initial required texts for this course included the film *Black Panther* (Feige, 2018) and Eve Ewing's book of poetry, *Electric Arches* (2017).

From our first sessions, we were immediately engaged with our first shared course texts, all of which used American Standardized English and also other codes. Through these initial texts, we engaged with literacy and texts as permeable, malleable, and powerful. Students also engaged in writing every week, participating in peer feedback where grammar comments were to be set aside in favor of comments that pertained to the flow and engagement of the text. In short, we were embodying what it meant to be readers and writers. Theories of literacy would come later and would make sense based on ontological experiences, not as texts written by intelligent scholars whose work nonetheless was often removed from urban and rural education realities.

READING AND WRITING LIVES IN A TIME OF CONSTRICTION

In our discussions of both the recent rendition of *Black Panther* by Coates (2016) and the film directed by Feige (2018), my students asked questions about the apparently magical promise of STEM presented in the film. They compared the savior-like ending to the political work of the Black Youth Project that presented their claim and evidence of "We Charge Genocide" to the United Nations in 2014. That class session in particular included hard, necessary, and reflective thinking about what forms of knowledge connect to freedom and liberation. We were engaged in critical literacy without having first read texts defining what it is.

Yes, we read some essential theories about literacy development, particularly works by Theresa Perry, Lisa Delpit, and Violet J. Harris. We also thought about the current activism of teacher leaders such as Dr. Kim Parker, whose community-building work has prioritized and created a structure for Black families with Black boys to come together on weekends to read, connect, read some more, and connect some more. In addition to the out-of-school spaces she has created, Dr. Parker's work also includes her own professional initiatives to teach the same curriculum designed for advanced students to her classes that were tracked with lower expectations. Practices such as these provided us with ways to bridge the disconnection many of my students had felt from reading and writing in school to their renewed understandings of themselves as readers and writers.

WHO IS A TEACHER NOW WHO IS NOT AN ACTIVIST?

As we read, wrote, and discussed the power of literacy and its foreclosure throughout history, my students posed blistering questions. They asked: What would literally happen if Standardized Academic English (SAE) were destabilized? Who would react and how? My students made parallels to how that question and its answers resonated in the rise of the 45th president of the United States through racist rhetoric, dating back to his full-page advertisement in the *New York Post* condemning the Central Park Five, a group of young Black men who were eventually exonerated from their criminalization, but not until after they had spent years in prison. These students posed the hard question that lies at the heart of abolition and liberation: What would all people need to unlearn and learn anew to exist in a connected way?

During one of our final class sessions, we read James Baldwin's (1997) essay, "If Black English Isn't a Language, Then Tell Me What Is?" During that session, with all of us by then deeply ensconced in the intertwined dynamics of literacy, power, and self-fulfillment, one student asked, riffing off the title to Baldwin's essay, "How could someone be a teacher now and not be an activist, at least to some extent?" This class knew of my interactions and the lessons I had learned from being part of the grassroots organization Education for Liberation. I had shared with them what I learned about collectivity from family and from organizing work. I shared these experiences not to induce them to do the same, but in my role as their teacher, I took seriously my responsibility to tell the various ways that literacy has been abused, taught, and used in formal and informal education settings. I did not need to guide them to the fact that formal schooling is individualistic and competitive. They had already lived and were still living that reality. We discussed what activism is, what "counts" as activism, and what strategies beginning, untenured teachers might use to educate for liberation in a time when the Federal Department of Education, helmed by Betsy DeVos, pursues privatization and the reduction of civil rights more than any other goal.

It is important to note that this class took place in southern California, 50 years after Chicanx students by the hundreds walked out of their schools as a direct action to demand an education that was relevant, emboldening, and pursuant to their needs. We met each week in the state where ethnic studies was first established as a legitimate university entity, and then as a required high school course. And we met not alongside expensive beach cities but inland, where unemployment, drought, and rising rents made life tenuous for so many of the region's peoples, most of whom are People of Color, including migrants and their children.

Upon reflection, perhaps it was precisely because of these conflicting realities that this class of students so readily embraced a literacy methods course that emphasized reading and writing texts well outside the academic canon.

Teacher education and literacy teacher education have had many high moments of brilliant work, and have also contributed to the perpetuation of a Eurocentric focus on achievement and which route will get young readers there fastest. Literacy education has conducted myriad experimental studies on Black and Brown children and poor white children, while middle- and upper-middle-class white children were spared these trials. For example, in a 1991 study by Blachman, Tangel, Ball, Black, and McGraw, a 2-year study of a phonological intervention was conducted on, as the study termed it, *low-income and inner-city children*. There are also hundreds of studies that compare the literacies of poor, often racially minoritized children to the literacy of white children. Arguably most infamous of these studies is Hart and Risley's 1995 study, which has been widely cited. It posited that African American children are exposed to millions fewer words than their white middle-class peers. This study has been debunked, time and time again, both directly and through studies that demonstrate the nuances of African American Vernacular English (see, for example, Lee, 2010) as well as how often these capacities are obviated through sanctioned standardized testing.

Experimental studies that implicitly and explicitly measure Black and Brown children's literacies do not only conduct research. They also convey a message of possibly scaling up interventions, but then collapse the proverbial intervention tent and leave after the funding ends. As with all of education, literacy education has contributed to the colonization of minoritized peoples, and it has had some high moments of truth telling. In the course evaluations from this class, one of the most resounding positive responses was that students had learned as much, if not more, from foundations courses that began with traditional scholarly texts, from the internal readings that social movements had used throughout history, including the Brown Berets, the Student Nonviolent Coordinating Committee, and the Dreamers movement. They learned explicitly from the texts, and they also learned about the strong ties that literacy has always had with the pursuit of justice.

From our literate practices with one another, we learned much about literacy, and we taught one another about the various ways literacy and power have intertwined. From this course, incredibly rich with wisdom from preservice teachers, it bears repeating the question from one of the students: "How could someone be a teacher now and not be an activist, at least to some extent?"

REFLECTIVE QUESTIONS

1. What are the ways that you were taught what counts as literacy?
2. What are the instances in which you have read and written under your own sovereignty, and by contrast, when have you engaged in literary practices that were decided for you by someone else?

REFERENCES

Acosta, C. (2014). Dangerous minds in Tucson: The banning of Mexican American Studies and critical thinking in Arizona. *Journal of Educational Controversy, 8*(1), 9.

Ahmed, S. (2012). *On being included: Racism and diversity in institutional life.* Durham, NC: Duke University Press.

American Library Association (ALA). (2018). Retrieved from ala.org/advocacy/bbooks

Baird, J. L. D. (2016). Wopanaak language reclamation program: bringing the language home. *Journal of Global Indigeneity, 2*(2), 7.

Baldwin, J. (1997). If Black English isn't a language, then tell me, what is? *The Black Scholar, 27*(1), 5–6.

Battiste, M. (2017). *Decolonizing education: Nourishing the learning spirit.* Vancouver, Canada: UBC Press.

Blachman, B. A., Tangel, D. M., Ball, E. W., Black, R., & McGraw, C. K. (1999). Developing phonological awareness and word recognition skills: A two-year intervention with low-income, inner-city children. *Reading and Writing, 11*(3), 239–273.

Bonilla-Silva, E. (2006). *Racism without racists: Color-blind racism and the persistence of racial inequality in the United States.* Lanham, MD: Rowman & Littlefield Publishers.

Bowles, S., & Gintis, H. (2011). *A cooperative species: Human reciprocity and its evolution.* Princeton, NJ: Princeton University Press.

Cabrera, N. L. (2011). Using a sequential exploratory mixed-method design to examine racial hyperprivilege in higher education. *New Directions for Institutional Research, 2011*(151), 77–91.

Coates, T. N. (2016). *Black Panther: A nation under our feet, book 1* (Vol. 1). New York, NY: Marvel Entertainment.

Ewing, E. L. (2017). *Electric arches.* New York, NY: Haymarket Books.

Ewing, E. L. (2018). *Ghosts in the schoolyard: Racism and school closings on Chicago's South Side.* Chicago, IL: University of Chicago Press.

Feige, K. (Producer) & Coogler, R. (Director). (2018). *Black Panther* [motion picture]. United States: Marvel.

Flores, N., & Rosa, J. (2015). Undoing appropriateness: Racioling uistic ideologies and language diversity in education. *Harvard Educational Review, 85*(2), 149–171. doi:10.17763/0017-8055.85.2.149

Gilmore, R. W. (2007). *Golden gulag: Prisons, surplus, crisis, and opposition in globalizing California* (Vol. 21). Berkeley, CA: University of California Press.

Grumet, M. R. (1988). *Bitter milk: Women and teaching*. Amherst, MA: University of Massachusetts Press.

Haddix, M. M. (2015). *Cultivating racial and linguistic diversity in literacy teacher education: Teachers like me*. New York, NY: Routledge.

Hart, B., & Risley, T. R. (1995). *Meaningful differences in the everyday experience of young American children*. Towson, MD: Paul H. Brookes Publishing.

Kinloch, V. (2018). Necessary disruptions: Examining justice, engagement, and humanizing approaches to teaching and teacher education. Retrieved from teachingworks.org/images/files/TeachingWorks_Kinloch.pdf

Lagemann, E. C. (2002). *An elusive science: The troubling history of education research*. Chicago, IL: University of Chicago Press.

Lee, H. (2010). *To kill a mockingbird*. New York, NY: Random House. (Originally published in 1960)

Meiners, E. R. (2010). *Right to be hostile: Schools, prisons, and the making of public enemies*. New York, NY: Routledge.

Oliveira, G. (2018). *Motherhood across borders: Mexican immigrants and their children in Mexico and New York City*. New York, NY: NYU Press.

Patel, L. (2015). *Decolonizing educational research: From ownership to answerability*. New York, NY: Routledge.

Patel, L. (2016). Pedagogies of resistance and survivance: Learning as marronage. *Equity & Excellence in Education (49)*4, 397–401.

Vizenor, G. (Ed.). (2008). *Survivance: Narratives of native presence*. Lincoln, NE: University of Nebraska Press.

Walker, V. S. (2018). *The lost education of Horace Tate: Uncovering the hidden heroes who fought for justice in schools*. New York, NY: The New Press.

Weems, C. M. (2012). *Carrie Mae Weems: Three decades of photography and video*. New Haven, CT: Yale University Press.

CHAPTER 2

"What Happens Here Can Change the World"

Preparing Literacy Teachers in the Digital Age

Detra Price-Dennis

Preservice teachers today are inducted into a field brimming with possibilities for developing curriculum and engaging in pedagogical practices that center digital epistemologies. Each academic semester, I engage preservice teachers in course readings and discussions that focus on digital epistemologies about race, equity, curriculum, and pedagogy. Sometimes, students ask difficult questions about how they perceive and interact with families who are racially, ethnically, economically, and/or linguistically different from them. These questions often raise more questions and concerns about how the institution of schooling is set up to support particular ways of being in the world that often leave Children of Color, children with rich linguistic repertoires, and children from economically fragile communities on the fringe. They begin to see inconsistencies in how resources are allocated, particularly when it comes to technology and literacy. As a class, we unpack which students have choice during writing workshop, which students have choice and access to digital tools, and which students are given prompts. As the semester unfolds, it becomes clear that certain children get a steady diet of skill-based worksheets, writing prompts, and reading materials that do not account for their home literacy practices or use of technology. Eventually, my preservice students wanted to do something about how these issues manifest in schools, typically in ways tied to their pedagogy. Because these students will be entering the final stages of their academic career after they leave my course, the most likely space for this disruption is student teaching. Thus, we set out as a community of learners to investigate ideas that work in diverse settings and then to create lessons and literacy events to engage their students in many of the practices they have learned in my course.

As a literacy teacher educator, I have also taken note of the types of questions and observations that my students discuss in class. Many of them shared observations from their field placements or student teaching that document the use of digital tools to surveil students (for example, Classroom Dojo), track their academic process, or provide literacy skill and repetition practice, particularly in schools that serve minoritized youth. During class discussions, they raised concerns about the disconnect between what they were observing and what they were learning about culturally responsive pedagogy and digital literacies from my course. Although they expressed great interest in incorporating digital literacy practices in their teaching in ways that honored their students' cultural knowledge and literacy practices, the absence of models in the field made it difficult for them to imagine how a pedagogy that blends technology and racial equity gets constructed and implemented in rigid teaching and learning environments. In response to my students' interest in learning how to teach with technology while also attending to race, language, and equity, I have designed multiple field-based language arts methods courses that integrate digital literacies into the curriculum, including a digital literacies camp. Both configurations provided a space for the preservice teachers in my courses to create a thriving educational environment that centered identity and equity to support digital ways of learning.

This chapter focuses on the emerging digital literacy practices and pedagogies that two preservice Teachers of Color developed to center issues of race, culture, and language with their 5th-grade students. Specifically, I detail how, over 2 years, two preservice teachers' understandings of teaching and digital literacies were rooted in a social justice stance that positioned the literacy curriculum as a site for intervention.

In what follows, I will unpack moments of success and tension that emerged for both preservice teachers as they learned to enact a curriculum that simultaneously addressed two theoretical constructs for teaching practices: (1) culturally responsive pedagogy and (2) digital literacies. I draw on both bodies of work to better understand the conceptual and practical tools that supported their emerging teaching philosophy and pedagogy that accounted for potential ways they saw race and equity shaping their students' digital literacies.

THE NEED FOR A CULTURALLY RESPONSIVE APPROACH
TO DIGITAL LITERACIES

Literacy research that focuses on equity has taught me a great deal about how to engage students from different cultural, racial, and linguistic backgrounds in academic learning (Blackburn, 2005; Blackburn & Smith, 2010; Gutiérrez, 2008; Kinloch, 2010; Kinloch, Burkhard, & Penn, 2017). When developing the syllabi for the language and literacy courses that I teach for preservice teachers, I draw upon literature rooted in culturally responsive teaching (Gay, 1995). I do so because this pedagogical framework serves to counter structural and educational inequities that marginalized groups experience in schools. The framework also positions teachers as having the capacity to honor students' lived experiences, home languages, literacies, and cultural practices. Similarly, Ladson-Billings's (1995, 2014) culturally relevant pedagogical framework makes the case for supporting preservice teachers as they learn how to work with culturally and linguistically diverse students to: (1) achieve academic success, (2) maintain and demonstrate cultural competence, and (3) develop critical consciousness to critique and push against dominant narratives. These frameworks stand in stark contrast to the typical experiences students from marginalized populations endure in school (Valenzuela, 2010).

For example, in literacy research, the dominant narrative constructs Students of Color from diverse cultural and linguistic backgrounds as struggling, "at risk," and not capable of high achievement. These narratives are sanctioned in reports, research, and federally funded programs (Hart & Risley, 2003; Reading First, 2001). Collectively, these narratives manifest in remedial programs that create a tiered system of education premised on a deficit view of students rooted in cultural biases that fails to recognize their capabilities. Although many efforts have been made, especially within literacy education, to incorporate and examine themes related to equity, achievement, and culture, there is far less evidence that suggests how these factors intersect with aspects of 21st-century or digital literacies education (NCTE, 2008).

Digital Literacies in Teacher Education

The National Council of Teachers of English (NCTE) published position statements and a framework outlining tenets for engaging in 21st-century literacy instruction (NCTE, 2004, 2008, 2010). These documents supported the creation of language arts curriculum informed by a digital literacies perspective. Such a perspective would foreground the following:

- Developing proficiency and fluency with digital tools
- Producing information to share with a variety of audiences
- Organizing and analyzing data from multiple sources
- Evaluating multimedia texts for multiple perspectives, accuracy of content, and reliability
- Developing an understanding of digital citizenship

The implications of this framework for teacher preparation programs imagine an engagement in multiple literacy practices for a variety of audiences and purposes. As one of the governing bodies for language arts educators, NCTE identifies what preservice teachers need to know and do in this digital age of education. At the same time, researchers also acknowledge that our teacher education programs are not adequately preparing candidates to teach digitally savvy students (Bauer & Kenton, 2005; Doering, Hughes, & Huffman, 2003; Koc & Bakir, 2010; Lei, 2009; Wright & Wilson, 2011). We are missing opportunities to draw on students' digital literacy practices to support their school-related tasks (Hagood, Provost, Skinner, & Egelson, 2008; Hull & Schultz, 2001; Mills, 2010). As a result, literacy educators indicated that a central goal for teacher education programs is to foster learning with their preservice teachers "about, through, and with" technologies (Cervetti, Damico, & Pearson, 2006, p. 383), as well as to create assignments that require preservice teachers to participate in "a new world of digital composition" (Hundley & Holbrook, 2013, p. 507). Collectively, this work suggests that future literacy teachers can learn to be more informed educators of digital age learners by writing and engaging in digital literacies (Hundley & Holbrook, 2013; Williams & Baumann, 2008).

In this chapter, I present how preservice Teachers of Color constructed a digital literacies curriculum that supported culturally and linguistically diverse learners. Teacher education programs, and especially literacy teacher education programs, face the challenge of preparing preservice teachers for increasingly technological, diverse, and multilingual classrooms. The majority of preservice teachers I work with lack the experiential knowledge to develop a digital literacies framework in their classrooms, particularly with students from marginalized populations. We cannot ignore this differential if we are intent upon reforming teacher education toward a framework that fosters culturally responsive digital literacies in purposeful and meaningful situations to transition preservice teachers to their future classrooms.

Creating space for preservice Teachers of Color to explore their identity. Before former preservice teachers Angela and Cody began working with their elementary students in the field-based course, they both spent time reflecting on their own identities and writing lives. Angela thought about the experiences she had as a K–12 student, as well as her emerging identity as a teacher of writing, and how those experiences impacted her decisions around curriculum development. For example, Angela began the course believing that it was the teacher's job to: (1) provide prompts each day for writing instruction, (2) focus on correcting grammatical errors in student writing, and (3) determine which materials and tools are available for writing. As she encountered different ideas from her readings and experiences working with students in the camp, she started to share how her initial conceptions of being a writing teacher were being challenged and how she had to rethink her positions in light of the new ideas she was learning in class. In a blog response to a course reading, Angela posted: "Students should be able to choose what they are interested in writing; choosing their own topics means voicing their opinions and perspectives through their pens and papers which in some cases can be more effective than oral communication." She was also beginning to envision the type of space that could support these ideas and to create digital responses to convey how her ideas about what was important to teach would find space to bloom in her classroom.

Cody also focused on how his identity and beliefs about the world were informing how he understood his role as a future classroom teacher. In a reflection he wrote, "I have started to find the writer who once was inside. I now use my journaling as an opportunity to write and get down ideas." In addition to journaling, Cody regularly made use of our class blog, which was a space where Cody and his classmates posted their thinking about what they were learning in class and in their work with students. For example, in one entry, Cody discussed his tattoos, explaining, "Each one tells a story," and reflected on how he, a Chicano man, will be perceived by others because of the "stories" he tells in displaying these images on his body. His understanding of teaching was rooted in his cultural knowledge. Cody explained: "In Mexico, the word for teacher is *maestro*; however, there, it is a word that is respected and honored. A child's maestro is one who leads them in life, teaching them what they need to know to be great people." He took that charge seriously and was excited about sharing his love of writing with his future students.

While preparing for his work with students in the field-based course, Cody began to imagine how the ideas he was reading about in class would inform the decisions he made on a weekly basis with his students. He pushed back on the representation of culture that he was subjected to as a K–12 student and shared, "We have heard that culture to most teachers means the three Fs: fun, festivals, and food. But we need to move away from that way of thinking. In order for us to teach to good culturally (relevant) pedagogy, we must have some competence in the culture of our students." This sentiment resonated in the work that both preservice teachers did with students in each field-based site.

Positioning elementary students as agentive writers who can make change in the world. In keeping with literacy teachers and researchers who advocate for the implementation of writing workshops in elementary classrooms, Angela and Cody voiced the importance of creating a classroom space where students are positioned as decisionmakers and are expected to make choices about what they read and write. During the field-based course, they put many of the ideas about student agency, choice, and authenticity that we had read and talked about into action. However, this group of preservice Teachers of Color distinguished themselves from their peers because of their commitment to developing socially conscious or "woke" writers who were well versed in a wide variety of genres and modalities to share their message with the world. This idea was not universal in the course. The majority of the other preservice teachers viewed teaching writing as a skill-based competency and the artifacts students generated from their lessons as evidence of academic aptitude.

Leveraging students' cultural and linguistic resources. During the course, each preservice teacher demonstrated that the cultural and linguistic practices of their students should inform their curriculum development. After talking with their young writers, both Cody and Angela expressed frustration at learning how infrequently the students were allowed to write in their home languages for their language arts assignments. This pushed both of them to be thoughtful about how to make sure the experiences they designed for students disrupted this pattern. For example, Cody spent a lot of time thinking, reflecting, and planning for ways to integrate his students' home literacy practices in the curriculum he developed. In his reflection, he described how his schooling experiences, language, culture, and identity as a Chicano influenced his thinking about culturally relevant pedagogy.

Angela also incorporated her growing knowledge about her students into the lessons she designed for them. When reflecting on her experiences teaching in the course, she wrote: "I find myself constantly trying to get my students' culture into their learning when what I should be doing is creating lessons inspired by their culture. This type of cultural competency will only take place if I fully commit to taking the time to learn about each and every one of my students. I have never had a teacher that has worked hard to get to know me; now I think about how much of a difference that could've made for my education." First, she incorporated multicultural children's literature by Maya Christina Gonzalez (2009) and Carmen Tafolla (2009) (both insiders writing about and illustrating their own culture) to help her students envision the possibilities for their digital stories. In one of her lesson plans, she wrote, "I chose this text *I Know the River Loves Me* (2009), because it has a Hispanic influence and describes the young girl's special place in such great detail. The illustrations are beautiful and really inspiring. I thought this would be a great introduction to talking about what our special place is, what it means to us, and how we would describe it." Because Angela listened to her students and got to know them as people and learners, she could use these texts to achieve academic goals as well as a larger goal of showing them how language and community can be sources of inspiration for their writing.

Toward the end of the course, Angela wrote about working with one of her students in her lesson plan reflection. She shared: "We practiced him reading the text in Spanish and I read in English. This was cool because every once in a while, we would stop and he would translate the Spanish to English for me. Then we talked about how we could incorporate Spanish into our final project." This moment was pivotal to Angela's development because she witnessed the power of integrating sound, image, and words in both languages. In her final class assignment, which was a portfolio project, Angela unpacked many of these ideas: "Every day, I found a way to match the lesson plan to his culture. This made the lessons so much more meaningful and relevant to his life. It allowed the content that I was trying to teach to stick and enabled his writing to flourish. I asked him to write in English and in Spanish, which really helped him create a very insightful, well-written narrative. In the end, my teaching allowed him to explore his culture and helped him grow academically. To me, these are the two most significant parts of the writing and learning process in a culturally responsive environment." Angela approached her work with her student from a capacities perspective that viewed his linguistic abilities as an asset. This approach helped her develop a pedagogy that accounted for multiple knowledge sources.

Angela and Cody recognized the need to center their students' cultural ways of knowing in both field-based courses. Both used mentor texts that affirmed students' home literacies and both created opportunities for students to use their emerging knowledge to compose multimodal projects that showcased their knowledge.

Creating space for students to write for real purposes and authentic audiences. During both courses, Angela and Cody demonstrated a commitment to developing confident writers who were capable of selecting their own topics, determining their audience, and evaluating their writing to make improvements to the content and the mechanics. It was that same commitment to growing writers that informed both of their decisions to introduce students to a wide variety of genres and authors, making transparent the options they had for sharing their work.

Cody shared a variety of digital tools with his students as choices for them to consider when it was time to present their writing. As a student in our university course, he developed ideas about student choice, writing resources, and how to create daily authentic writing experiences for his students. These ideas were informed by his writing life, course readings, and knowledge acquired through his weekly work with his students.

In Angela's case, she entered the class believing that the teacher was responsible for providing students with writing prompts, highlighting students' grammatical errors, and selecting for them specific writing tools. Many times in class, she would share how her initial conceptions of being a writing teacher were being challenged and that she had to rethink her positions in light of the new ideas she was learning in class. Her emerging teaching philosophy was beginning to advocate for time and space to think, share, and write for a variety of purposes, building on students' interests and linguistic repertoires.

Viewing technology as an intervention. In addition to thinking about writing as a print-based practice, the course was designed to focus on digital literacies and composing across modalities. Angela and Cody created lessons for their students that allowed them to explore technology. This was a departure from the ways in which technology was being used in the students' classroom. Typically, students in both field-based sites used technology to practice a skill. They had not used it as a tool to plan their writing, explore their ideas, examine their identities, or create multimodal representations of their thinking. Angela and Cody both expressed that our class was bringing in technology in ways that interrupted how it was positioned in the classroom. This provided an opportunity for them to play and reflect on how their use of technology in the course could inform their pedagogy.

For example, Angela relied on her use of technology in the course to inform what she would try out with her students. She decided to use Inspiration, a visual mapping, outlining, and brainstorming learning tool, as an entry point into their work together. She found this digital tool helpful in her writing and thought it could also benefit her students in organizing their writing. She wrote, "In Inspiration, we created three bubbles titled intro, body, and ending." Although Angela could have used paper and pencil to visually show her students how to organize their ideas for the narrative, she chose the Inspiration tool because it afforded a multimodal approach to writing and revising that allowed movement of ideas and connections that could be constructed with words, sounds, and images. It also provided fluidity of concepts, which helped her students rethink how their narratives could take shape digitally and could easily be revised as their writing project took shape. Once Angela had a plan in place, she began introducing students to different digital tools and sharing how she worked with these tools to create a digital story using iMovie. Her intention was to help students see technology as part of their writing process, not just the tool they used to create the final project. During each part of the writing process, Angela invited her students to consider using digital tools to support their thinking and composing of ideas (see Figure 2.1).

Her pedagogy moved seamlessly between print-based and digital literacy practices and reflects the perspective she shared on our course blog: "Living in the 21st century, we are such a technology-driven society, and that is passed on to our young people. It is important that we recognize how much students use such things and offer students as many chances as possible to use resources such as computers, laptops, iPads and other tablets, along with programs such as Inspiration, iMovie, iPhoto, Word, Excel, and others that will really aid writers in their learning process." Angela's case provides insight into how novice teachers who presume competence in their students can craft a responsive digital literacies curriculum that builds on their multiple literacies, strengths, and interests as learners.

The field-based course also helped Cody gain firsthand knowledge of how to negotiate the tensions of incorporating technology into the literacy curriculum. As part of the course, he had the opportunity to work with students on the creation of a digital poem. In reflecting on this experience, he explained, "In the beginning, I wasn't sure how I was going to get my students excited about writing poetry. Then, they heard that we were going to be using digital media to aid their writing. This was the moment that they were sold on the idea of using computers to do poetry." Throughout the experience of working with his students, Cody noticed how motivated his students seemed to be when they had the opportunity to compose using digital tools. In fact, he notes that his students seemed to think of the opportunity to use technology in the classroom as a "reward," rather than simply a tool to communicate. The goal in our course was to find a way to integrate digital tools into the process of writing; however, we learn through Cody's work that this task is not always easy to accomplish. This

Figure 2.1. Brainstorming ideas

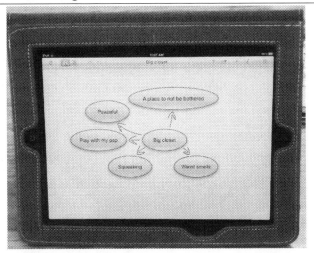

Angela's conceptual web created on Inspiration.

tension was felt by many preservice teachers in all of my courses, but Angela and Cody saw the potential that technology held in offering students the choice and freedom to explore different modalities to tell stories to a wider audience.

Developing reflective practitioners and advocates. Angela and Cody took advantage of every opportunity to blog, create visual responses to texts, and/or to share ideas in class as a means to engage with the material we were reading and working to make sense of as a community of learners. Angela spent time reflecting on these ideas throughout the course, and actively sought connections among the theories of writing we discussed and their potential applications with students. However, she also had to confront previous ideologies that were in conflict with the new ideas we were reading about in class. Before our class, she had experienced the writing process as a set of steps that each student followed to produce a piece of writing. However, after the first week of class, Angela learned that teaching the writing process requires flexibility and it is not a template that all students follow in lockstep fashion. She could trace how her process looked different depending on the genre and audience. At times, she wrote and revised for clarity and meaning, not worrying about spelling or grammar. At other times, she foregrounded mechanics. By developing her skill set as a writer, she was in a better position to understand what her students will actually experience, thus using her writing as a space to think about curriculum development. As a result, Angela came to understand that her writing life could inform her teaching and put her in a better position to meet the ever-changing needs of her students.

As the semester came to a close, Cody shared in class that he also began to encourage teachers in his field placement and his classmates at the university to recognize students' individual experiences, cultures, and languages as resources in order to develop a curriculum that is authentic, student-centered, and responsive to students' interests and needs. As he gained more access to colleagues in the field through the various field-based experiences he was participating in during our course, he noticed that many teachers fear teaching students to write because of their own negative experiences in the writing classroom. Cody was adamant that he would provide his students with a different experience. He wrote, "I promised myself I wouldn't be that teacher who destroys a child's love for writing, even if I have a fear of it." Cody voiced the need to rethink the role that writing might play in our own lives as well as in the lives of our students, commenting, "If they understand that they are in a safe environment that celebrates them as writers, then they become the writers we want." As the course progressed, Cody wrote about this issue more frequently in his weekly reflections. He also began to raise questions, such as "How do we become teachers who use good teaching and honor our students' use of their home language, while using pedagogy that is culturally relevant?" to consider how teachers might create a space in which students' funds of knowledge are valued and built upon. He was developing the stance of an advocate who understood the importance of creating a safe space for students to feel comfortable using their own voices.

CONCLUSION

Both Angela and Cody understood the benefits that came with teaching multicultural and multilingual learners. The course provided space for each of them to learn how to make adjustments to their teaching plans in real time to meet the needs of their students. Angela and Cody also connected the importance of knowing their students to planning for their learning. Grounding their understanding of curriculum development and digital literacies in a culturally responsive framework accounted for how both of them centered their students' linguistic preferences and cultural experiences in the assignments they developed.

A close examination of both student teachers' experiences emphasizes the need to teach preservice teachers about digital literacies in the context of their own teaching. In supporting preservice teachers in merging theory with practice, the field-based courses created a space for them to reflect on their readings and experiment with technologies before trying them out with student writers.

As I reflect on the lessons that I learned from teaching this preservice teacher education course and working with Angela and Cody, I offer specific questions for other literacy researchers and practitioners to consider.

REFLECTIVE QUESTIONS

1. What experiences with hybrid textual practices and multimodal composition do preservice teachers need in order to integrate digital literacies into their pedagogical repertoire?

2. What conversations should we be having with preservice teachers about data, privacy, and digital citizenship to prepare them for teaching about race and equity within sociotechnical spaces?

REFERENCES

Bauer, J., & Kenton, J. (2005). Toward technology integration in the schools: Why it isn't happening. *Journal of Technology and Teacher Education, 13*(4), 519–546.

Blackburn, M. V. (2005). Agency in borderland discourses: Examining language use in a community center with Black queer youth. *Teachers College Record, 107*(1), 89–113.

Blackburn, M. V., & Smith, J. M. (2010). Moving beyond the inclusion of LGBT-themed literature in English language arts classrooms: Interrogating heteronormativity and exploring intersectionality. *Journal of Adolescent & Adult Literacy, 53*(8), 625–635.

Cervetti, G., Damico, J., & Pearson, P. D. (2006). Multiple literacies, new literacies, and teacher education. *Theory into Practice, 45*(4), 378–386.

Doering, A., Hughes, J., & Huffman, D. (2003). Pre-service teachers: Are we thinking with technology? *Journal of Research on Technology in Education, 35*(3), 342–362.

Gay, G. (1995). Mirror images on common issues: Parallels between multicultural education and critical pedagogy. In C. Sleeter & P. L. McLaren (Eds.), *Multicultural education, critical pedagogy, and the politics of difference* (pp. 155–189). Albany, NY: State University of New York Press.

Gonzalez, M. C. (2009). *I Know the River Loves Me/Yo se que el rio me ama.* New York, NY: Children's Book Press.

Gutiérrez, K. D. (2008). Developing a sociocritical literacy in the third space. *Reading Research Quarterly, 43*(2), 148–164.

Hagood, M. C., Provost, M. C., Skinner, E. N., & Egelson, P. E. (2008). Teachers' & students' literacy performance in & engagement with new literacies strategies in underperforming middle schools. *Middle Grades Research Journal, 3*(3), 57–95.

Hart, B., & Risley, T. R. (2003). The early catastrophe: The 30 million word gap by age 3. *American Educator, 27*(1), 4–9.

Hull, G., & Schultz, K. (2001). Literacy and learning out of school: A review of theory and research. *Review of Educational Research, 71*(4), 575–611.

Hundley, M., & Holbrook, T. (2013). Set in stone or set in motion?: Multimodal and digital writing with pre-service English teachers. *Journal of Adolescent & Adult Literacy, 56*(6), 500–509.

Kinloch, V. (2010). *Harlem on our minds: Place, race, and the literacies of urban youth.* New York, NY: Teachers College Press.

Kinloch, V., Burkhard, T., & Penn, C. (2017). When school is not enough: Understanding the lives and literacies of Black youth. *Research in the Teaching of English, 52*(1), 34.

Koc, M., & Bakir, N. (2010). A needs assessment survey to investigate pre-service teachers' knowledge, experiences and perceptions about preparation to using educational technologies. *The Turkish Online Journal of Educational Technology, 9*(1), 13–22.

Ladson-Billings, G. (1995). Toward a theory of culturally relevant pedagogy. *American Educational Research Journal, 32*(3), 465–491.

Ladson-Billings, G. (2014). Culturally relevant pedagogy 2.0: aka the remix. *Harvard Educational Review, 84*(1), 74–84.

Lei, J. (2009). Digital natives as pre-service teachers: What technology preparation is needed. *Journal of Computing in Teacher Education, 25*(3), 87–97.

Mills, K. A. (2010). A review of the "digital turn" in the new literacy studies. *Review of Educational Research, 80*(2), 246–271.

National Council of Teachers of English (NCTE). (2004). "Beliefs about the teaching of writing." Retrieved from www.ncte.org/positions/statements/writingbeliefs%20

National Council of Teachers of English (NCTE). (2008). The NCTE definition of 21st century literacies. Retrieved from www.ncte.org/positions/statements/21stcentdefinition

National Council of Teachers of English (NCTE). (2010). Preparing, inducting and retaining English language arts teachers. Retrieved from www.ncte.org/library/NCTEFiles/Resources/Journals/CC/0193mar2010/CC0193Preparing.pdf

Reading First, No Child Left Behind Act, Public Law No. 107-110, Title I, Part B, Subpart 1 (2001).

Tafolla, C. (2009). *What can you DO with a Paleta?* Berkeley: Tricycle Press.

Valenzuela, A. (2010). *Subtractive schooling: US-Mexican youth and the politics of caring.* Albany, NY: SUNY Press.

Williams, T. L., & Baumann, J. F. (2008). Contemporary research on effective elementary teachers. In Y. Kim, V. J. Risko, D. L. Compton, D. K. Dickinson, M. K. Hundley, R. T. Jimenez, K. M. Leander, & D. W. Rowe (Eds.), *57th yearbook of the National Reading Conference* (pp. 357–372). Oak Creek, WI: National Reading Conference.

Wright, V. H., & Wilson, E. K. (2011). Teachers' use of technology: Lessons learned from the teacher education program to the classroom. *The Journal of the Southeastern Regional Association of Teacher Educators, 2*(2), 48–60.

CHAPTER 3

Students Developing Critical Language and Literacy Perspectives

Ijeoma E. Ononuju, BernNadette T. Best-Green,
and Danny C. Martinez

> The best tools for empowering students . . . are also the best tools for
> empowering teachers. (Watson, 2013, p. 400)

The journey toward helping preservice and novice literacy instructors develop critical perspectives defined by commitments to teaching and loving marginalized youth is not always easy. When we ask them to have an equal commitment to learn about and love the multiple literacies that marginalized youth bring with them into classrooms, we are often asking them to engage in an additionally complex and dynamic task. In fact, as Scholars of Color, we (a Black man, an African American woman, and a Chicano man) are often confronted with the arduous task of navigating our students' privilege and fragility, while also nourishing their capacity to be critical, to challenge the status quo, and to teach using a social justice praxis. The resurgence of historical injustices in this current time is real and cannot be understated. It generates conflict in the form of apathy within our classrooms as our students (preservice candidates and novice literacy instructors) sometimes fail to grasp the import of this resurgence or are unwilling to engage in dialogue that leads to understanding. We point to state-sanctioned violence against and overpolicing of Black and Brown communities, and the lack of tangible engagement within the curriculum for our students, as examples of the conflict of which we speak.

We come to this chapter as teacher educators and literacy scholars with a range of K–12 teaching and research experiences. Ijeoma spent much time working as a poet-mentor-educator (Watson, 2013) and as a youth justice liaison with middle and high school youth labeled "at risk." He also worked as a teacher educator in California and with school leaders in Arizona. A former school administrator, BernNadette currently works as a teacher and researcher of ethnically and linguistically diverse middle school youth in California's San Joaquin Valley. As a recently graduated doctoral student, she also teaches graduate courses for teacher credential and master's degree candidates at a research university in northern California. Danny was a middle and high school literacy teacher in San Francisco and Los Angeles. He has taught preservice teachers in Los Angeles, Chicago, and now in the Sacramento region of northern California. All of us engage in research that seeks to push the boundaries of traditional teacher education in ways that foreground social justice frameworks within a rigorous teacher development curriculum (Ukpokodu, 2007).

Collectively, we are concerned with the range of "social justice" commitments of our students. Thus, we come together to consider how Teacher Educators of Color do the cultural work of teaching in ways that facilitate the development of preservice and novice teachers' commitments to learning from and loving marginalized youth, and how these commitments materialize in their own practices. We specify that we are Teacher Educators of Color in order to acknowledge the different challenges we face when doing this work, in comparison to our white counterparts. Because the majority of our students are white, it can be personally challenging to go through the process of cultivating our students' commitment when we ourselves know firsthand the pain of being educated by white teachers who were not committed to justice and/or our well-being. The "doing" of the work, for us, is not merely an exercise of strategies and practices employed in the classroom, but also consists of the self-care work that reconciles our experiences on the margins.

We seek to facilitate the development of teachers who are reflexive about their subject positions and privileges, and who are aware that there is much to learn about the lives of the young people inside their classrooms. Also, we seek to facilitate the development of teachers who will disrupt the colonizing practices long seen as "best practices" in traditional classroom settings. To engage in this work, we acknowledge the limitations of the teacher education programs where we teach (Ijeoma teaches at a different institution, but serves as an adjunct in the program where Danny and BernNadette teach), whose demographics neither reflect the communities where we teach nor the lives of the children and youth who will be the students of the preservice teachers we are training.

FRAMING THE CHAPTER

This chapter will focus on how our students developed their commitment to a critical activist praxis, where activism is the real work they put into the pursuit of justice and justice is the reimagining of power—from "reckless and abusive" to corrective and restorative—in order to confront race and racism toward the goal of abolishment. We will also discuss the challenges of having an explicit curriculum that focuses on race, justice, and activism in teacher education and the importance of enduring the conflict (racism, disrespect, microaggressions, and so on) as Educators of Color, because truly that is where this work begins for us. Our purpose for doing this work is deeply personal. It is tied to our collective and individual responsibilities to our communities and to our children. The opportunity to teach, coach, and mentor others to have the same commitment to the children and communities we love is one that we don't take lightly. The process of enduring is of critical importance because it speaks to the ability to manage anger, disappointment, and frustration in ways that heal and not harm.

Enduring, however, does not mean that we have to adopt a pacifist approach in our classrooms. The self-reflection that our students require, self-reflection that holds them accountable to their privilege and the ethical implications of their participation in the current system, can only be facilitated by honest and courageous conversations about race and society. The discomfort of truth, of looking in the mirror, is essential for growth and the cultivation of a commitment that will value alternative literacies and youth practices. This process comes with loss. Inevitably, while we create courses and classrooms that encourage courageous conversations, some students will choose to disengage. They will choose to reject the call to embrace race, justice, and activism as part of their praxis, opting instead to continue reinforcing the status quo. But we accept this because the alternative of creating spaces where everyone is comfortable and *real talk* never occurs is unacceptable and harmful for our youth.

What we have found is that those students who buy into the process commit to doing the work. How they individually define their commitment is what we will explore throughout this chapter. In order to do this, we go through the process of "leveraging" to privilege youth practices, as a gateway toward building our students' commitments. For our students, "leveraging" leads to commitments defined by resistance, reeducation, and revolution. Although this is not an exhaustive list, we dive deeply into these three commitments to explore the range of answers our students give to our question: Will you love and are you committed? To start, we will provide a definition of race, justice, and activism that will guide the remainder of the chapter.

ADDRESSING STUDENT EXPECTATIONS

One of Ijeoma's students, a white male, expressed some of his frustration around "the lack" of social justice rigor that he had perceived in the teacher education program. He went on to explain that the reason he had chosen this particular program over the others he had been accepted into was because he believed our program had a stronger commitment to social justice. His disappointment stemmed from what he deemed as more of a commitment to perpetuating the status quo than a commitment to challenging it. The next time we (Ijeoma, BernNadette, and Danny) met to discuss this chapter, Ijeoma brought this student's concerns to BernNadette and Danny's attention. After ruminating over the conversation for a couple of days, Ijeoma concluded that what this student was looking for was discomfort. Not that our program was above critique, but from the way the student had expressed himself, it seemed he was looking for his Black and Brown instructors to carry a rebuke of white folks and white students in a way that would force his white peers to acknowledge their complicit participation in an unjust system. He wanted all of us to be forceful in our denunciation of an unfair and unjust system, invoking a call for rebellion or, better yet, an educational revolution that would save Black and Brown children from further academic isolation and failure.

Interactions like the one above are not strange to Scholars of Color. Whether during interviews, in staff meetings, in our classrooms, or in other social spaces where conversations about race, justice, and activism occur, we are expected to carry a righteous indignation that scorches the earth we stand on, all in the name of social justice. Or, at the very least, we are often seen as having the secret sauce for teaching folks who do not understand *how to understand* or for convincing folks who are not committed to justice *how to be committed* to a cause that they didn't know was their own (Baldwin, 2008). Surely, if we do not have the secret sauce, then we must have some proven strategies that have been effective in encouraging teachers to challenge institutional norms through literacy instruction. The work is not easy, and in many ways, it requires more of us to endure the side comments, the rolled eyes, the blatant disinterest and disrespect, the challenges to our authority as scholars, and the racism that is often hurled our way (Griffin, Pifer, Humphrey, & Hazelwood, 2011).

One of the challenges of being committed to preparing literacy instructors to become social justice advocates who are willing to become disrupters within the education system is that too many of our students are convinced that they "get it," even if they acknowledge that they don't actually "get it" at all (Kristof, 2014). These students are eager to learn but have predetermined their commitment to the work and readily espouse their understanding that the system is oppressive and that they are willing to reject their own privilege in the name of social justice. In their demands for a curriculum that exposes their privilege and is explicit about addressing race, justice, and activism, they are blinded to the ways their demands lack patience and perpetuate the primacy of race.

Another challenge is working with students who use literacy and language to articulate a pedagogy of inclusion and diversity, all in the name of disproving their racial biases. Such students are found across the spectrum, though the majority are white. Their fear of being labeled racist, and of the ostracism that accompanies that title, closes them off to acknowledging the primacy of race in the contexts of school, classroom, and life. In contrast to the first set of students, these students are interested in what we have to teach them until they are expected to acknowledge the consequences of race and racism within their own lives. Watson (2013) notes how in her literacy intervention, when the conversation around race and justice became too real, the room became divided, with some teachers choosing to remove themselves from the intervention as a result of the discomfort they felt from being white. According to Watson (2013), one of the teachers shared, "it felt very uncomfortable to be a White person in that room.... Even though I rarely see myself as a White person anymore" (p. 401).

As part of our discussions for this chapter, we contemplated the juxtaposition of these two groups of white students in our classes. We asked ourselves: How do we effectively teach students we feel "get it" while also addressing the fact that some students have chosen to deny their whiteness in such a way that they disengage when they are reminded of it? We also considered: How do we do this work while attending to the needs of our Black, Latinx, Asian, and Indigenous students, who have to endure having elementary conversations about race and justice, when their life experiences have prepared them for graduate-level dialogue?

As we contemplated these questions, BernNadette offered the following insights from her own experiences:

> In reflecting on my own growth as a teacher educator over the past 5 years, I realize that well-intentioned efforts to examine issues of race, diversity, and social justice in a minimized or "more palatable" fashion ultimately undermine our own efforts to support novice teachers' needed growth pertaining to these important issues. In my own experience, these efforts of minimizing or presenting topics in a "more palatable" way were introduced to avoid causing the dominant group to feel defensive about their own racial privilege, gender privilege, socioeconomic privilege, etc. In the end, however, I have concluded that though motivated from a place of compassion, these attempts to avoid courageous conversations and activities proved counterproductive to my goal of preparing students to advocate for equity in learning for all students.

As much as BernNadette's reflections captured the sentiment of our discussion, it brought up pressing questions of *why*: Why do we feel as though the best way to help our students is to make the conversation palatable? Why do we buy into their victimhood and fragility in such a way that it impacts our ability to "keep it 100" in the course of encouraging them to adopt this commitment? Although this chapter is about how students cultivate their commitment to race, justice, and activism through literacy instruction, it is equally about how we, three Scholars of Color, facilitate this process in a healthy way that does not succumb to our anger or to the fragility and victimization of our students. To do this, we contemplated our own experiences working within teacher education programs that claim to be oriented toward racial and social justice, yet fall short in providing a foundation steeped in what we outline as crucial components for teachers educating Children and Youth of Color. Below, we outline some of these reflections that help us work toward imagining and building teacher education programs that take up notions of race, justice, and activism as central organizing principles rather than peripheral topics cared for by one programmatic course. This work takes the language and literacy practices of Youth of Color as central for teacher learning.

STUDENTS' RIGHT TO THEIR OWN LANGUAGE

BernNadette's contributions to this chapter draw heavily from experiences she encounters on a daily basis as a teacher educator within a university-based teacher preparation program and as a teacher-researcher of multilingual and multidialectal middle school youth attending school within a contact zone (Pratt, 1991) in northern California. In the balancing of her dual roles, the justice she has committed herself to is the cultivation and sustaining of a praxis that affirms students' rights to their own language (SRTOL) (CCCC, 1974; Kinloch, 2010). At the core of BernNadette's commitment to affirming SRTOL is the primacy of race, and how language is understood through a racial lens. Her activism promotes the importance of K–12 educators, especially novice literacy teachers, who are invested in justice through the understanding of racialized dialects of English. Experiences shared with culturally and linguistically diverse 6th-, 7th-, and 8th-grade youth she has encountered inside the classroom have heightened her awareness of the linguistic dexterity of students who sometimes blend mainstream and nondominant Englishes. They also demonstrate the ethnolinguistic vitality of the languages they speak, including African American Language (AAL) (Smitherman, 1996), Spanglish (a hybrid dialect of Spanish and English) (Martínez, 2010), and Hmonglish (a hybrid dialect of Hmong and English) (Yang, 2010). The frequency with which she encounters such scenarios helps underscore why this learning must be centered within a race and justice curricula designed for preservice literacy teachers who are enrolled in our teacher preparation programs, as well as for novice literacy teachers who are candidates of education master's degree programs.

Like most K–12 teachers of English language arts who work in the United States, the preservice teacher candidates enrolled in BernNadette's teacher education courses and the first-year teachers enrolled in her master's degree courses are accountable to school-based administrators and instructional coaches who expect them to promote educational policies and practices that privilege Common Core State Standards (CCSS) conventions and learning objectives. In supporting these primarily monolingual novice teachers, the palpable ethnolinguistic vitality of AAL, Spanglish, and Hmonglish that their students bring into the classroom is frequently interpreted as students' inability to express their ideas using CCSS-aligned ELA conventions (Martínez, 2010; Yang, 2010). Unfortunately, deficit-oriented assumptions of multilingual and multidialectal youth routinely trigger unnecessary remediation of CCSS-aligned English language arts learning objectives for linguistically marginalized youth (Skerrett, 2012). These assumptions lack awareness of how language and literacy practices can be central to the establishment and maintenance of students' identities. The multidialectal youth whom BernNadette has observed do not view their nondominant Englishes from the same deficit perspectives with which teachers judge many youth. Further, the commonplace standards-aligned assessment protocols that teachers tend to use often lack a capacity to illuminate the dynamic and innovative ways we frequently hear youth with linguistic dexterity blend and alternate between the mainstream and nondominant Englishes within their linguistic repertoires. The challenge becomes how to confront deficit-oriented assumptions head on and in ways that provide preservice and novice teachers with the permission, tools, and strategies to ensure that students' right to their own language and literacy is a permanent part of the curriculum.

"LEVERAGING" TO BUILD THE COMMITMENT

In Danny's work with preservice teachers, he wants all students to think about the meaning behind the notion of "leveraging" language and literacy as a part of their activism and commitment to justice (Martinez, Morales, & Aldana, 2017). In research and in practice, he has found a range of interpretations of "leveraging," which can be subsumed under two primary goals:

Goal 1: "leveraging" to access dominant or "better" literacy practices
Goal 2: "leveraging" to privilege youth practices on par with dominant practices

In working with preservice literacy teachers, it seems normal for them to think of "academic" language as the goal, which aligns with Goal 1 above. In Danny's work, it is imperative for him to have all preservice teachers consider race and the real consequences of linguistic violence (Martinez, 2017) that Youth of Color experience when their home and community language and literacy practices are stigmatized, dismissed, and/or "corrected" in classroom interactions. It is a goal to articulate how classroom policies that insist that youth speak like white people do not guarantee that they will avoid violently racist and oppressive practices. Therefore, we take up notions of leveraging that privilege youth practices and work toward "leveling" (Zisselsberger, 2016) Youth of Color's language and literacy practices in ways that raise their prestige against dominant forms of language that are too often privileged in school classrooms, particularly in literacy learning contexts.

Across all of our work, but specifically as we engage with our preservice and novice literacy students, it is the first of these goals that is often prioritized within the process of effective culturally relevant instruction. That is, the confrontation between acknowledging students' right to their own language and literacy versus CCSS-aligned ELA conventions is often resolved through negotiating students' language and literacy as an access point to the preferred CCSS-aligned ELA standards. This leads to the conditional engagement of our students or tolerance for wading in the murky waters of race and justice, based solely on how they perceive that this approach to literacy instruction will help them get their students to access dominant practices. Thus, our challenge stems from how we convince our students that the second goal—leveraging to privilege youth practices—is of greater importance and is worth enduring the discomfort that arises from having to acknowledge one's own privilege and participation in an unjust system.

To face this challenge, we adopt and adapt Toni Morrison's ethos of motherhood, which positions teaching as a political undertaking with the explicit objective of empowering youth to survive and resist racism and sexism, as well as other isms, through the development of critical literacy practices. With our students, we explore how literacy is a tool for both domination and liberation (Leonardo, 2003), by developing a collective understanding of how literacy undergirds the relationship between race and power and then "leveraging" our language and literacy to critique and provide counternarratives that resist domination while empowering voices that remain unheard (Watson, 2013). Yet we acknowledge that this alone is not enough. Training programs often rely on appealing to the morality and personal biases of their teaching candidates, hoping that exposing them to the larger system of oppression in conjunction with cultivating their counternarratives will create a pathway toward enlightenment and critical consciousness (Hughes, Ononuju & Okoli, 2020). Despite this strategy, what persists is a privileging of not just dominant practices, but dominant interpretations of justice and morality. Hence, we end up producing literacy instructors who can feign enlightened and critical consciousness, by being able to speak to the issues, yet they remain adjusted to injustice and uncommitted to a social justice praxis as a tool of transformation. Their investment in utilizing literacy for justice is limited to being a strategy for assimilation.

We take this space and opportunity to present the approach of our teaching before getting into the development of our students' commitment because we feel that it is important to acknowledge the complexity of this work. On the surface, if we can demonstrate to our students the legitimacy of literacy instruction that explicitly examines race, justice, and activism, and how it will benefit them and their students, it seems clear that they will be moved (spiritually, morally, emotionally, and so forth) to adopt it as a primary focus of their instruction. But this is not always the case. Thus, our approach is of vital importance because it provides a pathway for moving and transforming our students.

Our approach privileges learning interactions that involve multiple stakeholders (administrators, teachers, teacher candidates, youth, community stakeholders, and so on) as part of the development of a learning ecology that emphasizes the richness of our youth's lived experiences (Moll, Amanti, Neff & Gonzalez, 1992). Chris Emdin (2016) claims that if we are truly committed to transforming of schools and meeting the needs of our youth, then we "must create safe and trusting environments that are respectful of students' culture" (p. 27). We intentionally embed the ideals of safety, trust, and respect in the learning interactions we facilitate for our students, where they are no longer reflecting on their literacy instructional practice within an echo chamber of their peers, but are confronted with the voices of their students, their students' families, and other stakeholders within a collaborative learning environment. It is at this point where our students contemplate the value of critical literacy instruction through our leveraging of youth, family, and community voices (bringing their voices into the university classroom spaces). One of the first lessons they learn is that when students choose to speak in their own language or engage in their own literacy practice, it is not evidence that they cannot access or translate their ideas into mainstream practices, but rather a choice to prioritize their own practices.

Zeus Leonardo (2003) reminds us that there is a difference between being an authority in your discipline and wanting to be an authority figure. In to-day's political climate, tackling the issue of authority exposes the undercurrent of power and oppression that plays out materially in the lives of our youth. Within the realm of authority, we cannot ignore the pervasiveness of race as a currency used for domination and the interplay of this currency in the govern-ing of the teacher–student relationship. What we find is that teachers privilege certain curricula and instructional praxis because doing so effectively empow-ers them while disempowering students. This is what Paulo Freire (1970) ad-dresses in the second chapter of his book *Pedagogy of the Oppressed*. We make sure we give our students his book to read. We take time to discuss the banking concept versus the problem-posing strategy he proposes. Yet how many of our students still choose to teach through a banking framework? What if the medi-ating factor for moving literacy instructors from goal 1 to goal 2 isn't an appeal to morality and injustice, but rather an appeal of power? Our belief is that by leveraging those excluded voices in our instructional spaces before we release our students into the full-time teaching world, we interrupt the traditional power dynamics that privilege dominant literacy narratives over those that are asking critical questions in a time when critical questions are needed. That is, we want to move our students away from viewing critical literacy as a threat to their authority by demonstrating how authority, as a byproduct of power and control, is a fallacy.

Bringing in the youth and community as equal partners in designed learn-ing interactions provides a safe space for our students to learn how to focus on the expansion of their authority within the discipline without threat to their authority as teachers. As an example, Ijeoma has invited community-based po-ets into his class to talk and work with students around culturally relevant lesson plans. These poets, in addition to leveraging youth literacy practice through the media of spoken word poetry and hip-hop, teach students about the value of community and developing authentic relationships. It is an op-portunity to observe how engagement with the literacy practices of our youth, who want to tackle critical issues such as police brutality, Kaepernick, Trump, collusion, and injustice, can lead to authority not defined by a teacher's ability to exert his or her will and control by force, but through a willingness to be vulnerable in the teaching, engagement, and examination of literacy informed by the critical issues of our time. In the words of James Baldwin (2008), "The obligation of anyone who thinks of himself as responsible is to examine society and try to change it and to fight it—at no matter what risk. This is the only hope society has. This is the only way societies change" (p. 1).

EXAMINING WHITENESS

The three of us explicitly address whiteness in our courses. We address whiteness (Roediger, 1999) because any conversation about race, justice, and activism is incomplete without explicitly addressing whiteness as a pervasive culture that validates and invalidates our understanding of justice and the question of what is just (Rawls, 1971/2009). Yet it is also not a cultural exploration, but an opportunity to expose students to critical language that effectively sows the seeds of critical thought. With critical thought comes a questioning of the hypocrisy that expects marginalized, underserved, and oppressed people to fight for justice and equity within the rules, language, and parameters of a system that is inherently inequitable. In the words of Audre Lorde (1984), "What does it mean when the tools of a racist patriarchy are used to examine the fruits of that same patriarchy? It means that only the most narrow parameters of change are possible and allowable" (pp. 110–111). In this sense, presenting whiteness to our students and providing them with the critical language to name and ruminate over their own racial identity as a social construction of a "racist patriarchy" is the cornerstone to defining and cultivating a personal commitment to critical literacy instruction.

Going back to the interaction between Ijeoma and his student, what we have is a student who is trying to hold his program accountable for delivering on what it promised. This student could articulate a surface-level understanding of the primacy of race, but was limited in his ability to effectively address it with the youth he teaches. Examining whiteness for this student became a very personal process of critical self-reflection where a cycle developed between him and Ijeoma that consisted of reading through the course material and dialogue exchanges through email, in-class discussions, and after-class reflections. Week after week for the duration of the class, the cycle would repeat itself. For Ijeoma's student, the explicit examination of whiteness brought up questions about fairness and justice, equity and equality, merit and discipline, and how race had moderated his perspective on these ideas, along with his relationship with his students. For the student, examining whiteness was the point in the course where his language, perspective, and question shifted.

Ijeoma's experience is neither unique nor exclusive to white students. We have all found that exposing our students to language and literacy that critically explores whiteness will inevitably turn some off, but for others it is the first stepping-stone to their full commitment to a critical literacy perspective that privileges nondominant literacies on par with dominant literacies. This is not to say that our students are relieved of their biases or that they don't still find themselves leveraging nondominant literacies as a pathway toward dominant literacies. But that committing to teaching through a framework of race, justice, and activism begins when one is willing to engage in a Socratic process with oneself.

Returning to Watson's (2013) account of her professional development work with literacy teachers, the most troubling part of the teacher's statement—"it felt very uncomfortable to be a White person in that room.... Even though I rarely see myself as a White person anymore" (p. 401)—was not that the teacher felt uncomfortable being white, but that he/she rarely saw him/herself as a white person. While whiteness, in effect, reduces people to their epidermis (Yancy, 2012) and creates a social hierarchy that unapologetically separates and sorts based on skin color, hair texture, as well as gender and sexual orientation, it also normalizes race and racial difference as part of American culture. Thus, the purpose of examining whiteness in our courses is not to villainize it, but to reveal the invisible way in which white customs, morals, values, political structure (democracy), and economics (capitalism), for example, become encapsulated under the umbrella of American (Bonilla-Silva, 2012; Kincheloe, Steinberg, Rodriguez, & Chennault, 2000). It is here that the language of whiteness, to which our students are exposed, begins to plant those seeds of critical thought because they are confronted with the question: What is American and what is not?

The rebranding of white and whiteness as *American* serves as a block to literacy instructors who do not recognize the ruse. Here, we are not referring to *American* as an identity, but as a culture and ideology. This leaves little recourse for literacy instructors in the classroom to be able to connect with students in meaningful ways. The lack of critical language and perspective associated with *American* means that teachers who want to have a discussion with students about, for instance, the merits of Kaepernick's protest of the NFL are handcuffed by the superficial ideology of allegiance and the implicit bias that excludes People of Color from the true essence of what is American. For People of Color, *American*—our access to this ideology—hinges on our ability to align, pledge allegiance, and assimilate in the face of injustice, oppression, and enslavement. Yet, for teachers who bring with them the language of whiteness and the exposure to critical literacy as presented in our courses, the commitment to utilizing this perspective in classrooms hinges on their ability to empathize and their moral discontent with injustice.

CULTIVATING COMMITMENT

There are certain things in our nation and in the world which I am proud to be maladjusted and which I hope all men of goodwill will be maladjusted until

> the good societies realize. I say very honestly that I never intend to become adjusted to segregation and discrimination. I never intend to become adjusted to religious bigotry. I never intend to adjust myself to economic conditions that will take necessities from the many to give luxuries to the few. Leave millions of God's children smothering in an airtight cage of poverty in the midst of an affluent society. (Dr. Martin Luther King, Jr., 1963)

Readers may recall that the authors of this chapter all work with both preservice teaching credential candidates as well as novice literacy instructors. The demographics of our students is roughly 70% white; 20% Asian; and 10% Latinx, African American, and other combined. In our work with our students, one common characteristic that tends to emerge as they begin to cultivate their commitment to race, justice, and activism is the orientation of their morality. In the same sentiment as Martin Luther King, Jr., our students—once exposed to injustice, once given access to the language and critical thought associated with injustice—become maladjusted in a way that spurs action. Students begin to "examine carefully the dissonance between what presently occurs in schools that perpetuates the status quo and what could happen in schools that would bring about marked change in these institutions" (Dantley, 2003, p. 14). These were also the students who found indignation in idleness. Whether it be from themselves, from their instructors, or from the schools in which they worked, their exposure to critical perspectives and the awakening of sorts that occurred was one that emanated from a disruption in their spirit, based on how they were inclined to be maladjusted.

Generally speaking, we found that our students defined their commitment in three distinct ways: resistance, reeducation, and revolution. For the remainder of this chapter, we will explore what these three types of commitment looked like for our students.

Resistance

For the students who have participated in our courses, the cultivation of their commitment begins with two fundamental questions: What am I willing to do? and What am I willing to risk? Inevitably, those students who embark on this path will acknowledge that these two questions are interconnected and that what they are willing to risk often dictates what they are willing to do. Those students who define their commitment through resistance understand risk through the lens of the love and commitment they have toward their students. They are restrained in what they are willing to do because they are unwilling to risk their position as teachers. This is not a function of their own self-preservation, but rather is born out of an understanding of the privileged positions they occupy. The students who adopt this path of commitment often exclaim how few teachers there are who are willing to take on a commitment to critical literacy and to embrace literacy instruction that explicitly empowers students. Thus, they prioritize the preservation of the space and positions they hold. They question who would replace them if they weren't there, and who would be the teacher to work with their students? They also question whether that teacher would carry the same love and commitment they have for the youth, and if that teacher would be willing to take a critical literacy approach to better serve the youth. Not knowing the answers to these questions propels them to moderate their actions as they work toward change in their individual classrooms.

Taking into consideration the two goals that Danny laid out earlier in this chapter, our resistant students vacillate between goal 1—leveraging to access dominant practices—and goal 2—leveraging to privilege youth practices. In balancing these two goals, those in this category often expressed their indignation at how the system currently works and rail at how the system constrains the goals they choose to prioritize as well as how literacy and literacy acquisition are evaluated. Nevertheless, their commitment is defined by a willingness to engage in race, justice, and activist literacy, and a leveraging of these literacies to help their students access more mainstream practices. Their prioritization of accessing mainstream practices does not come at the expense of critical literacy, as much as it comes to its benefit. Their goal is to be the silent resistance, to push the boundaries of what they can expose their students to, and to engage in action in their classrooms without rocking the boat. But they also acknowledge the tug of war between two masters that occurs with this commitment. Their vacillation between goals is ultimately the consequence of trying to meet the objectives of an oppressive system while also trying to challenge that system through an activist praxis.

Reeducation

The second group of students can be defined by their willingness to risk more, to sacrifice more in order to more explicitly embrace a critical literacy agenda. The members of this group live out their commitment by fully embracing the privileging of youth literacy and critical literacy on par with mainstream practices. Yet, instead of taking the path of resistance, they up the ante by taking the path of reeducation. Reeducation is defined by a shared belief across this group of students that our youth have been lied to and miseducated in order to propagate dominant history, culture, and values. Thus, they personally commit to ensuring that their students are reoriented into the power of their own history, culture, language, and community.

A commitment cultivated and defined by reeducation is one that, at its core, embraces the justice and activist components of critical literacy. These teachers grapple with questions of justice and how to enact justice in their curriculum and classrooms. Their answer is to prioritize the various critical and alternative literacies of their students, while marginalizing mainstream practices. Yet they also understand that by doing this, they are making an explicit political stance, one that directly challenges the legitimacy of the American educational system and all its tenets. The inclusion of mainstream practices, as part of the curriculum, is only for its value within the code-switching milieu (Wheeler & Swords, 2004), which reframes them as essential skills for survival and navigation in a white-dominant world. Yes, these are the teachers who explicitly teach their students about code-switching because their intention is not to prepare students to leave and abdicate their responsibility to their community, but to use the tools and skills of the system to uplift their community. Although examining race, justice, and activism is a component of their literacy instruction, their ultimate goal is for their instruction to empower their students through the process of legitimizing their literacy practices, which have traditionally been characterized as deficient.

Revolution

Members of the final group define their commitment through their willingness to devote their career as literacy instructors to overthrowing the current standards and system in favor of one that is more equitable for their students. Different from the other two subgroups of students, these students have calculated that the maximum consequences are within the acceptable risks of revolution, given that the disruption they create leads to wholesale system changes that benefit their students. They ask questions. They demand answers. They make folks confront the discomforts of injustice and ask them why they remain adjusted. They attend stakeholder meetings and they are purposeful in how they empower students. They encourage unrest and protest. And they make it impossible for kids to fail.

Whereas the resistance group vacillates between privileging mainstream practices and youth practices, and the reeducation group minimizes mainstream practices in favor of youth practices, the revolution group rejects mainstream practices altogether in favor of youth practices. But what is unique about this rejection, particularly for our white students, is that it's not merely a rejection of mainstream practices but a rejection of self. What is tied into cultivating a commitment for all of our students is how they reconcile their own literacy practices with the alternative literacy practices of the youth with whom they work. It is a self-reflection process where our students have to reconcile how they privilege mainstream practices, which are intimately tied to their own identities, over the practices and literacies of their students. Our students also wrestle with their privilege, how to accept their privilege and how to use it within the cultivation of their commitment to embrace alternative literacies and explore complex issues that may make them uncomfortable. The rejection of the mainstream for those who choose revolution is a recognition of how these practices, of which they are products, have caused harm for their students. In this way, they understand how they can use their privilege toward reparation.

What distinguishes those who adopt a revolutionary mindset from the others described previously is that they see it as their responsibility to lend their voice to those who are traditionally silenced. To put it bluntly, they often adopt a savior's mentality. Though saviors, particularly white saviors, can be problematic within literacy instruction, these students remain open to the exploration of alternative literacies that are often disregarded in order to create a more inclusive learning environment. We find that this particular group of students is willing to risk more because they perceive their position and privilege to be tenable. Yet it is because they accept their own tenability and because they remain maladjusted to injustice that they are intent on wanting to overthrow the system. The blind spot for these students is that they often lack understanding of how the consequences of revolution impact those who may not enjoy the same privileges they do. As much as they are all in on the commitment, choosing to explore the meaning of race, justice, and activism within their own classrooms, they also lack vision as to the collateral effects of their commitment on students. Their privilege has sheltered them from the hidden fangs that exist in the shadows of democracy and their tenable stature ensures that they are able to recover when the tides of revolution are met with resistance. This represents one of the biggest challenges they face: how to challenge tradition while also protecting their students.

The three commitments explored in this chapter—resistance, reeducation, and revolution—are by no means an exhaustive list. Nor were these commitments mutually exclusive for our students. We find that many of them vacillate among the three commitments we identified in this chapter and others we weren't able to discuss. For our students, a key variable in defining their commitment was the context in which their commitment was required. By context, we are referring to the school where they work, the needs of their students, and current events, all variables that play an important role in how they respond to our questions and cultivate their commitment. But across all commitments is a determination to expand the traditional conception of literacy in their classrooms. In our estimation, this is a win.

REFLECTIVE QUESTIONS

1. How have you endured when it comes to the challenges of working with students who have apathy toward issues pertinent to race, justice, and activism? How has it impacted how you work with students?

2. What does it mean when our students challenge the commitment of our courses and programs to holding them accountable to a social justice commitment? How do we hold ourselves accountable to ensuring that our courses and programs "keep it 100"?

REFERENCES

Baldwin, J. (2008). A talk to teachers. *Yearbook of the National Society for the Study of Education, 107*(2), 15–20.

Bonilla-Silva, E. (2012). The invisible weight of whiteness: the racial grammar of everyday life in contemporary America. *Ethnic and Racial Studies, 35*(2), 173–194.

Conference on College Composition and Communication. (1974). Students' right to their own language. Special Issue. *CCC 25*(3), 1–32.

Dantley, M. E. (2003). Purpose-driven leadership: The spiritual imperative to guiding schools beyond high-stakes testing and minimum proficiency. *Education and Urban Society, 35*(3), 273–291.

DeBose, C. (2006). The Ebonics controversy as language planning. *International Journal of Learning, 13*(7), 89–95.

Emdin, C. (2016). *For White folks who teach in the hood . . . and the rest of y'all too: Reality pedagogy and urban education.* Boston, MA: Beacon Press.

Freire, P. (1970). *Pedagogy of the oppressed.* New York, NY: Bloomsbury Publishing USA.

Griffin, K. A., Pifer, M. J., Humphrey, J. R., & Hazelwood, A. M. (2011). (Re) defining departure: Exploring Black professors' experiences with and responses to racism and racial climate. *American Journal of Education, 117*(4), 495–526.

Hughes, T., Ononuju, I., & Okoli, G. (2020). Reinforcing administrator cultural consciousness during the social media revolution. *Oxford Encyclopedia of Administration.* Oxford, UK: Oxford University Press.

Kincheloe, J. L., Steinberg, S. R., Rodriguez, N. M., & Chennault, R. E. (Eds.). (2000). *White reign: Deploying whiteness in America.* Basingstoke, UK: Palgrave Macmillan.

King, M. L., Jr. (1963, December 18). Speech at Western Michigan University. Speech presented at West Michigan University in Kalamazoo, MI. Retrieved from: wmich.edu/sites/default/files/attachments/MLK.pdf

Kinloch, V. (2010). "To not be a traitor of Black English": Youth perceptions of language rights in an urban context. *Teachers College Record, 112*(1), 103–141.

Kristof, N. (2014, August 30). When whites just don't get it. *New York Times*, Section SR (p. 11). Retrieved from www.nytimes.com/2014/08/31/opinion/sunday/nicholas-kristof-after-ferguson-race-deserves-more-attention-not-less.html

Leonardo, Z. (2003). Discourse and critique: Outlines of a post-structural theory of ideology. *Journal of Educational Policy, 18*(2), 203–214.

Lorde, A. (1984). *Sister outsider: Essays and speeches.* Berkeley, CA: Crossing Press.

Martinez, D. C. (2017). Imagining a language of solidarity for Black and Latinx youth in English language arts classrooms. *English Education, 49*(2), 179–196.

Martinez, D. C., Morales, P. Z., & Aldana, U. S. (2017). Leveraging students' communicative repertoires as a tool for equitable learning. *Review of Research in Education, 41*, 477–499.

Martínez, R. A. (2010). "Spanglish" as literacy tool: Toward an understanding of the potential role of Spanish-English code-switching in the development of academic literacy. *Research in the Teaching of English, 45*(2), 124–149.

Moll, L. C., Amanti, C., Neff, D., & Gonzalez, N. (1992). Funds of knowledge for teaching: Using a qualitative approach to connect homes and classrooms. *Theory into Practice, 31*(2), 132–141.

Pratt, M. L. (1991). Arts of the contact zone. *Profession*, 33–40.

Rawls, J. (2009). *A theory of justice.* Cambridge, MA: Harvard University Press. (Originally published 1971)

Roediger, D. R. (1999). *The wages of whiteness: Race and the making of the American working class.* New York, NY: Verso.

Skerrett, A. (2012). Languages and literacies in translocation: Experiences and perspectives of a transnational youth. *Journal of Literacy Research, 44*(4), 364–395.

Smitherman, G. (1996). African-American English: From the hood to the amen corner. In L. Bridwell-Bowles (Ed.), *Speaker Series, 5.* Minneapolis, MN: University of Minnesota Press.

Ukpokodu, O. N. (2007). Preparing socially conscious teachers: A social justice-oriented teacher education. *Multicultural Education, 15*(1), 8–15.

Watson, V. M. (2013). Censoring freedom: Community-based professional development and the politics of profanity. *Equity & Excellence in Education, 46*(3), 387–410.

Wheeler, R. S., & Swords, R. (2004). Codeswitching: Tools of language and culture transform the dialectally diverse classroom. *Language Arts, 81*, 470–480.

Yancy, G. (2012). *Look, a white!: Philosophical essays on whiteness.* Philadelphia, PA: Temple University Press.

Yang, P. (2010). Hmomglish [sic] in urban high school classes: A code mixing case study of four Hmong high school students. *School of Education Student Capstone Theses and Dissertations*, 413.

Zisselsberger, M. (2016). Toward a humanizing pedagogy: Leveling the cultural and linguistic capital in a fifth-grade writing classroom. *Bilingual Research Journal, 39*(2), 121–137.

CHAPTER 4

Rethinking Curriculum and Pedagogy in Schools

Critical Literacies and Epistemologies in Theory and Practice

Limarys Caraballo and Lindsey Lichtenberger

According to Noguera (2009), "students often possess insights into their educational experience that adults either do not understand or simply are not privy to" (p. 18). He argues, "In most research into policy and school reform initiatives, particularly in education, youth are treated as the passive objects" (p. 18). Without students' own voices and perspectives, educational reform may continue to miss the mark, leading to waves of initiatives that only partially address the complex issues educators face in schools today, and at worst, may create a wider gulf between students and the educators who shape their academic trajectories. Similarly, in this increasingly standardized and high-stakes accountability context of teaching, in which teachers may be deemed highly effective (or not) based strictly on students' test scores (Achieve, 2009) and where literacy is often narrowly defined as "neutral" skills in reading comprehension and composition (National Governors Association, 2013), teachers are often excluded from initiatives that are designed to improve learning outcomes. It is therefore crucial for current and future teachers, and their students, to engage in collaborative inquiries to address the educational issues that affect them.

In this chapter, the first author (Limarys) draws upon qualitative data from a long-term study of Cyphers for Justice, an after-school program that centers youth culture, multiple literacies, and critical social theory grounded in a youth participatory action research (YPAR) framework. As a preservice teacher and co-researcher, the second author (Lindsey) examines her engagement with YPAR in the after-school program, and her more traditional student teaching experience, reflecting on how both inform her perspectives about curriculum and pedagogy. Building from this analysis of preservice teachers' identities and experiences in a space in which students and educators engage in dialogue and critical analysis on key social and educational issues, we propose a (re)framing of literacy teacher education that centers justice and activism as integral to culturally sustaining curricular and pedagogical stances (Paris, 2012; Paris & Alim, 2014).

THEORETICAL ORIENTATIONS FOR YPAR IN THE CONTEXT OF TEACHER PREPARATION

Policies and mandates such as No Child Left Behind and Race to the Top, along with various state and local accountability measures, have increasingly limited teachers' autonomy and breadth of experience with curriculum and pedagogy as a result of the pressure of high-stakes assessments, particularly in urban schools (Costigan, 2008; Tanner, 2013). This narrowing of curriculum and assessment exacerbates the disconnect between a predominantly white and monolingual teaching force (Zumwalt & Craig, 2008) and an increasingly diverse, multicultural, and multilingual student population (Aud et al., 2012) whose rich cultures (Moll & Gonzalez, 2004), languages (Martinez, 2010), and literacies are frequently overlooked in mainstream educational contexts (Guerra, 2008).

In contrast, YPAR builds on decades of participatory action research and consists of the collective investigation of a problem. Also, it relies on the knowledge of those most directly affected or involved, is driven by a desire to take action, and engages youth in addressing issues of social inequality (Morrell, 2004, 2006). In the first study to document PAR with youth, McIntyre (2000) argues for the power of "engaging in a process that positions youth as agents of inquiry and as 'experts' about their own lives" (p. 126). YPAR projects can engage students and their teachers in rigorous research as part of a radical effort to broaden the field's understanding of inquiry-based knowledge production. Such projects must be led not just by scholars in academic institutions, but also by the students and teachers who directly experience the educational contexts that scholars, practitioners, and policymakers endeavor to understand.

However, such research is often excluded from teacher education in favor of debates regarding state certification requirements (Darling-Hammond & Youngs, 2002), instructional "best practices" (Morrow, Gambrell, & Duke, 2011), strategies to increase students' performance on standardized assessments (Heck, 2007), mainstream readings of course texts (Haddix & Rojas, 2011; Kinloch, 2011), and essayist "academic" literacies (Burroughs & Smagorinsky, 2009). This chapter draws from interdisciplinary areas of research and scholarship that broaden conceptualizations of teaching and learning in teacher education, to include participatory and action research (Cochran-Smith & Lytle, 1992; Fine, Roberts, & Torre, 2004; Rubin & Jones, 2007); multicultural fieldwork experiences (Brayko, 2013; Whipp, 2010); and the interrelatedness of curriculum experiences, identities, and literacies (Luttrell & Parker, 2001). Building upon these alternative critical approaches, YPAR privileges the firsthand experiences and knowledge production of students, teachers, and communities, positioning them as agents of social change (Fine et al., 2004; Morrell, 2008).

Similar to participatory action research (PAR), YPAR represents "a new paradigm, a challenge to existing epistemologies, and, thereby, a competing (or complementary) entry into the political economy of knowledge production" (Noffke, 1997, p. 307). Thus, YPAR is both a critical research methodology that carries specific epistemological commitments regarding who is "allowed" to conduct and disseminate research in actionable ways, and also a pedagogical framework based on a conception of teaching and learning through collaborative inquiry. Morrell (2006) traces the roots of PAR and YPAR to Brazilian educator Paulo Freire, who argued that meaningful transformation and change must occur in collaboration with everyday people who make a "conscious effort to disrupt or call into question this paradigm of knowledge production" (Freire, 1990, pp. 6–7).

Our approach to YPAR draws from critical sociocultural theories and cultural studies, framing identities and literacies as constructed in the context of practice within figured, or cultural, worlds (Caraballo, 2011; Holland, Lachicotte, Skinner, & Cain, 1998). Through an identities-in-practice lens, which encompasses practice theories from various disciplines such as anthropology, sociology, linguistics, and cultural studies, identities are constructed continuously as individuals act upon and are acted upon in given cultural realms or figured worlds (Holland et al., 1998). A figured world is a "realm of interpretation" in which "a particular set of characters and actors," such as teachers or students, "are recognized, [where] significance is assigned to certain acts, and particular outcomes are valued over others" (Holland et al., 1998, p. 52). Like a cultural world, which is defined by cultural norms in particular settings, a figured world may be conceptualized as the interpretive realm that permeates a given context. As a figured world, the context of critical participation in the YPAR after-school program is not just a physical space but also a culturally mediated environment in which youth and preservice teachers may construct identities and literacies as researchers and as agents of change. As documented in the preservice teachers' narratives shared throughout this chapter, these situated identities and literacies are critical tools with which to address the power relations outside as well as within the YPAR space.

CYPHERS FOR JUSTICE: A MULTIMODAL RESEARCH COLLABORATIVE

Led by a collaborative of researchers and teaching artists, Cyphers for Justice (CFJ) is an intergenerational YPAR program situated across multiple sites. One of the sites is an early college YPAR seminar course for high school students offered as part of the College Now program at Queens College, City University of New York (CUNY). The second is an after-school program hosted by the Institute for Urban and Minority Education at Teachers College,

Columbia University (IUME). In both sites, the curriculum focuses on YPAR as method and praxis, framed by multiple rhetorical modes such as hip-hop, spoken word, and digital media. In this seminar, youth have opportunities to explore a topic and communicate their perspectives in ways that expand ideas about literacy, and they learn about research alongside preservice teachers who observe and assist in the seminar as part of their fieldwork requirements. The seminar is co-facilitated by teaching artists who support youth in using their home literacies and preferred forms of creative expression to shape their re-search and engage others in social action about issues they care about. Once their projects are complete, students have the opportunity to present their re-search at multiple venues, including professional development workshops and academic conferences. Both youth and future educators participate in a figured world that is very different from the typical classroom (Caraballo & Lyiscott, 2018). As part of the YPAR course and after-school program, students and pre-service teacher facilitators read about critical social theory and participatory action research methods. Thus, the seminar deliberately seeks to disrupt some of the hierarchies that tend to regulate mainstream classrooms.

With preservice teachers as collaborators, CFJ engages youth in every phase of inquiry, from design, implementation, and critical reflection to analysis and performance. As Luke (1995) argues, "every text is a kind of institutional speech act—a social action with language with a particular shape and features, force, audience, and consequences" (p. 15). Agreeing with Luke's understanding of "text" allows us to situate literacy as social practice and to center the intersec-tion of identities and literacy experiences as they inform the consumption and creation of oral and written texts. In this way, the YPAR curriculum introduces students and preservice teachers to traditional research methods and explores opportunities for them to report and act on research results by using a range of rhetorical modes, from digital literacies to hip-hop and spoken word. As Freire and Macedo (1987) succinctly stated, literacy is that which pertains to students' readings of the "word" and the "world"—their responses to texts and the texts that they create offer insights into students' identities and positionalities as situated in racialized contexts, whether they be in schools or beyond.

RESEARCH DESIGN, DATA COLLECTION METHODS, AND ANALYSIS

The long-term qualitative study[1] that informed this chapter addressed iden-tities, literacies, and discourses as interrelated, inviting students and preser-vice teachers' cultural and experiential perspectives on education and social change into ongoing debates in curriculum, pedagogy, and teacher education across multiple educational contexts. Drawing from both the College Now and IUME research sites, all members of our research collaborative partici-pate in the qualitative examination of the experiences of high school students and preservice teachers in the context of the YPAR seminars. The purposes of this ongoing inquiry are to (1) engage students and undergraduate preservice teachers in critical participatory action research projects that recognize and develop their multiple literacies to enact social change, and (2) examine how the students and preservice teachers' YPAR experiences inform their perceptions about identities, literacies, curriculum, and achievement.

PRESERVICE TEACHERS' EXPERIENCES IN THE YPAR SEMINAR

As part of the weekly after-school YPAR seminars, the students and preservice teachers were introduced to participatory action research theory and methods in order to support the development of critical, culturally sustaining perspectives. In the figured world of the YPAR seminar and the academic institutions in which they are nested, students' and preservice teachers' narratives about their experiences with YPAR addressed how their perspectives on curriculum, pedagogy, and social action were mediated by their own multiple identities, as well as by their work as researchers in schools and communities. Their engagement in the YPAR context disrupted some of the divisions between various roles (student, educator, institution) within this cultural world, and also disturbed hierarchies of power and knowledge in and beyond institutions. Themes that emerge from the data indicated that students, preservice teachers, and researchers experienced the YPAR seminars as an empowering context in which all participants, regardless of their role, constructed new knowledge(s).

One key theme was the connection between preservice teachers' collaborative work with students in the YPAR seminars and their ideas about mainstream classroom instruction. For example, Jazmine, a preservice English teacher, constructed an identity as a researcher fairly early in the program, recognizing that "students' engagement with critical social issues shapes literary curriculum and instruction by allowing students the opportunity to discuss and research questions we as educators are continually asking ourselves." For Jazmine, these experiences led to generative dialogue about the roles and purposes of curriculum, pedagogy, and teacher preparation with other team members and, eventually, with her new colleagues when she began her full-time teaching position.

Having participated in a YPAR project as a preservice teacher, as a new teacher Jazmine began to seek ways to establish a YPAR group in the school where she was hired. In one of the YPAR sessions Jazmine shared with her students that she decided to co-facilitate the group, despite all the pressures of being a first-year teacher. She wanted the students to know that she cared about their lives and experiences outside of school would help create a context of participation and engagement. During a warm-up activity, Jazmine shared her own racialized high school and college experiences with the group. She made explicit how she came to understand that her experience as a Latina from an underprivileged background contributed to her teachers' low expectations. She also underscored that there were key teachers and professors who cared about her and did not let her give up when she felt overwhelmed. Ana (pseudonym), one of Jazmine's high school students, who joined the newly formed group, commented that it was "helpful to have opportunities like this YPAR group because it's an opportunity to focus on things we wouldn't be able to focus on in our regular classes." Jazmine later reflected on how the YPAR seminars not only offered her students individual support, but also encouraged them to begin engaging with the issues that shaped teaching and learning at their school, such as the stratifying effect of course scheduling and the exclusion of critical and relevant cultural and racial perspectives from the humanities curricula.

A second strand of the inquiry focused on how teachers engaged with students in the YPAR space to develop research tools for youth to learn more about issues that are relevant to them, especially when these issues are not recognized or discussed in school. For example, teachers' theoretical orientations, beliefs, and practices tend to be steeped in normative whiteness that guides instructional decisions and expectations about student behavior, especially because teacher evaluation frequently normalizes whiteness (Salazar, 2018). Furthermore, the experiences of Students of Color from lower socioeconomic backgrounds are more likely to be informed by teachers' low expectations (Goodwin, 2010). Focusing her analysis specifically on student work and recordings from 24 YPAR sessions during the period from September 2014 through February 2015, Yeila, a preservice Spanish language teacher and co-researcher in the project who identified as Latina, saw a direct link between her research and her future as an educator:

> While talking to some of the youth apprentices working on their particular project, I realized the power teachers have to change students' lives. I have to admit that my initial clinical experience in middle school has made me rethink about my philosophy of teaching. . . . However, the passion and commitment demonstrated points toward an issue that is rarely addressed in classrooms settings either in college or high school, the ability youth have to explore, investigate, and to put into action the results they obtain. I was in awe just by listening to the amazing ideas young people have about the issues that affect their communities and how eager they are to make a difference in their communities. . . . This experience means a huge change in how I look at my work not only as a teacher but also as researcher. . . . I learned . . . that true education is situated within a reciprocal relationship between the community, the classroom, and the university. I have realized that learning is not a one-way action; that teachers can learn from their students in the same way students learn from their teachers, based on experiences, mutual interaction, and respect for other people's opinions.

Thus, beyond its role as a critical research methodology that carries specific epistemological commitments regarding who is invited to conduct and disseminate research in actionable ways, preservice teachers found direct connections to their own education philosophy and pedagogy. As a result, YPAR can be a lens that informs pedagogical and research frameworks (Caraballo & Lyiscott, 2018).

A third theme suggests that preservice teachers construct identities as researchers and develop dispositions toward teaching in the context of the YPAR space. These dispositions and commitments, as addressed in Lindsey's inquiry below, extended beyond the figured world of YPAR as they informed her perspectives on curriculum and pedagogy as well as her relationships with students.

LINDSEY'S INQUIRY WITH/IN YPAR

Adolescents are often depicted in movies, television shows, and real life as having bad attitudes and being lazy, self-involved, and disengaged from learning (Lesko, 1996). But in my experience, the youth in the YPAR program seemed to want to learn *more* than what was being taught to them. They wanted to learn about their civil rights, their heritage and cultures, current events, and more—areas that are sometimes left out in a typical school curriculum.

As an undergraduate education student, I spent 3 and a half years studying "best practices" for teaching secondary students. While we were introduced to many different teaching methods, the most prevalent were using visuals, incorporating technology, having students figure things out for themselves rather than lecturing, and so on. But what was missing were ways to learn about what youth themselves want and need. What we did not master, as prospective educators, was how to incorporate the topics that individual students wanted to learn about within an already-predetermined curriculum. We tend to teach students that what they say matters, that they can be whatever they set their minds on, but our actions as educators don't always match our message of self-efficacy. How do we follow a curriculum that is designed based on the state tests, address students' questions about what they find important, and still complete the lesson prepared?

Inquiry Phase I: Student Teaching

At the time of this writing, I had completed my first student teaching semester in an English language learners (ELLs) class, teaching world history. My cooperating (mentor) teacher assured me that teaching to the test was most important when creating a lesson plan, stating, "If it's not on the test, we don't teach it." To me, that made no sense—teaching to a state-mandated test explicitly seems to deprive students of things that can offer them a new perspective or even help them once they leave the classroom. It can limit what questions they can ask, and what opinions they may voice if given the chance.

As educators, we teach students life skills, theories, facts, and things that have happened before, assuming these things will help students understand their current and future world. As a white woman, I was especially interested in how we teach about literacy and historical texts, as people in power dictate history and nondominant groups and women have been left out. There were so many notable events (and from varying perspectives) we could have discussed during my student teaching practicum, which occurred in the spring of 2016 during the U.S. presidential campaign, but most of them were ignored in the classroom where I co-taught. One monumental event that did get discussed was the presidential debate, and most students were fearful because the majority of them were immigrants, but their status and concerns were ignored. While the ethical and racial questions raised in the debate could have been incorporated and connected to racial issues already within the curriculum, because there wouldn't be a question about this on the Regents exam, these issues had no place in the curriculum.

Although my first classroom experience was with English language learners, and my students had traveled from all over the world to come to America for various reasons, I felt that they were not positioned to teach one another. Because it was a world history class, we learned about countries around the world, so it would only make sense to ask the students the history they knew from their countries. Each time students heard the history of their birthplace, they perked up and participated. But their firsthand knowledge and personal experience were also ignored because those subjects were not going to be on the test.

The teacher–student relationships took a toll as well. The overcrowded classrooms and state tests made it almost impossible to build any type of trusting connection with students. From my own experience of student teaching in a classroom of 30 ELL students, I can say that I was able to form a close bond with each of the students only because I was there for a double period with the same students every day. When I got there a few weeks into school, my cooperating teacher was struggling to remember their names—but she also taught six different classes, with more than 100 students to remember. As the second teacher in the classroom, with only one class to worry about, it was easier for me to focus on the students and figure out what worked best for them.

When my time with my first high school class came to an end, I wanted to give them a meaningful good-bye. I wrote each of my 30 students a personalized letter; I spent a few weeks writing them, each only a page long, but I wanted to make sure what I said mattered to each individual student. After I handed them out, I told them the letters were unique, just like all of them. They didn't believe me; they didn't believe that I would spend that much time on something for them. One profound moment for me was when one of my ELL students, whose letter I had translated into Spanish, came up to me with a tear in his eye and said thank you, and gave me a hug. I felt that was my first accomplishment as an educator.

Students told me they felt that no one showed them they cared about what they had to say—and they were 10th-graders. That was one of the most depressing statements I had ever heard. Because of their different home languages, they had few opportunities to experiment or choose their literacy projects, and they had limited opportunities to share their perspectives about social issues or the curriculum. In many schools, where "newcomer/new American students are too often exposed to programs that neither value their cultural and linguistic richness nor embrace their identities as assets for their learning" (Gee, cited in Dover & Rodríguez-Valls, 2018, p. 60), culturally responsive relationships between students and teachers can help change the course of students' lives and enrich our own experiences as educators. These examples helped me focus on why I wanted to be a teacher in the first place, and aim to work toward a system that allows all to thrive.

Inquiry Phase II

In 2015–2016, I participated in two after-school YPAR seminars. Both classes followed YPAR frameworks, but each seminar was different because of the location, time constraints, and the priorities of the youth involved. The youth were assured that what they had to say mattered, that their voices and ideas could lead to change—that it was up to them to transform society. Below, I focus mainly on the YPAR seminar that was taught on my college campus as an enrichment course for high school students via the CUNY College Now program in New York City.

As a teaching strategy, YPAR can create opportunities for students' voices to be heard. It allows them to speak and act openly on social issues. Some topics may make youth feel uncomfortable: racism, bullying, violence, standardized testing, LGBTQ rights, and others. YPAR makes the conscious effort to enact change, to stop the tireless lecturing that has been common in classrooms. These students form their own projects surrounding a social issue that they feel most strongly about, along with other students who feel the same. They then collect their own data after learning multiple strategies on how to do so. Their ideas are backed up with evidence, whether it be statistics or interviews. This means that what they are saying not only matters, but is also based on facts and actual experiences.

The YPAR college course was designed to allow high school students to experience a typical college-level workload, while also being exposed to completely new teaching methods and classroom expectations. The class was based on one semester where the students learned about coding data, presentation techniques, and how to collect data properly, which they combined into an engaging presentation on their research. They were also able to learn about spoken word and the power it can have in moving an audience when it is incorporated into a presentation. Then they learned how to analyze videos and make their own movies to communicate their perspectives and share research findings. In creating these multimodal projects, which included their own short films, they accomplished what many of them thought they would not be able to do when they began the course. Also, they learned that just having a standard PowerPoint may not be enough to convince someone of what they have to say. Convincing someone that change is necessary sometimes takes more than just words.

During my time in the College Now YPAR seminar, I was not only observing but also co-facilitating. There were multiple preservice teachers in attendance who were able to complete their observation requirements prior to student teaching, while also helping actual students. Each of the preservice teachers was matched with a group of students working on a group project centralized around one issue related to educational justice. Some of the examples from this particular class included overcrowding, bullying, and standardized state testing. My own group explored violence in schools. The preservice teachers' role was to help the students brainstorm and design the inquiry.

As one of five preservice teachers who served as co-facilitators in the YPAR class, I was there to support students who had never conducted research in this way before, and also to learn about YPAR along with my peers. I was an extra support for both the students and the YPAR instructor. This is something uncommon in public schools today because in many cases the student–teacher ratio is 1:30 or more students. This makes it harder for students to get the help they need, to ask the questions they have, and for a teacher–student relationship to form. In this class, however, each group of students worked with a preservice teacher throughout the entire project. Because I worked with one group closely, I will draw on that group for evidence to support my claims about the importance of YPAR.

I worked with three young women in high school: Emily, Alondra, and Nicole, two sophomores and one senior, respectively (all names are pseudonyms). The group was formed because all of them were interested in the root causes of violence. All three went to the same high school in Queens, New York, so their experiences with violence in schools were all very similar. They were especially interested in the psychological issues that might provoke students to resort to violence, such as abuse at home, the desire to feel superior, and the need to "fit in." This was the groundwork for their project. I was having a discussion with the group about the psychological factors behind why someone would want to bring a gun to school. Being that over the past few years, mass shootings and school shootings had frequently been in the news, my students asked me if this had ever happened before, and I mentioned the Columbine shootings of 1999. They looked at me perplexed; they had never heard of the Columbine shootings before. I was surprised that this was the first time they were hearing about it, but I explained what happened and then we searched for news articles and investigative journals about the incident. Soon, they found that, statistically, mass shootings are not new; they are just more frequently televised these days. The students were able to embed new decisive evidence into their own projects. This consisted of environmental or external factors as well as the notion of mental illness playing a role in violence.

Each group was tasked with coming up with research questions, a goal, and a mission statement. This was daunting at first glance, but with the help of the preservice teachers, it was able to come together smoothly. There were certain difficulties along the road, as is typical with group-work. Emily and Alondra were already friends, and when they became overwhelmed with personal issues, the third group member was working on her own until facilitators were able to help them get back on track. Ultimately, their project was highly successful and the course instructor shared with me that their "paper was [on] the level of a college student, and their project was moving and entertaining." They succeeded in using methods they never used before. They created a PowerPoint and used statistics to support their ideas, but they also included short video clips, images, and a film they created themselves. This led them to feel like they could successfully try new things, even those that seem daunting.

I believe these students were successful because they were able not only to engage in a project of their choosing, but because they were able to ask as many questions as they needed. They were guided when they needed to be, and the classroom flowed better because the students didn't have to wait in line to get help or more instruction. They were able to come out on top because they were told they had something to contribute.

As its own class, the YPAR program was able to focus just on what the students wanted, just on what they found interesting. Other researchers and teachers have written about integrating youth culture, especially hip-hop culture, into classroom practices and school-sponsored extracurricular activities, with some similarities to the work we did in our YPAR program (King, 2013). From my perspective as a history and humanities teacher, I know that drawing from literacies that build upon students' own experiences and forms of communication can create a connection between a past they'll never personally experience and their own lives. This type of project can be infused into a curriculum that is already in place, perhaps focusing on racial issues in schools and communities while using a historical basis and current statistics as well as personal statements from community members. Youth who have grown up reading mainly about the accomplishments of middle- and upper-class white people would have the opportunity to expand their knowledge and present their own viewpoints, essentially writing their own historical truths. This would be a project I could develop in my own classroom after students have some background knowledge about a particular topic. There needs to be a balance—educators can't ignore the state tests, but students can't pretend to be excited about something when they are not. In both my student teaching course and YPAR seminar, the one thing in common was that young people felt passionately about the world they live in, and wanted a chance to show what they were capable of doing.

Making "Sense" of Preservice Field Experiences in YPAR Contexts

As Jazmine, Yeila, and Lindsey reflected, their experiences with YPAR challenged them to expand their perspectives regarding their students and their teaching. They found that working through the key stages of a YPAR inquiry, and engaging with youth in the collaborative figured world of YPAR, can challenge existing perceptions about literacy education. On one hand, the opportunity for preservice teachers to experience the figured world of YPAR with youth as fellow learners and co-researchers interrupts and disrupts existing binaries between teacher/learner and researcher/participant, as Lindsey describes above. Our findings support the development of a working model for undergraduate preservice fieldwork in seminars that incorporate YPAR theory and methods to contribute to the curricular and pedagogical knowledge base in teacher education.

Second, by juxtaposing their own participation in traditional classrooms and in collaborative YPAR seminars, preservice teachers can also begin to expose false dichotomies between academic readiness and the literacies claimed and practiced by Youth of Color. These dichotomies bear witness to the pervasiveness of racial and linguistic prejudice, as well as its impact on students' academic and social identities. For example, in her work with 6th-grade Mexican-origin girls in an after-school participatory action research (PAR) project on teen pregnancy, Martinez (2006) notes that although the girls in the study were high achievers in a magnet program, their participation in the classes she observed was unenthusiastic and somewhat peripheral. Ana, a student with one of the highest averages in her class, expressed that "she was not sure about her academic abilities" (p. 163). Another student, Maria Elena, was often upset when her teacher scolded her for using Spanish. By contrast, in the YPAR project, the girls demonstrated that they "took up school-sanctioned literacy activities of reading and writing competently" and were "readers and writers in the school sense" (p. 161). These 6th-grade high achievers, engaged in the ongoing process of constructing their academic, linguistic, and ethnic identities in practice, were arguably unsupported in the more overtly racialized figured world of the classroom, in part perhaps because the teachers were unaware of their experiences. Though teachers cannot address every issue that students face, literacy educators should feel prepared to recognize tensions related to students' experiences with languages and literacies, broadly defined, and reflect on how the curriculum and their own pedagogies can exacerbate them.

Beyond introducing students and preservice teachers to participatory action theories and methods and supporting the development of critical, culturally sustaining perspectives, our seminars engaged preservice educators in conversations about epistemological, curricular, and pedagogical issues—such as what counts as "literacy" learning, whose knowledge matters in curriculum, how teaching nurtures or inhibits students' agency, and how educators' positionalities inform teaching—that are typically debated only by educational scholars. In particular, the figured world of YPAR offered a generative space in which preservice teachers could interrogate their own racial identities, which is seldom discussed by white teachers, despite their demographic majority in the U.S. teaching force (Zumwalt & Craig, 2008). Rather than addressing race as if it pertained only to People of Color, we must, as Kinloch argues, leverage "what we know about whiteness (the superficiality of whiteness as a checklist) and center on how to better engage in antiracist practices by focusing on racial identities, social context, and power" (Kinloch & Lensmire, 2019, p. 123). Furthermore, in the midst of current polarizing and dehumanizing rhetoric about race and immigration in the United States and other globalized societies, teachers' interrogation of their own identities and positionalities is crucial to exposing the normalization of whiteness in educational structures and institutions.

Because YPAR can expose these and other complexities of collaborative spaces and intersections among youth, preservice teachers, and teacher educators from various backgrounds, it can also decentralize existing norms that constrict learning, creativity, and voice. These complexities are central to the work of YPAR in its capacity to decolonize educational spaces in order to learn from the authentic interactions between youth and the educators who care for and about them (Lyiscott, Caraballo, & Morrell, 2018). Via YPAR, the process of conscientization (Freire, 1970), a necessary counternarrative against the neoliberal rhetoric of colorblindness, is shared among students, teachers, and teacher educators.

IMPLICATIONS FOR TEACHER EDUCATION AND BEYOND

Educational "reforms" increasingly limit teachers' autonomy and breadth of experience with curriculum and pedagogy as a result of the pressure of high-stakes assessments, particularly in urban schools (Costigan, 2008; Tanner, 2013). Parallel to Ball's (2009) theory of generative change in professional development, engaging preservice teachers and students in YPAR projects disrupts hierarchies among cultural and experiential knowledge(s) and "official" or disciplinary knowledge(s), and contributes to authentic learning for students from all backgrounds and contexts (Milner, 2013). It also (re)frames teacher education and ongoing teacher development as a project of educational justice. In the long term, rethinking curriculum and pedagogy through a YPAR lens can advance the development of literacy teacher preparation and professional development programs to equip future and current teachers not only to meet the curriculum standards of districts and states, but also to incorporate the cultural and community resources of students from marginalized communities via culturally sustaining curriculum and pedagogies (Paris, 2012; Paris & Alim, 2014).

As a critical research methodology that carries specific epistemological commitments regarding who is invited to conduct and disseminate research in actionable ways, YPAR can be a lens that informs pedagogical frameworks. Our analysis promotes a critical broadening of preservice teachers' conceptions of youth, literacies, and social action, and extends the current scope of research and scholarship in teacher preparation by rethinking curriculum, pedagogy, and teacher education as collaborative and democratic endeavors with, rather than for, youth (Caraballo & Lyiscott, 2018). More broadly, this line of inquiry extends and problematizes the current scope of research and scholarship in teacher education and professional development and addresses deeper questions about the role of student voice in curriculum and pedagogy (Cook-Sather, 2017; Cook-Sather, Bovill, & Felten, 2014). This work illuminates frequently overlooked complexities at the intersection of classroom instruction, social justice, and schooling, and introduces preservice teachers to the possibilities of critical research.

Although such intersections enrich the curricular experiences of students from all backgrounds in a global society, there is particular urgency in incorporating such experiences for teachers preparing to enter diverse classrooms. While YPAR can expand pedagogical possibilities in general (Cammarota & Fine, 2008), access to YPAR experiences is particularly impactful for youth from historically marginalized populations whose rich experiences, identities, and literacies are often excluded in traditional and increasingly standardized educational contexts. By creating spaces in which students and teachers may engage in dialogue and critical analysis on key social and educational issues, our work builds upon recent critical youth research (Kinloch, 2012; McIntyre, 2000) to catalyze a (re)framing of literacy teacher education that promotes culturally sustaining curricular and pedagogical stances and facilitates students' construction of identities and literacies as researchers and agents of change—all in the interest of educational equity and social justice.

REFLECTIVE QUESTIONS

1. In what concrete ways can youth research and activism transform literacy curriculum and pedagogy in schools?

2. How can educators be supported to reflect on their own identities and positionalities, especially amid the constraints of state certification requirements and/or mandatory teacher evaluation frameworks?

NOTE

1. The study has been approved by the institution's Internal Review Board.

REFERENCES

Achieve. (2009). Teacher effectiveness. *Race to the Top: Accelerating college and career readiness in states.* Retrieved from achieve.org/RacetotheTop

Aud, S., Hussar, W., Johnson, F., Kena, G., Roth, E., Manning, E., . . . National Center for Education Statistics (Eds.). (2012). *The condition of education 2012.* NCES 2012-045. National Center for Education Statistics.

Ball, A. F. (2009). Toward a theory of generative change in culturally and linguistically complex classrooms. *American Educational Research Journal, 46*(1), 45–72. doi:10.3102/0002831208323277

Brayko, K. (2013). Community-based placements as contexts for disciplinary learning: A study of literacy teacher education outside of school. *Journal of Teacher Education, 64*(1), 47–59. doi: 10.1177/0022487112458800.

Burroughs, R., & Smagorinsky, P. (2009). The secondary English curriculum and adolescent literacy. In L. Christenbury, R. Bomer, & P. Smagorinsky (Eds.), *Handbook of adolescent literacy research* (pp. 170–182). New York, NY: Guilford Press.

Cammarota, J., & Fine, M. (Eds.). (2008). *Revolutionizing education: Youth participatory action research in motion.* New York, NY: Routledge

Caraballo, L. (2011). Theorizing identities in a "just(ly)" contested terrain: Practice theories of identity amid critical-poststructural debates on curriculum and achievement. *Journal of Curriculum and Pedagogy, 8*(2), 155–177. doi: 10.1080/15505170.2011.624939

Caraballo, L., & Lyiscott, J. (2018). Collaborative inquiry: Youth, social action, and critical qualitative research. *Action Research,* 1–18. doi: 10.1177/1476750317752819

Cochran-Smith, M., & Lytle, S. (1992). Communities for teacher research: Fringe or forefront. *American Journal of Education, 100*(3), 298–324.

Cook-Sather, A. (2017). Students as co-creators of teaching approaches, course design, and curricula: implications for academic developers. *Journal of Educational Innovation, Partnership and Change, 4*(1), 1–4.

Cook-Sather, A., Bovill, C., & Felten, P. (2014). *Engaging students as partners in teaching & learning: A guide for faculty.* San Francisco, CA: Jossey-Bass.

Costigan, A. T. (2008). Canaries in the coal mine: Urban rookies learning to teach language arts in "high priority" schools. *Teacher Education Quarterly,* 85–103.

Darling-Hammond, L., & Youngs, P. (2002). Defining "highly qualified teachers": What does "scientifically-based research" actually tell us? *Educational Researcher, 31,* 13–25. doi: 10.3102/0013189X031009013

Dover, A. G., & Rodríguez-Valls, F. (2018). Learning to "brave up": Collaboration, agency, and authority in multicultural, multilingual, and radically inclusive classrooms. *International Journal of Multicultural Education, 20*(3), 59–79.

Fine, M., Roberts, R. A., & Torre, M. E. (2004). *Echoes of Brown: Youth documenting and performing the legacy of* Brown v. Board of Education. New York, NY: Teachers College Press.

Freire, P. (1970). *Pedagogy of the oppressed.* New York, NY: Continuum International Publishing Group.

Freire, P. & Macedo, D. (1987) *Literacy: Reading the word and the world,* New York, NY: Bergin and Garvey.

Goodwin, A. L. (2010). Globalization and the preparation of quality teachers: Rethinking knowledge domains for teaching. *Teaching Education, 21*(1), 19–32

Guerra, J. C. (2008). Cultivating transcultural citizenship: A Writing across Communities model. *Language Arts, 85*(4), 296–304.

Haddix, M. M., & Rojas, M. A. (2011). (Re)Framing teaching in urban classrooms: A poststructural (re)reading of critical literacy as curricular and pedagogical practice. In V. Kinloch (Ed.), *Urban literacies: Critical perspectives on language, learning, and community* (pp. 111–124). New York, NY: Teachers College Press.

Heck, R. H. (2007). Examining the relationship between teacher quality as an organizational property of schools and students' achievement and growth rates. *Educational Administration Quarterly, 43*, 399–432. doi:10.1177/0013161X07306452

Holland, D., Lachicotte, W., Skinner, D., & Cain, C. (1998). *Identity and agency in cultural worlds*. Cambridge, MA: Harvard University Press.

King, J. M. (2013). *Expanding literacies with students: Youth participatory action research (YPAR) in a school-based setting*. Unpublished doctoral dissertation, University of Rochester, Rochester, New York.

Kinloch, V., & Lensmire, T. (2019). A dialogue on race, racism, white privilege, and white supremacy in English education. *English Education, 51*(2), 116–125.

Kinloch, V. F. (Ed.) (2011). *Urban literacies: Critical perspectives on language, learning, and community*. New York, NY: Teachers College Press.

Kinloch, V. F. (2012). *Crossing boundaries: Teaching and learning with urban youth*. New York, NY: Teachers College Press.

Lesko, N. (1996). Past, present, and future conceptions of adolescence. *Educational Theory, 46*(4), 453–473.

Luke, A. (1995). *Educational policy, narrative and discourse*. New York, NY: Routledge.

Luttrell, W., & Parker, C. (2001). High school students' literacy practices and identities, and the figured world of school. *Journal of Research in Reading, 24*(3), 235–247.

Lyiscott, J. J., Caraballo, L., & Morrell, E. (2018). An anticolonial framework for urban teacher preparation. *The New Educator*, 1–21. doi:10.1080/1547688X.2017.1412000

Martinez, L. R. (2006). *Mexican-origin girls as researchers: Exploring identity and difference in a participatory action research project*. Doctoral dissertation, University of Texas at Austin, Austin, Texas.

Martinez, R. A. (2010). Spanglish as literacy tool: Toward an understanding of the potential role of Spanish-English code-switching in the development of academic literacy. *Research in the Teaching of English, 45*(2), 124–149.

McIntyre, A. (2000). Constructing meaning about violence, school, and community: Participatory action research with urban youth. *The Urban Review, 32*(2), 123–154.

Milner, H. R. (2013). Rethinking achievement gap talk in urban education. *Urban Education, 48*(1), 3–8.

Moll, L., & Gonzalez, N. (2004). Engaging life: A funds-of-knowledge approach to multicultural education. In J. A. Banks & C. A. M. Banks (Eds.), *Handbook of research on multicultural education* (2nd ed., pp. 699–715). San Francisco, CA: Jossey-Bass.

Morrell, E. (2004). *Becoming critical researchers: Literacy and empowerment of urban youth*. New York, NY: Peter Lang.

Morrell, E. (2006). Critical participatory action research and the literacy achievement of ethnic minority groups. In J. V. Hoffman, D. L. Schallert, C. M. Fairbanks, J. Worthy & B. Maloda (Eds.), *55th yearbook of the National Reading Conference* (pp. 1–18). Oak Creek, WI: National Reading Conference.

Morrell, E. (2008). Six summers of YPAR: Learning, action, and change in urban education. In J. Cammarota & M. Fine (Eds.), *Revolutionizing education: Youth participatory action research in motion* (pp. 155–187). New York, NY: Routledge.

Morrell, E., Duenas, R., Garcia, V., & Lopez, J. (2013). *Critical media pedagogy: Teaching for achievement in city schools*. New York, NY: Teachers College Press.

Morrow, L. M., Gambrell, L. B., & Duke, N. K. (2011). *Best practices in literacy instruction* (4th ed.). New York, NY: Guilford Press.

National Governors Association Center for Best Practices & Council of Chief State School Officers. (2013). *Common Core State Standards*. Washington, DC: Authors.

Noffke, S. E. (1997). Professional, personal, and political dimensions of action research. *Review of Research in Education, 22*, 305–343. doi: 10.3102/0091732X022001305

Noguera, P. (2009). Special issue foreword. *New Directions for Youth Development* (123), 15–18. doi: 10.1002/yd.311

Paris, D. (2012). Culturally sustaining pedagogy: A needed change in stance, terminology, and practice. *Educational Researcher, 41*(3), 93–97.

Paris, D., & Alim, H. S. (2014). What are we seeking to sustain through culturally sustaining pedagogy? A loving critique forward. *Harvard Educational Review, 84*(1), 85–100.

Rubin, B. C., & Jones, M. (2007). Student action research: Reaping the benefits for students and school leaders. *NASSP Bulletin, 91*(4), 363–378. doi: 10.1177/0192636507310316.

Salazar, M. C. (2018). Interrogating teacher evaluation: Unveiling whiteness as the normative center and moving the margins. *Journal of Teacher Education, 69*(5), 463–476.

Tanner, D. (2013). Race to the top and leave the children behind. *Journal of Curriculum Studies, 45*(1), 4–15.

Whipp, J. (2010). Developing socially just teachers: The interaction of experiences before, during, and after teacher preparation in beginning urban teachers. *Journal of Teacher Education, 64*(5), 1–14. doi: 10.1177/0022487113494845.

Zumwalt, K., & Craig, E. (2008). Who is teaching? Does it matter? In M. Cochran-Smith, S. Feiman-Nemser, & J. McIntyre (Eds.), *Handbook of research on teacher education: Enduring questions in changing contexts* (3rd ed., pp. 404–423). New York, NY: Routledge/Taylor & Francis Group and the Association of Teacher Educators.

CHAPTER 5

Arlene's Actionist Work
A Case Study of Writing and Self-Activism

Maneka D. Brooks and Arlene M. Alvarado

I'm glad that I dropped out of Big Green University.[1] I had to deal with stereotypes and prejudiced comments from a few of the students and professors. Particularly this one professor that I took a writing course failed me because she couldn't accept the fact that I wrote an A++++ paper, she quickly judged my character and claimed that I'd plagiarized, and she gave my essay an F. Everything was going well, I was passing my classes, enjoying being a college student until this professor. FUCK YOU! I worked on that paper to prove to you that I can be an excellent writer. I hated going to your office hour because you were not helpful, you made me feel ashamed of myself. . . . I remembered I sucked in my tears because I never met anyone so cruel. I wanted you to be proud that I took your advice and wrote a college level paper, and I did that and you took my glory away. So I packed my bags and went back to LA, defeated. Honestly, it took me a while to go back to school. When I finally did, I was scared to fail. However, I wasn't failing. I was passing and my professors at La Familia Community College were so motivating and helpful. Transferred to Lilac University, took 18 units for three semesters and now I am graduating.

The above epigraph is a Facebook post that Arlene wrote in April 2016. In it, she explicitly detailed what occurred and the coinciding emotions that led her to "drop out" of a large public university along the coast of California and return home to South Central Los Angeles. Arlene did not just highlight the way she felt defeated by the circumstances she encountered while pursuing a bachelor's degree at Big Green University (BGU). Within the same post, she also described how enrolling in La Familia Community College allowed her to eventually transfer to and graduate from Lilac University. The discrimination that Arlene described in her Facebook post is not an anomaly. Many students who belong to racially and linguistically minoritized groups encounter discrimination from students, faculty, and staff in institutions of higher education (Franklin, Smith, & Hung, 2014; Garcia & Johnston-Guerrero, 2015; Griffin,

Cunningham, & Mwangi, 2016; Hurtado & Ruiz Alvarado, 2015; McGee & Bentley, 2017; Museus & Park, 2015).

When I (Maneka) read Arlene's Facebook post, my anger only allowed me to focus on the atrocious ways in which Arlene was treated. I had been Arlene's 9th-grade social studies teacher and we had stayed in contact over the years; reading Arlene's post about how an educator violated her enraged me. In the midst of this response to Arlene's post, I realized that by focusing on my own anger with regard to how Arlene was treated, I was centering myself. I overlooked the ways Arlene talked about her own pursuit of justice in higher education. To draw on the words of San Pedro and Kinloch (2017), I was *re-storying* Arlene's educational journey by "hypervisualiz[ing] pain as hopelessness and ignor[ing] the transformative power that exists within" (p. 375S).

A passage from an essay by Audre Lorde (2007) provided a pathway to reframe how I engaged with Arlene's post. Lorde writes: "And where the words of women are crying to be heard, we must each of us recognize our responsibility to seek those words out, to read them and share them and examine their pertinence to our lives" (p. 43). Through her Facebook post, Arlene was making her words, feelings, and what she endured visible to a portion of the world. In this chapter, Arlene and I seek to amplify who sees her story and how it can be used to help the lives of others. Specifically, we focus on those who are involved in the literacy education of high school students who belong to groups that are both linguistically and racially minoritized in higher education. This, by extension, includes those who teach and work directly with high school students (teachers) and those who work with their teachers (teacher educators). Drawing on Lorde's (2007) framing, we ask readers to examine the pertinence of Arlene's words and experiences to their lives as literacy educators.

This chapter's audience is literacy educators because the flashpoint of discrimination that Arlene had to navigate was in her first-year writing classroom at BGU. The language and literacy practices of linguistically and racially minoritized college students are frequently the axis on which they are attacked (e.g., Baker-Bell, Paris, & Jackson, 2017; Kinloch, 2005; Kynard, 2010; Martínez, 2016; Valdés, 1999). Importantly, Kynard (2015) encourages writing practitioners and researchers not to position these racist acts as merely the "meanness" of individuals, but as endemic of systemic racism. Specifically, she documents how pedagogies of racism often go unchecked in the departments that produce instructors of writing in higher education.

Given the battleground that is the writing classroom for many linguistically and racially minoritized students, Arlene and I contend that it is important for literacy educators (both high school teachers and teacher educators) to prepare their students to navigate the minefield that they may encounter upon entering higher education. The focus on preparing students to navigate discrimination is not to remove the burden from institutions or from educators to address these issues systemically. It is to provide another weapon in the arsenal for linguistically and racially minoritized students to be able to defend themselves. Our personal experiences as Women of Color—Arlene is Latina and I am Black and South Asian—have taught us the importance of these types of defense systems. Moreover, we build upon research that documents the significant role of high school faculty and staff in Latinx students' college-going trajectories (Acevedo-Gil, 2017a; Martinez, Vega, & Marquez, 2018; Pérez & McDonough, 2008).

In thinking and writing about Arlene's experience of higher education, we recognize that Arlene engaged in what Butler (2016) terms *actionist work*. Drawing on her collaborative research with teenage Girls of Color, Butler arrived at this term as a result of the confusion about what being an activist meant; a participant, Chika, offered the actionist terminology. Butler (2016) defines "'actionist work' as critical acts of unmasking inequities, challenging injustice, and dismantling oppressive structures" (p. 314). This chapter is actionist work and documents actionist work. Arlene and I reflect upon the multiple roles that Arlene's actionist work played in her experiences of higher education: We unmask the numerous inequities that Arlene encountered and highlight the multiple ways in which she challenged injustice. Then, we propose ways for literacy educators to prepare students to name and reject the many forms of discrimination they may encounter. Together, this chapter represents a culmination of Arlene's actionist work to dismantle oppressive structures and an invitation to literacy educators to join in this fight.

Although our process of creating and organizing this chapter was collaborative, we were not able to write this chapter in the traditional collaborative sense. As a result, beyond direct quotations, Arlene is referred to in the third person and Maneka uses *I*. We made this decision to maintain authorial integrity and the authenticity of how we constructed the final text.

COLLABORATIVE ACTIONIST LITERACY RESEARCH

After Arlene made the initial Facebook post, we had a telephone conversation in which we discussed what we hoped to achieve from writing this chapter. We decided that this chapter would be written to support other students in accomplishing their college-going aspirations. Then, we engaged in a process of discussion and revision, which allowed us to arrive at the following questions:

- How does Arlene describe the experiences that "pushed" her out of Big Green University?
- What resources did Arlene use to facilitate her successful completion of her degree at Lilac University?

In order to answer these questions, we co-constructed interviews that replicated Seidman's (2013) three-interview series: focused life history, details of experience, and reflection on the meaning. The three 90-minute interviews took place approximately 2 weeks apart. These interviews occurred over Skype and were audio-recorded. Then, the interviews were transcribed. In total, this chapter draws on information from Arlene's initial Facebook post, a written reflection, and the transcriptions of three interviews. Finally, I used member-checking (Cresswell & Miller, 2000) to ensure that the results of the analytic process and final written document were accurate and coincided with Arlene's interpretations.

Although literacy education is central to this chapter, the two fundamental questions that guide this work do not explicitly mention reading, writing, or literacy. Instead, they focus on how Arlene makes meaning of her 6-year journey through higher education that involved three distinct institutions. The absence of explicit references to literacy highlights the fact that it is not a neutral skill set that occurs in isolation from the social world (Street, 1984; Willis, 2015). Literacy is embedded within day-to-day life and the power systems that govern the other aspects of our lives (Martinez, 2017a; Rogers, 2018). As will become evident later in this chapter, literacy is central to Arlene's encounters with discrimination and to her pursuit of justice in higher education. The justice that Arlene sought was a classroom where she had the ability to focus on learning new information because the instructor created and sustained an environment in which her academic, linguistic, and cultural backgrounds were respected. In this just educational setting, Arlene would be able to learn from others, be seen as able and provided with the opportunities to make meaningful intellectual contributions, and be provided with pathways to redress violations that occurred within the learning environment. She desired an instructional space where she was treated by the instructor and her classmates as an equal member of the learning community.

In addition to the previously described conceptualization of literacy, three other theoretical underpinnings form the backbone of this chapter. Specifically, we reject deficit thinking, normalize nonlinear postsecondary trajectories, and name the violence that pushes minoritized students out of higher education. Below, we describe how each of these underpinnings is central to the actionist work of this chapter.

Rejecting Deficit Thinking

As the bilingual child of immigrants from El Salvador and a first-generation college student from the economically marginalized community of South Central Los Angeles, Arlene belongs to several groups that are underrepresented in U.S. higher education. In talking about the twists and turns of Arlene's journey through higher education, it could be easy to fall into a narrative that reinforces individual deficits (for instance, limited motivation) about underrepresented students. This type of narrative is commonly referred to as deficit thinking: "Deficit thinking, an endogenous theory of school failure, 'blames the victim' rather than examining how schools and the political economy are structured to prevent students from learning optimally" (Valencia & Black, 2019, p. 4). Unfortunately, as Rios-Aguilar and Kiyama (2018) document, this way of thinking reflects a predominant perspective within the research on higher education. In creating this chapter, Arlene and I committed to actively resisting the deficit lens because it is theoretically limiting and inaccurate. As Women of Color, we also reject this lens because by using it, we would be complicit in reproducing stereotypes about groups to which we belong and with whom we stand in solidarity.

Normalizing Nonlinear Postsecondary Trajectories

To avoid the trap of the deficit lens, we build on the scholarship that recognizes that the transition from high school to college is not a linear 4-year journey for all students (Acevedo-Gil, 2017b; Solórzano, Datnow, Park, & Watford, 2013). Students like Arlene, who belong to multiple groups that are marginalized within institutions of higher education, often have more twists and turns in this journey that may delay or prevent their graduation. It is true that some of these difficulties may occur because of the result of systemic inequalities in Pre-K–12 education that may lead to students being academically underprepared (e.g., Kibler, 2013; Murillo & Schall, 2016; Ruecker, 2013). However, solely focusing on perceived underpreparation of students overlooks the ways in which interpersonal, institutional, and systemic inequalities endemic to higher education and other social settings impact students' journeys. For example, students often change their educational trajectories because of their experiences with racism, limited financial aid, family commitments, and/or misinformation about college processes (Cox, 2016; Martinez, 2013; Vega, 2018). Therefore, within this research, we begin with the presumption of nonlinearity of postsecondary academic trajectories.

Pushed Out and Pulled In

The last aspect of the analytic lens that guides this research is our rejection of the positioning of Arlene as a dropout of BGU. Admittedly, *dropping out* was the term Arlene used to reference her own schooling experiences in the initial Facebook post. Instead, we use the term *pushout*. We draw on Tuck (2011) and her co-researchers' use of this term "to describe the experiences of youth who have been pressured to leave school by people or factors inside school, such as disrespectful treatment from teachers and other school personnel, violence among students, arbitrary school rules, and the institutional pressures of high-stakes testing" (p. 818). Like Tuck (2012), we are aware of the problems with this terminology. She notes that the term *pushout* can be seen as a way to strip students of agency; can be interpreted as euphemism for students being "squeezed, kicked, punched, sliced out" of school (p. 61); and can be antithetical to participants' self-identification. In acknowledging the problematic use of *pushout*, Arlene and I still chose to use it because it moves attention away from Arlene's individual decision to leave BGU. It casts a spotlight on the roles of the institution and those who worked for the institution. Moreover, throughout this chapter, we are intentional in highlighting Arlene's agency. We draw upon Arlene's own words to express how she makes meaning of her own educational trajectory. This centering of Arlene's agency allows for the recognition of her actionist work. Together, the theoretical lenses that inform this research did not privilege institutionalized understandings of "dropping out" or "college success."

ARLENE'S JOURNEY THROUGH HIGHER EDUCATION

The words of Professor Spring, Arlene's second writing professor, whom Arlene references in the epigraph, echoed in her mind as she made the decision to leave BGU: "I was mostly thinking about I'm not a good student. I was just repeating the words Professor Spring was repeating towards myself. I was like, I'm not a good writer. I'm not a good writer because I didn't get these amazing opportunities while other American-born parents would have for their American-born children." Throughout the winter quarter, she had listened to Professor Spring talk about the limited abilities of immigrant students. Although Arlene was born in the United States and did not identify as an immigrant student, Professor Spring's personal attacks during class and office hours made it evident that she did not differentiate between Arlene and her classmates who were international students. The fact that Arlene was born, raised, and educated in the United States did not protect her from Professor Spring's prejudice.

Given Arlene's explicit discussion of the consequences of Professor Spring's xenophobic racism that occurred during class and in office hours, it would be easy to solely highlight this professor's specific actions as what led to Arlene being pushed out of BGU. However, Arlene recounted other systemic and institutional factors that lay the fertile soil for her to be isolated and targeted in this manner. These factors included Arlene's disparate educational experiences, biased understandings of language proficiency, and the absence of institutional processes to redress injustice.

Factors That Pushed Out

Disparate Educational Experiences. Prior to encountering Professor Spring, Arlene recognized the disparate access to educational opportunities between herself and many of her classmates at BGU. In looking specifically at writing instruction, Arlene recounted that she was never asked to write more than a paragraph throughout middle school. It was not until 9th grade that she wrote her first essay. Although in high school she was challenged to write in what she described as "college-level ways," she quickly realized that many of her classmates at BGU had distinct educational backgrounds and resources. Not only did they have more opportunities to practice writing, but they had access to tutors, parents who assisted them with their work, and a whole range of privileges that Arlene had not imagined. As a result, Arlene was acutely aware that she had a different set of instructional experiences with writing for academic audiences. Arlene explained that these differences, at times, could make her feel as if she did not belong at BGU. However, she did her best to focus on what she could do to make sure that she was successful. For instance, she worked diligently with Professor Christy, who taught the first writing course Arlene took at BGU, to show that she belonged at this institution of higher education.

Arlene noted that Professor Christy had the uncanny ability to recognize her strengths and areas of growth: "I remember she told me, but nicely, she was like, 'Here, I want you to read this book. I think it will help you.' It was a book for writers. However, it was for grammar. She was like, you're really good. Your writing is strong; however, you have some grammar errors.'" Importantly, Professor Christy believed in Arlene's abilities as a writer. At the end of the quarter, Arlene had passed the course, but not the portfolio component. As Arlene shared: "Professor Christy told me I still had small grammar issues. She was like, 'But, I think you will pass your second portfolio.' I believed her." In spite of having to take a second writing course, Arlene was proud that she was able navigate the demands of an academic curriculum like students who had educational privileges and supports that she had never had throughout her life.

Biased understandings of language proficiency. The second writing course was not the same supportive environment that Arlene experienced with Professor Christy. One of the first things Arlene noted about the new writing class with Professor Spring was that the rest of her classmates were international students from Asia and Latin America who had learned English later in life. Arlene's placement in this particular class indicated that Professor Christy attributed Arlene's "small grammar issues" to her English language ability. Arlene's placement in this class was inappropriate because she was neither an international student nor a student who had recently learned English. She had been speaking both English and Spanish since early childhood. In fact, Arlene described herself as having more confidence in her English abilities because she had been educated solely in English in U.S. schools. Arlene's placement in Professor Spring's class was not the first time she was placed in an unsuitable class. In 6th grade, she was incorrectly placed in an English as a Second Language course, but transferred to a regular English language arts class within the year. Arlene had a similar plan to work hard and transfer out of this second writing class. She was going to follow the rules, listen, and work hard to continue with her educational trajectory. Unfortunately, she encountered the xenophobic racism of Professor Spring.

Explicit xenophobic racism. Prior to entering Professor Spring's class, Arlene had racist interpersonal interactions with various students. For example, students would make what she described as "prejudiced and stereotypical remarks" to her. However, these incidents were miniscule in comparison to what she would encounter in Professor Spring's writing class. Arlene's memories about that class center on the things that Professor Spring would say while teaching: "I remember she would make really sassy remarks about immigrants, how they don't know English, they don't really succeed in college. She would be like, 'Oh, this is the reason why lots of immigrants don't graduate or finish college because they're not good writers or good speakers. They have lots of issues that you can't be really taught well or good enough.'" These types of comments were not limited to classroom time; her attacks on Arlene continued during the office hours that she was required to attend.

In spite of this hostile learning environment, Arlene continued to attend class and office hours. She explained that she was doing her best just to survive the course and move on with her undergraduate education. One day, she decided to fight back after hearing that Professor Spring was an immigrant herself. Arlene recounted with pride:

I found out that she was an immigrant, and that she came here to study, and that she's a really, really good writer. Then, I was like, wow, she's just a hypocrite. I was like, but you're not born in America. Well, I'm born in America. Yeah, I remember I was like, "But you're not born here. You're born somewhere in Europe." She was like, "How do you know?" I was like, the Internet. I think she was taken aback and surprised that I did research on her.

Yet Arlene's verbal identification of Professor Spring's hypocrisy did nothing to change Professor Spring's behavior.

Throughout the quarter, Arlene was determined to prove Professor Spring wrong. So she used the writing center to support her journey as a writer. Although Arlene's grades on papers were improving, she lost all hope at the end of the quarter when she read the feedback on her final paper. Professor Spring had written the word *plagiarized* on it. Arlene was deeply hurt that a paper she had put so much effort into completing had been labeled as the work of someone else. When Arlene asked Professor Spring to run the essay through the computer system to check for plagiarism, she refused. Arlene shared that Professor Spring said: "I don't need to because I already know that you plagiarized because you don't write like this." As an example, she pointed out Arlene's use of the word *provocative*. Professor Spring claimed that Arlene had copied her use of the word *provocative* in class. When Arlene pointed out that using the same word in a different context is not plagiarism and that an entire section of the paper was about Arlene's younger sister, Professor Spring accused Arlene of paying someone to write it for her. To add insult to injury, on the final day of class, Professor Spring announced to the entire class that only one student did not pass the portfolio, which further singled out Arlene.

Absence of support to redress injustice. Talking about Professor Spring and leaving BGU still brings tears to Arlene's eyes. In reflecting on this moment in her life, she shared: "Yeah, she made me cry that whole quarter. Then, I came back home defeated. I never told my mom. I never told my family. I just felt like I didn't wanna relive it, re-talk about it. It kinda still hurts me." Her family, who had been so consequential to every other aspect of her life, was hundreds of miles away. She could not share with them what she had endured because she did not want them to worry about her. Unlike at high school, which Arlene described as a very supportive setting with multiple caring adults, at BGU, she did not have interpersonal supports with faculty and staff. Lastly, she did not have close friends on campus. Arlene was feeling ashamed and isolated from any previous interpersonal support network in a new environment.

In spite of Arlene's feelings of isolation, Arlene sought out the assistance of the one professor with whom she had developed a trusting relationship: Professor Christy. Professor Christy suggested that Arlene appeal the decision; however, Arlene's hopes for recourse were dashed when she heard that Professor Spring received the appeals. It was at this moment that Arlene realized she was "put in a corner." If there were any other institutional supports to redress injustice, they were hidden from Arlene. She had no protection from Professor Spring's xenophobic racism—those negative behaviors that positioned Arlene as deficient because she was viewed as a "foreigner" who belonged to a racially stigmatized group. Professor Spring, in fact, was an immigrant, but her whiteness allowed her to function as an unmarked "American" who was free from the deficiencies of those she saw as non-white immigrants. She was able to hide her immigrant status until Arlene revealed it to the class. Like Bajaj, Ghaffar-Kucher and Desai (2016), we are committed to examining, naming, and challenging how xenophobia and racism intersect within the context of bullying and other forms of aggression within schools.

Resources to Sustain

After she was pushed out of BGU, Arlene enrolled as a part-time student at La Familia Community College, but her perception of herself as a student shifted dramatically across the two experiences. She recalled:

I was kind of in my own world. I was depressed. I kind of felt ashamed as a student because I thought, "Oh. Well, look at me. I'm going to this top-notch university." And I just felt like I didn't fit in because I felt like I wasn't a top-notch student. Then how the professors were treating me and believing that I probably paid someone to write my essays. That really hurt. I was just in shock right there. You're assuming that the way how I

look I'm not that smart that I can write a paper like that— a good paper?
I kind of felt that way. Once I went to La Familia, I still felt depressed, and
I was just like, "I don't know if I can do this."

Professor Spring's xenophobic racism, biased understandings of her language proficiency, and absences of institutional support to redress injustice
shattered Arlene's confidence in what was already a difficult transition from
high school to college because of the disparate educational histories of Arlene
and her classmates. Arlene's classmates' previous educational experiences had
provided them with more opportunities to practice writing, access to tutors,
parents who assisted them with their work, and other privileges. Nevertheless,
Arlene was able to accomplish what her experiences at BGU had made her
think was impossible: earning a bachelor's degree. After attending La Familia
Community College, she transferred to Lilac University from which she graduated with a bachelor of science degree in criminology. Arlene described family
and neighborhood support, interpersonal and institutionalized support within La Familia, and her ability to create a space for personal reflection as helping
her regain the confidence she needed to graduate.

Family and neighborhood support. Returning to South Central Los Angeles
and moving back into her mother's home with her sisters meant that she returned to the support network that had gotten her through other challenging
situations in life. Arlene shared how her sisters encouraged her in their own
unique ways when she returned from BGU doubting her academic abilities.
While she was at La Familia, her sisters would talk to her about her career
goals, ask about her classes, and celebrate her small accomplishments. For example, her younger sister bought her a cupcake for doing well in a class. Moreover, her family served as motivation to push her to take steps toward being
able to transfer from community college. Arlene initially enrolled "part-time"
at La Familia. Yet she told her mother that she was a full-time student. After the
first session of classes, Arlene's younger sister revealed the truth to their mother. This truth telling and the resulting conversations with her mother pushed
Arlene to become a full-time community college student. Arlene's mother and
sisters banded together to remind her of the importance of finishing on time
and transferring to a 4-year college. Although Arlene did not feel comfortable
sharing her struggles from afar, she had a strong support system when they all
lived together.

Arlene shared other information about living in her neighborhood that
gave her comfort and strength. For example, she described how a homeless
man at Church's Chicken restaurant encouraged her to continue with higher
education after sharing his story of struggles with employment. This and other
seemingly small moments of encouragement from community members were
reminders that there was a broader network of people invested in her success.
Moreover, she talked about having more resources within her community to

engage in self-care. She could get the foods that she liked from local street vendors. In addition, she had access to her many pets, which were a great source of comfort and stress relief. As Arlene shared, "Well, for some reason, animals, they take away my pain." Over the course of her life she had lived with chickens, lizards, rabbits, turtles, dogs, and birds. While living in the dormitory at BGU, she was unable to have pets. Arlene was separated from a frequently relied upon self-soothing resource.

Returning to her family and neighborhood allowed Arlene to engage in various types of self-care and to rely on support from which she was barred at BGU. Arlene shared that this type of support made her realize she was not alone. At BGU, she felt isolated and overwhelmed by all the new adjustments she was expected to make. Now that she was back with her family and in her neighborhood, everything was familiar and she could focus her energy on learning to do school differently. Moreover, the support she received made her feel stronger when it came to navigating the various obstacles that might occur.

Interpersonal and institutionalized supports. Arlene not only found support at home and in her neighborhood; she also found academic supports in the professors and courses at La Familia. She found an education that reflected a belief in her abilities and her potential. She received the type of education that she needed as a student. Arlene described the manner in which the majority of the professors engaged with students at La Familia as fundamentally different from what she encountered at BGU. She felt like much of this difference was based in the fact that many of the La Familia professors were alumni of the institution who went on to pursue advanced degrees at elite universities. These individuals returned to La Familia because they wanted to work with community college students, and they frequently shared this mission and their personal educational journeys in class. Arlene talked about many of the professors at La Familia as being an inspiration for one of the several pathways on which she could choose to embark. She saw how people with life trajectories similar to hers could attain success.

Yet it was more than just the way in which she saw professors that were visions of what she could be. There were courses explicitly designed to meet the needs of students like her. Arlene was not placed into a writing course designed for recently arrived international students. Instead, she was put into an accelerated writing course at La Familia, which was co-taught by Professors Cooper and Sosa. In this course, Arlene was able to get practice writing the longer papers with which she was unfamiliar. However, and Arlene argued most importantly, Professors Cooper and Sosa taught Arlene the importance of maintaining her own voice and making her writing accessible to multiple audiences:

All I need to do is just stick to what I'm good at, and that is simplicity, but yet, I'm so foreign to it. I was like, wow, no one ever told me that. They were always telling me you have to be a college-level writer. You have to speak this way or all this. [Professors Cooper and Sosa] were like, no, you don't need to be like that. Simplicity will take you so much further from talking so prestige. Sometimes not everyone can read prestige words. I was like, you're right. Something simple, you can make it sound even much more prestige. They gave me hope, and they reassured me, those two professors.

In her other classes, Arlene was able to build upon the study skills that she learned in high school to understand how to succeed in college classes. La Familia's institutionalized support services, along with professors who believed in her voice and abilities, helped rebuild the foundation that her experiences at BGU and with Professor Spring had destroyed.

Space for self-reflection. Arlene described the safety and support that she found at La Familia and by returning to her family and neighborhood as allowing her to heal. As a result of this environment, Arlene could better recognize the strength and abilities that had always resided within her. Distance from the incident with Professor Spring, along with a series of positive interactions with multiple professors, allowed her to contextualize this experience. She recognized that she was in a particularly vulnerable space when she encountered Professor Spring's xenophobic racism. She was an 18-year-old, first-generation college student from an inner-city community and she was living on her own for the first time at a remote university. She asked one person for help and they could not offer any assistance; so, Arlene recognized that she did what was best for her at the time, and that was to leave. Several years later and with more perspective, Arlene talked about how she better understood the resources of a university. She realized that she could have shared her struggles with her family, talked to a counselor, or just communicated to more people. Nevertheless, Arlene recognizes that she is not to blame for having to leave BGU. There were factors outside of her control that pushed her out of this institution: Professor Spring's xenophobic racism, biased understandings of her language proficiency, and the absence of institutional support to redress injustice.

Also, transitioning from a full-time to a part-time student at La Familia allowed Arlene a new space for exploration. When she first attended BGU, she took a full load of classes on the quarter system. The number and pace of classes overwhelmed her; she did not have the opportunity to explore what she wanted to get out of a college experience. As a part-time student, she was able to take interesting classes and relax on campus. This time to explore her options helped her recognize her career goal. Her zoology professor mentioned that her husband was a fish and game ranger. This career tied together a focus on wildlife and human interaction that piqued Arlene's interest. With her newfound career goal as a fish and game ranger, she was better able to position any obstacles that occurred as temporary hiccups. For instance, when she was about to transfer to Lilac University, a La Familia professor submitted the wrong grade and went on vacation. As a result, Arlene's transfer did not go through until the professor could correct it several weeks later. Instead of allowing this mishap to derail her overall trajectory, Arlene just pushed back her transfer date. She recognized that certain obstacles were out of her control and focused on the goals of receiving her degree in criminology and becoming a ranger.

The final lesson that Arlene shared that she learned from her schooling at BGU and La Familia was that attending a prestigious institution was not the most important aspect of higher education. Arlene explained that having a personalized learning experience, being around family, and being in a supportive environment were of primary importance. These goals guided her decision around transferring to a small private institution, Lilac University, to complete her bachelor's degree. Notably, Arlene revealed that she understood these things about herself as a high school student. She wanted a college that could re-create the close-knit, supportive setting that she felt in high school. She knew that a large school could not provide her with that type of education. In fact, Lilac University had been her first choice as a high school senior. However, at that time, the university did not give her enough financial aid. Arlene decided to listen to the advice of school-affiliated adults who told her to select the most prestigious institution. Her initial second choice was a larger public school that was close to home. With hindsight, her experience at BGU and La Familia taught her that her initial instincts and priorities were correct. Arlene learned to regain her voice to advocate for what she saw as the best for her own future. Her ultimate success at Lilac University bolstered this understanding.

Refusing Dehumanizing Schooling

At BGU, Arlene independently engaged in the actionist work of naming and rejecting discrimination and attempting to dismantle oppressive structures (Butler, 2016). Each of her attempts to rectify the racism and discrimination that she endured at BGU was shut down. As a lone student, Arlene did not have the power to create a just learning environment in which she was treated as an equal and valued member of the learning community. Arlene was pushed out of BGU by multiple dehumanizing schooling experiences. The dehumanizing experiences that Arlene recounted are not new, unique, or isolated (Baker-Bell et al., 2017; Kinloch, 2005; Kynard, 2010; Martinez, 2016; Valdés, 1999). Like other pushouts (Fine, 1986; Tuck, 2011, 2012), she described leaving school as a way to maintain dignity and as a form of "self-care."

Arlene returned to and was successful in higher educational environments that affirmed her multidimensionality (and thus, her humanity). Pivotal in the journey toward receiving her degree were the supports available at La Familia Community College. At La Familia, there were clear and readily available institutional supports to sustain a more just educational environment. The fact that La Familia was a supportive space in which Arlene was able to flourish does not make it an anomaly among community colleges. Research illustrates that community colleges can be a place for students from minoritized backgrounds find the support that they need to thrive academically (Baber, 2018; Dowd, Pak, & Bensimon, 2013; Rendón, 2002). This learning environment was complemented by the fact that a community of supportive individuals who valued her goals and feelings surrounded Arlene at home and in her neighborhood. Moreover, it was in this affirming educational environment that Arlene was provided with a space for self-reflection and goal setting. As a result of her experiences at La Familia, she was able to confidently select Lilac University as the appropriate place to finish her higher education journey.

Upon graduating from Lilac University, Arlene transferred the focus of her actionist work from herself to others. Like other young people in her generation (Stornaiuolo & Thomas, 2017), she used social media to share her story and contribute to the dismantling of oppressive structures. In her initial post and the multiple conversations that followed, she made visible for others within her online social network a counterstory (Solórzano & Yosso, 2002) that rejected a deficit framing of underrepresented students in higher education. Arlene called attention to the fact that higher education is a place where some students from minoritized backgrounds encounter racism from professors and where pathways to graduation can be nonlinear.

Arlene's decision to collaborate with me to share this story is another example of expanding the reach of her actionist work. Her experiences provide others with examples of resistance, community, and survival. Below, we propose a way for high school educators to collaborate with students in extending Arlene's actionist work through literacy teaching. In particular, for first-generation Latinx college students like Arlene, high school faculty and staff play an important role in providing information for students that can shape their understandings about the possibilities of college (Acevedo-Gil, 2017a; Martinez et al., 2018). Therefore, we argue that high school faculty and staff have a unique responsibility to arm students with weapons to fight for a more just higher educational experience. Indeed, literacy education is a space where this can happen.

High School Literacy Education for College Justice: Implications for Teaching and Teacher Education

Scholars, practitioners, and scholar-practitioners within literacy research illustrate how the ways in which literacy is taught can contribute to justice inside and outside of classrooms (Johnson, 2018; Kinloch, 2012; Martinez, 2017a; Rosario-Ramos, 2018; Winn, 2013, 2018). Although the particulars of how justice is conceptualized can vary within various pedagogical approaches, they are focused on healing, critical analysis, and social transformation. Importantly, these pedagogies require a fundamental respect for students' existing capabilities and their ability to learn (and do) more. It is within this spirit of these actionist- and justice-oriented pedagogies that we propose text types and writing activities that can be used to explicitly talk and teach about racism in higher education. Reflecting our initial goal of supporting minoritized students' college-going aspirations, we describe the assignment as it can be used with high school students themselves. However, it can also be adapted so that literacy teacher educators can have pre-/inservice teachers design lessons for a high school classroom. The overarching goal is to extend Arlene's actionist work through explicitly talking and teaching about racism in higher education.

Actionist Teaching

The false perception that institutions of higher education are racial utopias or free from bias can harm students who may be unaware of the discrimination that they encounter. The ways racism is embedded in and a part of higher education is absent from dominant narratives about higher education in media and research (Patton, 2016). As Arlene shared, she was not "prepared" for the racism. Like other students from the urban centers in southern California (Martinez, 2017a, 2017b), Arlene had endured the brunt of systemic racism and the policing of her languages. However, she had always attended neighborhood public schools in which the majority of students were Latinx and almost all students were Students of Color. This student population and the experiences of discrimination to which she was accustomed was distinct from what she found at the predominantly white institution of BGU. The need for literacy educators to talk about these incidents with high school students is not to frighten them away from higher education, but to provide pathways for surviving and thriving.

Readings. Three different text types that are useful in creating a forum to discuss the realities of life on a college campus are newspaper articles, academic articles, and (auto)biographical narratives. Literacy educators could also use videos, podcasts, maps, graphs, and other multimedia resources. These three text types are merely popular and easy-to-access exemplars. In addition, these three text types, which can be used to meet English language/literacy standards, are, in fact, some of the texts that students will encounter in their postsecondary instruction (Holschuh, 2014).

Popular Media Articles. Newspaper, magazine, and internet articles can be used to provide up-to-date information about racist events at local institutions of higher education and community responses to those events. These types of locally focused readings allow for more direct connections to schools that students may have heard of or where alumni of the students' high schools may attend. The use of current events illustrates that these events are not relics of the past. They color current college students' experiences of higher education.

Academic Articles. There are two key ways high school literacy educators can use articles and other publications from academic journals. First, the analysis provided in certain academic articles can help students understand the pervasiveness of racism on campus. Garcia and Johnston-Guerrero (2015) analyzed "all news-making racially biased incidents that occurred on college and university campuses over a period of five academic years" (p. 54). The depth of this analysis and findings demonstrate the diverse ways racism occurs across different types of institutions. Second, academic articles can be used as a forum for educators to learn more about these topics in order to introduce them to students. Literacy educators can read about various programs that have been successful in creating just educational experiences for students, find a glossary of key terms about racism and racial equity, learn the intersections of linguistic and racial discrimination, and familiarize themselves with the ever-shifting dynamics of placement practices for linguistically minoritized students.

Notably, academic articles can be difficult to access because many are behind paywalls. However, abstracts that describe content and list authors are readily available through free online databases, like Google Scholar, or other sources. If educators find articles that pique their interest but to which they do not have access, they can directly email authors to ask for a free copy of their work. Academic articles are meant to be used and fees should not prevent access.

Autobiographical and Biographical Works. It is important for students to read narratives written by or in collaboration with current and/or former students of higher education about their experiences with racism and discrimination. These can be formally published pieces or more informal pieces like the blog post written by Tiffany Martinez (2016) about her experiences with writing and racism (see vivatiffany.wordpress.com/2016/10/27/academia-love-me-back/). The narratives that students read should not only be damage-centered (Tuck, 2009), but should also explicitly discuss how students navigated racism and discrimination. This does not mean all narratives must entail descriptions of success in creating more just educational conditions. This would not be an accurate representation of reality. Nevertheless, these narratives need to model for students how individuals like themselves engage in actionist work.

Writing Activities. The previously discussed text types create many opportunities for students to write. As Arlene vocalized, opportunities to write were not always presented to her in school. Therefore, we wanted to be sure that we explicitly highlighted how these texts, along with other sources, can be used to create (among other tasks) annotated bibliographies, encyclopedia entries, personal reflections, and (auto)biographical narratives. These various writing activities provide pathways for having students critically analyze the racial dynamics of higher education and envision their pursuit of justice in higher education. At the same time, these writing activities connect to normative conceptions of "college-preparatory" writing.

There are two important goals of writing activities as they relate to extending Arlene's actionist work. The first is to call attention to ideas or concepts in texts that might not be immediately salient to students. For example, if students were assigned to read Arlene's story, then they may focus on Arlene's overt experiences with Professor Spring's xenophobic racism. However, a prompt can be used to call attention to other aspects within Arlene's story that are evidence of more subtle and systemic discrimination. Arlene shared that both in middle school and at BGU she was placed into courses designed for students who were learning English. Although Arlene is bilingual, she is not learning English, and is not best served by these courses. In this sense, writing can be used as an activity to have students think deeply about a concept or situation before it is addressed in class. The second goal is to have students use texts to identify strategies and brainstorm new possibilities of how they can identify and create more just learning environments. Through a writing activity, a teacher could ask students to consider what they would do if they found themselves in the same situation as Arlene and were placed in a class that was not appropriate for them. They could use Arlene's story, personal experiences, and other texts they have read to brainstorm who they could talk to in order to change the situation. This second goal of the writing assignment provides a pathway for students to identify how they can draw on their own agency and community and institutional resources to fight injustice. It makes explicit the tools of justice that are accessible to students.

Moving Forward

Arlene's story speaks to the importance of literacy educators preparing students to name and reject the discrimination they may encounter. We understand that high school educators cannot protect future students from being discriminated against by others. Our desired outcome for writing this chapter is that students do not have to experience isolation as they engage in this type of actionist work, especially as they are supported by caring, engaged teachers. We hope more teachers will engage in this work and join in the battle for justice.

REFLECTIVE QUESTIONS

1. How can educators support students in recognizing and naming the multiple signs of discrimination that persist in higher educational context?

2. How can students be supported to use available resources to create and participate in a more just educational environment?

NOTE

1. All identifying institutional names are pseudonyms.

REFERENCES

Acevedo-Gil, N. (2017a). College-going facultad: Latinx students anticipating postsecondary institutional obstacles. *Journal of Latinos and Education*. doi: 10.1080/15348431.2017.1371019

Acevedo-Gil, N. (2017b). College-conocimiento: toward an interdisciplinary college choice framework for Latinx students. *Race Ethnicity and Education, 20*(6), 829–850.

Baber, L. D. (2018). "Living in the along": Validating experiences among urban community college students in a college transition program. *Community College Review, 46*(3), 316–340.

Bajaj, M., Ghaffar-Kucher, A., & Desai, K. (2016). Brown bodies and xenophobic bullying in US schools: Critical analysis and strategies for action. *Harvard Educational Review, 86*(4), 481–505.

Baker-Bell, A., Paris, D., & Jackson, D. (2017). Learning Black language matters: Humanizing research as culturally sustaining pedagogy. *International Review of Qualitative Research, 10*(4), 360–377.

Butler, T. T. (2016). "Stories behind their hands": The creative and collective "actionist" work of girls of color. *English Teaching: Practice & Critique, 15*(3), 313–332.

Cox, R. D. (2016). Complicating conditions: Obstacles and interruptions to low-income students' college "choices". *The Journal of Higher Education, 87*(1), 1–26.

Creswell, J. W., & Miller, D. L. (2000). Determining validity in qualitative inquiry. *Theory into Practice, 39*(3), 124–130.

Dowd, A. C., Pak, J. H., & Bensimon, E. M. (2013). The role of institutional agents in promoting transfer access. *Education Policy Analysis Archives, 21*(15). Retrieved from epaa.asu.edu/ojs/article/view/1187

Fine, M. (1986). Why urban adolescents drop into and out of public high school. *Teachers College Record, 87*(3), 393–409.

Franklin, J. D., Smith, W. A., & Hung, M. (2014). Racial battle fatigue for Latina/o students: A quantitative perspective. *Journal of Hispanic Higher Education, 13*(4), 303–322.

Garcia, G. A., & Johnston-Guerrero, M. P. (2015). Challenging the utility of a racial microaggressions framework through a systematic review of racially biased incidents on campus. *Journal of Critical Scholarship on Higher Education and Student Affairs, 2*(1), 48–66. Retrieved from ecommons.luc.edu/jcshesa/vol2/iss1/4

Griffin, K. A., Cunningham, E. L., & Mwangi, C. A. G. (2016). Defining diversity: Ethnic differences in Black students' perceptions of racial climate. *Journal of Diversity in Higher Education, 9*(1), 34–49.

Holschuh, J. P. (2014). The Common Core goes to college: The potential for disciplinary literacy approaches in developmental literacy classes. *Journal of College Reading and Learning, 45*(1), 85–95.

Hurtado, S., & Ruiz Alvarado, A. (2015). *Discrimination and bias, underrepresentation, and sense of belonging on campus*. Los Angeles, CA: Higher Education Research Institute.

Johnson, L. L. (2018). Where do we go from here? Toward a critical race English education. *Research in the Teaching of English, 53*(2), 102–124.

Kibler, A. (2013). "Doing like almost everything wrong": An adolescent multilingual writer's transition from high school to college." In L. C. de Oliveira & T. Silva (Eds.), *L2 writing in secondary classrooms: Student experiences, academic issues, and teacher education* (pp. 44–64). New York, NY: Routledge.

Kinloch, V. (2012). *Crossing boundaries: Teaching and learning with urban youth*. New York, NY: Teachers College Press.

Kinloch, V. F. (2005). Revisiting the promise of" students' right to their own language": Pedagogical strategies. *College Composition and Communication, 57*(1), 83–113.

Kynard, C. (2010). From candy girls to cyber sista-cipher: Narrating Black females' color consciousness and counterstories in and out of school. *Harvard Educational Review, 80*(1), 30–53.

Kynard, C. (2015). Teaching while black: Witnessing disciplinary whiteness, racial violence, and race-management. *Literacy in Composition Studies, 3*(1), 1–20.

Lorde, A. (2007). The transformation of silence into language and action. In A. Lorde (Ed.), *Sister outsider: Essays and speeches by Audre Lorde* (pp. 40–44). Berkeley, CA: Crossing Press.

Martinez, D. C. (2017a). Imagining a language of solidarity for Black and Latinx youth in English language arts classrooms. *English Education, 49*(2), 179–196.

Martinez, D. C. (2017b). Emerging critical meta-awareness among Black and Latina/o youth during corrective feedback practices in urban English language arts classrooms. *Urban Education, 52*(5), 637–666.

Martinez, M. A. (2013). (Re) considering the role familismo plays in Latina/o high school students' college choices. *The High School Journal, 97*(1), 21–40.

Martinez, M. A., Vega, D., & Marquez, J. (2018). Latinx students' experiences with college access and preparation at college preparatory charter schools. *Journal of Latinos and Education*. doi: 10.1080/15348431.2017.1418353

Martínez, T. (2016). Academia, love me back [Blog post]. Retrieved from vivatiffany. wordpress.com/2016/10/27/academia-love-me-back/

McGee, E. O., & Bentley, L. (2017). The troubled success of Black women in STEM. *Cognition and Instruction, 35*(4), 265–289.

Murillo, L. A., & Schall, J. M. (2016, October 26). "They didn't teach us well": Mexican-origin students speak out about their readiness for college literacy. *Journal of Adolescent & Adult Literacy, 60*(3), 315–323.

Museus, S. D., & Park, J. J. (2015). The continuing significance of racism in the lives of Asian American college students. *Journal of College Student Development, 56*(6), 551–569.

Patton, L. D. (2016). Disrupting postsecondary prose: Toward a critical race theory of higher education. *Urban Education, 51*(3), 315–342.

Pérez, P. A., & McDonough, P. M. (2008). Understanding Latina and Latino college choice: A social capital and chain migration analysis. *Journal of Hispanic higher education, 7*(3), 249–265.

Rendón, L. I. (2002). Community college Puente: A validating model of education. *Educational Policy, 16*(4), 642–667.

Rios-Aguilar, C. & Kiyama, J.M. (2018). Introduction: The need for funds of knowledge approach in higher education contexts. In J. M. Kiyama & C. Rios-Aguilar (Eds.), *Funds of knowledge in higher education: Honoring students' cultural experiences and resources as strengths* (pp. 3–6). New York, NY: Taylor and Francis.

Rogers, R. (2018). Literacy research, racial consciousness, and equitable flows of knowledge. *Literacy Research: Theory, Method, and Practice, 67*(1), 24–43.

Rosario-Ramos, E. M. (2018) "Why aren't there enough of our stories to read?": Teaching autoethnographies for radical healing. *English Teaching: Practice & Critique, 17*(3), 213–227.

Ruecker, T. (2013). High-stakes testing and Latina/o students: Creating a hierarchy of college readiness. *Journal of Hispanic Higher Education, 12*(4), 303–320.

San Pedro, T., & Kinloch, V. (2017). Toward projects in humanization: Research on co-creating and sustaining dialogic relationships. *American Educational Research Journal, 54*(1_suppl), 373S–394S.

Seidman, I. (2013). *Interviewing as qualitative research*. New York, NY: Teachers College Press.

Solórzano, D., Datnow, A., Park, V., & Watford, T. (2013). *Pathways to postsecondary success: Maximizing opportunities for youth in poverty*. Retrieved from pathways.gseis.ucla.edu/publications/PathwaysReport.pdf

Solórzano, D. G., & Yosso, T. J. (2002). Critical race methodology: Counter-storytelling as an analytical framework for education research. *Qualitative Inquiry, 8*(1), 23–44.

Stornaiuolo, A., & Thomas, E. E. (2017). Disrupting educational inequalities through youth digital activism. *Review of Research in Education, 41*(1), 337–357.

Street, B. V. (1984). *Literacy in theory and practice*. Cambridge, UK: Cambridge University Press.

Tuck, E. (2009). Suspending damage: A letter to communities. *Harvard Educational Review, 79*(3), 409–428.

Tuck, E. (2011). Humiliating ironies and dangerous dignities: A dialectic of school pushout. *International Journal of Qualitative Studies in Education, 24*(7), 817–827.

Tuck, E. (2012). *Urban youth and school pushout: Gateways, get-aways, and the GED*. New York, NY: Routledge.

Valdés, G. (1999). Nonnative English speakers: Language bigotry in English mainstream classrooms. *ADFL BULLETIN, 31*(1), 43–48.

Valencia, R. R., & Black, M. S. (2019). "Mexican Americans don't value education": On the basis of the myth, mythmaking, and debunking. In E. G. Murillo, Jr. (Ed.), *Critical readings on Latinos and education* (pp. 3–25). New York, NY: Routledge.

Vega, D. (2018). Navigating postsecondary pathways: The college choice experiences of first generation Latina/o transfer students. *Community College Journal of Research and Practice, 42*(12), 848–860.

Willis, A. I. (2015). Literacy and race: Access, equity, and freedom. *Literacy Research: Theory, Method, and Practice, 64*(1), 23–55.

Winn, M. T. (2013). Toward a restorative English education. *Research in the Teaching of English, 48*(1), 126–135.

Winn, M. T. (2018). A transformative justice approach to literacy education. *Journal of Adolescent & Adult Literacy, 62*(2), 219–221.

CHAPTER 6

Pardon This Disruption

Cultivating Revolutionary Civics Through World Humanities

Tamara Butler, Jenell Igeleke Penn, and Johnny Merry

One group of students discusses their plans to build a trebuchet. Another group pushes their desks together as a makeshift conference table to discuss pencil-drawn sketches of their proposed roller coaster. Large sticky-note paper covers the classroom walls as another group outlines how to explain different forms of energy to stakeholders. This was Jenell Penn's classroom at a STEM-centered high school, where students consistently engaged in an array of design challenges, which were a staple of the school's curriculum. However, it was Jenell's final mini-design challenge, centering on social justice in relation to the larger context of STEM education, that is important to highlight.

Thus, this is where our story begins—with two high school educators and teacher collaborators (Johnny Merry and Jenell Penn) who share an interest in graphic novels, hands-on curricula, and combating social inequities, and with an educational researcher (Tamara Butler) who is passionate about youth activism. As doctoral students, Johnny and Tamara often spoke about their connections to South Carolina and their deep commitments to working with/in marginalized communities. It is here—around the "tree [that] ain't even been planted . . . yet" (Jordan, 2007, p. 149)—that the three of us gather to reflect upon our own understandings of social justice and the spaces it occupies in K–12 and teacher education. It is here that we ruminate on Eve Tuck and K. Wayne Yang's (2018) reminder that "social justice is not the other of the field of education, it *is* the field" (p. 6). In fact, Tuck and Wang state that "there is no future of the field of education without the contributions of people who are doing their work under the rising sign of social justice" (p. 6). Their assertion guides the work that we do, as it provides us with an understanding that it is not so much about social justice's fit into education as much as it is about how education is grounded in how we come to name oppressive ideologies, challenge unfair educational practices, and dismantle inequitable structures. Such an education, then, focuses on teaching, learning, and engagements that transform our understandings of and interactions with one another. Additionally, this type of education pushes us away from practices that are rooted in fear, ignorance, and desire to dominate, and moves us toward practices that center humanity, reciprocity, respect and responsibility (Torrez, 2018).

Before entering into the World Humanities class that brought the three of us together, we pause to think about how justice operates as "a catalytic concept" that "circulates as a placeholder for actions and stances against dispossession, displacement, and death" (Tuck & Yang, 2016, p. 4). Although we might not share the exact vision of what justice can do, we agree with Tuck and Yang's (2016) belief that "even if the desire for justice is unrequited, it produces futures beyond the current political moment" (p. 8), which leads us to grapple in this chapter with the following questions:

- What is required of educators and students for them to intentionally engage social justice issues inside classrooms?
- How can students and educators collaboratively imagine "futures beyond the current political moment"? In other words, what kinds of generative spaces can manifest when educators and students challenge one another to engage with local communities around local (and global) issues?

To address these questions, we reflect on practices in a high school World Humanities course. In the first section, we consider theories and practices that emerged from the class that shaped what we refer to as revolutionary civics, or engagements where students, teachers, and community members collectively discuss, analyze, and challenge longstanding forms of oppression and injustice. The second section discusses the partnerships, evaluations, and evolution that made the student projects, which we refer to as Social Justice Capstone projects, possible. The third section is a disruption. It is here that we interject moments from different iterations of the Social Justice Capstone projects to think about a key element of the work: sustainability—that is, how the lessons, conversations, and projects from the course shaped the emerging and ongoing social justice commitments of the students and, by extension, of us (Tamara, Jenell, and Johnny). To bring the parts of our chapter together, we close with reflective questions for teachers and teacher educators to consider when engaging in the work of revolutionary civics in K–12 education.

JUSTICE IN THE FIELD: TOWARD REVOLUTIONARY CIVICS

When we began working together, Barack Obama was in the middle of his first term as the 44th president, and the first Black president, of the United States. Public media narratives suggested that the election marked a new level of racial equality, even postracial or colorblind status for the United States. Our lived and professional experiences told a different story. In our classrooms and communities, we found ourselves living in the counternarratives (Rankine, 2015). In February 2012, Trayvon Martin was murdered by George Zimmerman, and in June, CeCe McDonald was imprisoned for defending herself during a racist and transphobic attack. All along, President Barack Obama's birth status was still being questioned by those involved in the "birther" movement, a racist conspiracy effort that emerged during his 2008 presidential campaign and that claimed Obama was not born in the United States, is not a naturalized citizen, and is not qualified to be president.

During this same time, most of the high school students we worked with were African American students in a segregated district and the majority were enrolled in the free or reduced-price lunch program. Despite being an arts magnet school and one of the best high schools in the state, our school's facilities and resources still had room for improvement—they were underresourced and in poorer condition than many suburban schools. Our students did not have access to one-to-one technology. In fact, only approximately 75% of the computers that were available in the school building worked. Many of the rooms were so cold that students had to wear their winter coats in the classrooms, and there was little to no academic or social support outside of the school day. Although it was important to celebrate this country's capacity to elect a Black commander-in-chief, we reminded ourselves that there was still a lot of work left to do, especially with regard to educational equity.

Therefore, Jenell and Johnny's teaching efforts to think with students about "actions and stances against dispossession, displacement, and death" (Tuck & Yang, 2016, p. 4) were driven by two core beliefs that the three of us share: (1) that as teachers and students, we could do something now to fight for equity, and (2) that none of us could afford to be bystanders in the face of racial and gender violence, transphobia, homophobia, and other lethal forms of xenophobia. We were interested in challenging ideas of youth learning and living in urban communities as solely service recipients, apathetic consumers, and as individuals striving to be "good citizens." We were neither interested in romanticizing young people's knowledges nor painting their lived experiences with broad brushstrokes that erased their struggles, failures, and questions. Instead, we saw (and continue to see) young people as innovators, inquirers, and human beings striving "to be recognized as human, levelly human" (Combahee River Collective Statement, 1971). We were interested in disrupting the curriculum in ways that would transform our thinking about justice, equity, and of course, humanity—for students, community members, educators, and various stakeholders within and beyond the classroom.

In their work on civic education in the Trump era, Garcia and Dutro (2018) encourage us to "locate the political in our work, and locate ourselves within it" (p. 382). Therefore, we return to Jenell's stance to think about what is possible when we locate the political within ourselves and our classrooms. During a writing/brainstorming session, Jenell began her reflection with, "Teaching is a political act. It is revolutionary." She went on to talk about why she and Johnny wanted to focus on social justice with their ninth graders and why they wanted to teach using an arts-integrated curriculum. The main goal was to challenge students to become change agents in their communities through the power of activism and art. As a result, art became a way for students to stand and work for justice. Relatedly, the various media functioned as megaphones for students to speak with communities about issues that they identified as important, critical, and relevant.

REVOLUTIONARY CIVICS: FUSING THE DISRUPTIVE AND ARTISTIC

Our concept of revolutionary civics is informed by three conversations about transformative education: (1) youth civic engagement and learning, (2) artivism, and (3) necessary disruptions. We are drawn to these three conversations because they address teaching, learning, and engagement as political acts, with an emphasis on politics that moves beyond the American dream, romanticized notions of democracy, and complacency with current systems of oppressions and marginalization (Mirra & Garcia, 2017). When we use these three strands to reach beyond, we can reassess the political for its transformative elements, which include intergenerational coalition building, creative responsiveness, and collaborative grassroots approaches. Below, we briefly describe these three conversations and their connections to transformative education.

Youth Civic Engagement and Learning

Urban teacher educators, literacy researchers, and education scholars who focus on youth participation and engagement are advocating for a form of civic education that operates beyond the confines of what being a "good citizen" and citizenship have meant historically. In an era when the federal, state, and local governments across America cannot come to consensus on the value of Black/trans/Indigenous/womxn, immigrant (undocumented and documented) and refugee lives, teaching for and enacting a stance toward civic education becomes difficult. In their review of research on youth participation and civic education, Mirra and Garcia (2017) highlight the tensions around the type of "knowledge, skills, and identities" young people use to "understand and participate in . . . community life" (p. 139). They found that scholars are still debating the type of political participation that current civic education programs and curricula promote. Acts such as voting, union participation, religious activity, and community service are rooted in exclusionary notions of belonging (for example, citizenship status, age, dis/ability, literacy level). As a result, "educators face the daunting task of instead developing an alternative vision of civic engagement with students that can inspire hope and action" (Mirra & Garcia, 2017, p. 144). This chapter joins these conversations about the possibilities and futurities of civic education (Garcia, Mirra, Morrell, Martinez, & Scorza, 2015;

Johnson & Vasudevan, 2012; Love, 2019; Mirra, Coffey, & Englander, 2018; Torrez, 2018) that are interested in sustainable and responsible engagements.

Artivism

One way that educators can develop "an alternative vision of civic education" is by turning to arts-integrated approaches to teaching, learning, and engagement. Because Johnny and Jenell worked at an arts magnet school, they were drawn to the justice-oriented work of artivism. In her work with LGBTQ+ youth, Rhoades (2012) describes artivism as a way of "synthesizing arts-based and social justice-centered pedagogies [that] may capitalize on youth's assets by fostering creative, engaging, challenging, and transformative discourses that can impact the consequences of being LGBTQ" (p. 320). Artivism, as she notes, "has allowed such youth to transform from oppressed victims into community-based artists, educational activists, and agents of change" (p. 320).

Rhoades's (2012) focus on artivism builds on Asante's (2008) positioning of the arts in a "crucial and critical space" (p. 203) insofar as understanding how art has the ability to impact the multiple ways people address inequities, inequalities, and oppressions throughout the world. More specifically, for Asante (2008), the role of art is to "shed light, to encourage all life-forms, to promote growth, to provide warmth, to let us imagine and dream . . ." as well as "to create and to have a palpable impact in the real world" (p. 205). We turn to art because we recognize it as a longstanding consciousness-raising medium, playing a vital role in historical and contemporary social movements. We bring to this space our memories of the artwork of Aminah Robinson, who relied on family and community stories to create her artwork, and Emory Douglas, who helped cultivate the visual identity of the Black Panther Party. Additionally, we rely on the photographs of Kojo Kamau, known for his photographs that documented the lives and cultures of people across the world, and Carrie Mae Weems, who uses art to explore family relationships, cultural identity, and power. In addition to these important artists, we also consider the significance of pamphlets, buttons, shirts, and paraphernalia (all as art forms) from the United Farm Workers, Black Panther Party, Women of Color Feminist movements, and LGBTQ movements, among others.

In the course, we used music and film because of their potential for highlighting inequities. Because we were not as familiar with other media, we partnered with a local arts center to help us understand how students can use different media for empowerment and as a way to share stories. It was through this partnership that we began to consider storytelling an act of resistance that can encourage teachers and teacher educators to make space for students to bring their visions, lived experiences, and questions not only into classrooms, but also into conversations about justice and equity. As a result, we began to think about resistance, sociopolitical change, and student voice at the center of classrooms and how each represents a different form of disruption.

Necessary Disruptions

"To affirm the lives and literacies of young people inside schools," Kinloch (2018, p. 4) calls for disruptive approaches in teaching and teacher education. She conceptualizes "teaching as acts of necessary disruptions" (p. 5). In other words, to teach is to engage in intentional practices that push back against xenophobic, classist, homophobic, transphobic, racist, sexist, and patriarchal rhetoric and behaviors within and beyond classrooms. She centers "the high-leverage practice" of "explaining and modeling content, practices, and strategies" to include "Teaching as examinations and interrogations into sociopolitical, sociocultural, economic, and educational contexts that perpetuate oppression, hatred, and violence" (Kinloch, 2018, p.6). In asking students to think about "humanity" in a humanities course, to develop projects that call attention to oppressive acts, and to analyze creative texts for their sociopolitical commentary, educators begin to engage in such "high-leverage practices."

Necessary disruptions, in our work, focus on various "high-leverage practices," including supporting students to explain the practices and strategies they use in their projects, encouraging students to facilitate group presentations, and working with students to partner with community groups. Collectively, we (Jenell, Johnny, Tamara, and students) were building upon Kinloch's (2018) notion of disruptions as necessary to transforming classrooms, communities, and society. In this way, the work happening inside our classroom represented attempts to engage in necessary disruptions in teaching and learning, which impacted how students interacted with people inside community spaces. Such necessary disruptions were manifested through our attention to coalition building, consciousness raising, and policy changes in education. Embracing the activist work of art alongside the belief that young people can use art as a form of civic engagement offers us opportunities to imagine classrooms as spaces for inquiry-driven engagements rooted in social justice. Through these lenses, the inner workings of revolutionary civics can emerge.

Revolutionary Civics

We conceptualize revolutionary civics as engagements where students, teachers, and community members collectively discuss, analyze, and challenge longstanding forms of oppression and injustice. Through this lens, teachers, students, and community members are co-conspirators in the work toward justice, equity, and liberation. The lens of revolutionary civics emerges from the theoretical space between the preceding frameworks. First, it takes seriously Kinloch's (2018) "necessary disruptions" to consider how young people's inquiry-driven, social justice art disrupts our understandings of teaching, learning, and youth engagement. It also takes love, commitment, and solidarity as indispensable to working with youth and marginalized communities. By reimagining youth civic engagement, we take up Mirra and Garcia's (2017) call to consider the "modalities of youth participation" (p. 144) to understand how young people have and use their agency in participatory ways. While they are interested in digital technologies, we turn to Rhoades's (2012) and Asante's (2008) conceptions of artivism to consider the type of artistic disruptions young people engage in as they work toward justice.

Teachers' practices can become disruptive when they destroy the walls between classroom and community and drastically alter the relationships between schools and communities (centering engagement). As a result, community members and youth learn to hear and see one another. In classrooms, disruptive students occupy school spaces in ways that challenge the body regulating rules of school. Such students speak at a louder volume than their teachers and/or classmates, answer different questions from the one the teacher posed, stand rather than sit, do not walk in single-file lines, dance in the hallways, hold conversations about music, television shows, and anything other than what the current lesson is covering. The overpolicing of such students is disruptive. School violence is disruptive. Thus, we are pushing for a different conception of disruptive beyond the assumed "negative" occupying acts that young people engage in when the lessons become mundane, routine, and irrelevant; when young people feel dismissed; and when school authorities want "professional/middle-class" behaviors from non-middle-class Black, Brown, gender diverse, and multilingual youth.

Disruptions are wrecking balls to the current societal norms of standardization, monolingualism, and monoculturalism. Disruptions are fugitive and futurity moves. They work in the present toward futures to ensure that educational equity becomes realized in theory and in practice. As we think deeply about disruptions, we rely on the framework of revolutionary civics to reassess our teaching philosophies and pedagogical approaches, and to consider how students responded to classroom activities and justice projects that reflected engagement, artivism, and necessary disruptions.

WHAT DOES IT MEAN TO BE A HUMAN BEING?

Journeys to (Social) Justice (Capstones)

The social justice focus of the World Humanities class began as a district initiative. Though we had a pacing guide, we realized that we needed to do more to disrupt traditional notions of what it means to teach social studies and language arts. The course began as a way to better coordinate a district-mandated freshman social justice capstone project that students completed at the end of the school year. Johnny developed the 9th-grade course with one other teacher and two intervention specialists. Originally, the team sought to integrate into the curriculum visual literacies (including using graphic novels) with traditional social studies and English to serve as a scaffold between films and books. They chose graphic novels that connected to the world history themes in the course and focused on essential questions (as provided by district curriculum), such as these:

- How can citizens change their government?
- Why do people move?
- What happens when cultures collide?
- Who were the "winners" and who were the "losers" in the age of imperialism?
- What is the impact of genocide? Who is responsible for the Holocaust?

These essential questions were meant to encourage students to use literary elements and rely on historical events to question, interrogate, and discuss meanings of social justice and injustice. However, many of the 9th-graders enrolled in the course initially resisted this curriculum and our approach to teaching and learning because the design of the course was different from how most had previously experienced learning in school. More specifically, the course did not focus on rote memorization or concrete answers to standardized curriculum; instead, it was student-led, dialogic, and, with Jenell and Johnny now co-teaching the course, full of multiple literacy experiences (such as historical and literary texts, images, music, film, guest speakers, presentations). The course design included an explicit attention to arts-integrated social justice projects, students as agents of change, questions about humanity, and discussions on learning as/for social justice.

The Social Justice Capstone: Bringing Learning to Life

After being approached by the outreach/education coordinator from the Wexner Center for the Arts—a multidisciplinary center connected to a local university that emphasizes exploration and advancement of contemporary art, arts education, and community outreach—Jenell and Johnny designed a unit in their course on "Explore. Explain. Empower: Art in Action" (2011–2012) and, in subsequent school years, a unit on "Explore. Establish. Explain. Empower: Art in Action." We wanted students to choose social justice topics that were relevant and critical to their lives. We wanted students to see (and engage with) what daily activism looked like, as opposed to the romanticized versions with which they were familiar. Through our partnership with the Wexner Center for the Arts, students were able to get up close and personal with the artist community in central Ohio and throughout the nation (for example, Noah Purifoy and Alexis Rockman). The partnership also helped us connect students with local Black artists and organizations and was instrumental in shaping our students' capstone projects.

Establish (added in second iteration): The focus of the first quarter was to emphasize the importance of not only establishing a topic of interest, but also establishing relationships with one another and with activists and organizations in our central Ohio community. Using a graffiti board, we had students build a working definition of "social justice" and revisited this graffiti board multiple times throughout the quarter to revise our class definition. We also had students choose an independent reading book from a list of about 30 nonfiction, social justice–focused books, such as *Sugar in the Raw* by Rebecca Carroll, *Fast Food Nation* by Eric Schlosser, *The Slave Next Door* by Kevin Bales and Ron Soodalter, and *The Other Wes Moore* by Wes Moore. Toward the end of the quarter, students grouped themselves into teams of four to select roles (project manager, data manager, documentation manager, and relationship manager) and a social justice topic. It was important for students to see that social justice activism happens with multiple hands on deck. It was also important that our students' concerns and experiences were always affirmed and that they were provided with opportunities to locate their bodies and voices within our shared humanity.

Explore: During the second grading period, students explored their chosen social justice topics through research and contacted activists and organizations already doing important work to address these social justice issues. It was imperative that students sought out local folks in the struggle to emphasize that justice work isn't solely the work of large, generational organizations, such as the NAACP, but the work of everyday people on the ground like them. At the end of the quarter, students presented their findings to the rest of the class in the format of an informal panel and received feedback in the form of questions, notes, and suggested resources. It was crucial for students to understand the importance of relying on one's community to help push along the work.

Explain: During the third grading period, students reviewed the classroom community's feedback and expanded on their initial research. They narrowed down their research questions and developed presentations and short handouts (print and/or digital) to share what they learned. Through social media (some groups) and during Art in Action Night (all groups), the students shared their experiences and learnings with their classmates and the greater community. Additionally, students practiced presenting to one another and to adults in the building.

Empower: In the final grading period, each student group created an art piece and an artists' card to communicate a message about their social justice issues. During this phase, students wrote grants to request art materials, consulted with professional artists, and worked in teams to construct art pieces that raised awareness, expressed a message, and/or disrupted assumptions about their social justice topics. We emphasized the need to connect with professional artists, disrupting the notion that the classroom teacher holds all the answers. At the end of the grading period, the students' art pieces were displayed in an art space during what we called Art in Action Night. We shared with students that we were inviting people and they should invite people, too, especially the community activists and artists who helped them along the way in order to thank them. We also told students, "We're going to tell people to ask you about your project." Therefore, Art in Action was not a night of notecards and prepackaged presentations. Instead, students had their art projects, which they worked on for months, and were expected to walk attendees through the pieces.

DISRUPTING NOTIONS OF SUSTAINABILITY

We saw art as an avenue for sustainability. In one of our writing sessions, Jenell shared: "We've seen this happen: Art is a form of activism; what emerged still shocked us." Equally shocking was that the projects became sustainable in ways we hadn't initially considered. We wanted students to engage in research projects around social justice topics that were critical to their lives. Initially and at the beginning of the school year, we envisioned sustainability to be a project that would just keep going. Sustainability for students meant going into the community to talk about why they did this project and what it meant to them. Some student projects were selected by local museums for display to reach a larger audience. Some students engaged in trainings and later trained other individuals beyond our high school. In fact, some of the students' relatives became involved in the projects and helped spread awareness to their families and community members. Other students created and sold T-shirts, while others went to middle schools to talk about their social justice issue. As a result, sustainability manifested in ways divergent from anything we could have ever planned for or imagined. Here, we share a few moments from students and their projects that still resonate with us and have reshaped our understandings of sustainability. These examples, we believe, represent a broader, more promising uptake of sustainability—as efforts people engage in during a defined time (for a lesson, within a school year) *and* as efforts that have a long-term impact on people's individual and collective engagements across space and time (the dissemination of projects outside of the classroom, the connections forged between classroom and community literacy engagements).

Example I

Marquan, one of our students, struggled freshman year with school work and social pressures. April Martin, filmmaker for *Cincinnati Goddamn*, a documentary about riots, worked with the students who wanted to create films as part of their Social Justice Capstone projects. Marquan's group worked with April to create a film about the social pressures and violence that LGBTQ youth face in schools. Once he began filming with April, Marquan came alive in the class. After working with April, Marquan realized his great interest in film (but did not work with any of the teachers in our school's film program). During his sophomore year, he became deeply involved in the high school's Gay-Straight Alliance (now named the Genders and Sexualities Alliance) and contacted April again, this time on his own, to gain advice on another film he was producing on LGBTQ rights. Unwilling to continue to subject himself to the violence of heterosexism and transphobia, Marquan eventually left the school during his junior year, but he became an ambassador with a local organization for queer youth and engaged in discourse with others in the city around LGBTQ issues. Marquan chose not to wait until he was an adult to engage in justice work against the oppression he was facing in the now.

Example II

After months of working on an art piece, one of Shayla's group members declared, "We don't have anywhere to store this." At the end of the Art in Action night, her group destroyed their artwork. To be honest, we thought that maybe this destruction indicated that they weren't as invested in the work and completed the assignment just for a grade. Never would we have imagined that 4 years later, Shayla would be drawing on her 9th-grade experiences doing justice work around domestic violence and even pursuing a career that would allow her to continue doing the work. For part of her 12th-grade writing portfolio, Shayla wrote a college entrance essay about domestic violence. In her essay, she detailed her commitment to this issue and all the work she had done and was still doing. She knew how to talk to survivors. She took her skills and wanted to pursue a career in social work and counseling. The topic and her passion for fighting for justice for victims of domestic violence had stuck with her throughout her high school career. Maybe it was something she witnessed or maybe it was having space in school that led her to do such work, but while we were wishing that the artwork would be the avenue through which their message would be sustained, it was the justice work that was sustained.

Example III

One group of students worked with a local activist on the city's near–East Side to investigate how and why neighborhoods change. By exploring a historically Black neighborhood, they learned how the space had evolved from an ethnic enclave to a vibrant, prosperous community, to a neglected shell, and finally to an "urban renewal project" undergoing gentrification and rebirth. Students studied the art of Aminah Robinson and worked with the King Arts Complex and with Kojo Kamau, a celebrated local artist and photographer, who gave students photographs of the neighborhood. Students compared Robinson's work and Kamau's photographs and to current realities. The students' cardboard sculpture sought to capture the current neighborhood in the style of Aminah Robinson's vibrant celebration of the neighborhood of her youth. Before graduating, the students donated their piece to a traveling exhibit curated by a local activist, and the art piece was circulated through the community (Riffe Center and King Arts Complex).

Example IV

Annie's group created a film titled *Vivian*, which focused on the human trafficking of young women close to home. At the end of her sophomore year, Annie chose to enter a 2-year welding career center program. By the time she needed to decide on a senior capstone, she combined her 9th-grade work about young women trafficked for labor and sex work with her experience as a young woman disrupting and challenging the rules of a male-dominated workplace. Annie's long-term plan was to work as a welder before entering college. Once in college, she planned to major in women's, gender, and sexuality studies and eventually write about her experiences as a woman in the welding industry as well as the experiences of other women in similar industries. Olivia's mother also worked as a welder and she hoped to raise awareness about women's struggles in male-dominated workplaces.

Example V

After watching Majora Carter's TED Talk "Greening the Ghetto," Mackenzie and her group chose to focus their capstone project on an environmental justice issue: radon poisoning in homes. Mackenzie's group found that radon gas emissions disproportionately impact poor and marginalized communities. Mackenzie and her group mates identified areas around central Ohio that were at the greatest risk of radon poisoning, contacted companies, sought out costs for testing kits, and developed a multitiered campaign to raise awareness and advocate for change. This project extended to Mackenzie's family, who tested their own homes and the homes of others in their communities. Additionally, her father (an MD) learned with his daughter and communicated the knowledge to his patients. Following her freshman year, Mackenzie went on to develop a schoolwide diversity club to address issues of equity and justice. During her junior year, she presented her own TEDx Talk about the history and importance of natural hair to various cultural groups. Mackenzie did not wait for another school project to engage in justice work. She took matters into her own hands by building a coalition of students to continue to address inequalities and inequities and used her powerful voice to disrupt oppressive narratives about the natural hair of Black and Brown peoples.

Through these stories, we learn that teaching and learning about social justice through art and, relatedly, creating and disseminating ideas as artwork, are not so much about the art itself. These things are also about the potential lessons and engagements that can result from the art-making process. Reflecting on Shayla's story, we realize that although the group destroyed the art piece at the end of Art in Action night, they all confessed to storing the artwork mentally and to having taken pieces of it with them into their ongoing thinking about domestic violence. Shayla, her group members, and the various students featured here disrupt our conceptions of what art can do by disrupting and moving beyond limited notions of sustainability. Students may destroy and/or donate artwork, part ways with their mentors, or leave the school altogether, but they continue to carry the ideas. It is through these stories that we have become more aware that we were cultivating revolutionary civics by encouraging students to engage in artivism and necessary disruptions with courage, in collaboration, and through risk-taking. We were teaching students and students were teaching us "how can you get the answers you want," which is evident in how they created, produced, and presented their capstones and engaged in learning interventions in both the present and in the future. This is an example, we argue, of revolutionary civics.

IMPLICATIONS FOR MOVING FORWARD WITH REVOLUTIONARY CIVICS

We close this chapter by returning to a question that guides this book: "What needs to happen inside schools in relation to race, justice, and activism in literacy teacher education?" We believe that revolutionary civics needs to happen inside all K–12 classrooms and in teacher education programs. However, before enacting these practices, teachers and teacher educators must be willing to engage in the reflexive and dialogic processes of becoming disruptive. In other words, what are you willing to risk to become a justice-oriented educator, agitator, or co-conspirator (Love, 2019)?

As educators, we must sit with a few questions that bring into focus who we are, who we are working for and with, and what we are working toward. These questions include the following:

Who we are: Why should we take a revolutionary civics approach in our classrooms? What are our individual and collective understandings of community and engagement? How will these engagements impact students, communities, and me? Who are we in this sociopolitical moment?

Who we are working for and with: Are we working for ourselves or for others? How are we envisioning those with and for whom we are working? What roles are we playing and willing to play? In other words, are we allies, advocates, or accomplices and co-conspirators? To answer the last question, we must consider risk: What are we willing to risk in order to do this work and to work with (and for) community members and/or students? How are they included in the work?

What we are working toward: Tuck and Yang (2016, 2018) remind us that justice is in flux, its position is ever-changing. Therefore, to work *toward* justice means that we, too, are constantly in motion and in conversation, recognizing that justice is not a destination. We recognize that each community and individual has varied definitions of what justice looks like, requires, and wants. We ask of you the same question that Tamara posed to students enrolled in her African American and African Studies course: "How will we know that we have attained justice?"

In answering these questions, we begin to reassess our classrooms, practices, and dispositions. We are then able to confront our biases, name our limitations, and chip away at our hesitations to make room for new ways to learn, collaborate, and confront injustices. For Mirra and Garcia (2017), "Deep exploration of the root causes of racial inequality in this country requires that education refuse to force youth to conform to dominant systems of civic participation and instead create space for interrogation and innovation" (p. 144). However, we believe this to be true for racial inequality as well as racial and gender violence, classism, sexism, transphobia, anti-Blackness, anti-Indigenous, anti-immigrant, and other forms of xenophobia. It is only then that we make room for imagination, collaboration, futurity, and humanity.

Making room requires a commitment to intentional and necessary disruptions in the curricula and classroom. To make room for imagination (Greene, 1995) requires that we design classroom activities, readings, assignments, and discussions with the belief that students are and will continue to become learners, teachers, and innovators. This requires that students be invited to envision themselves as learners, teachers, and innovators. To make room for collaboration requires that we all learn how to develop sustainable partnerships. Students, practicing teachers, and preservice teacher education candidates should all be included in processes of working with and listening to community partners. Doing so would further encourage them to also learn about why changes in partnerships are acceptable, healthy, and often necessary to maintain the integrity of a project or partnership. To keep people (most importantly students) at the center is to make room for humanity. This connects with the previous point about collaboration, in that we have to learn to make decisions with students that are best for students, not just for community partners and/or teachers.

Revolutionary civics requires knowing when to move. For example, there are times when adults must get out of the way, even if students don't request it. When adults move to the sidelines, students have opportunities to imagine alternate, innovative ways for civic engagement that embrace futurity, hope, and action. Moving does not mean abandonment; instead, moving opens up space for students to collaborate with community members and other students. Moving suggests a reciprocated level of respect, as in teachers and students respecting one another's decisions and contributions. Moving also suggests a reciprocated level of trust—teachers trusting that students will make ethical decisions as they engage in artivism through responsible inquiry and develop creative interventions. As a result, the spaces that emerge in revolutionary civics are grounded in disruptions. More specifically, we must uproot and/or unhinge the way we see and interact with one another in the work toward social justice. When we open our classrooms and communities to young people's inquiry and art, we disrupt closed-circuit approaches to teaching, learning, and youth engagement. With these openings, we began to access, create and imagine routes to liberation and humanity for all.

REFLECTIVE QUESTIONS

1. Who are our students and why should we use a revolutionary civics approach in our classrooms?
2. What are we working toward (for example, justice) and in what ways will we know that we have attained it, especially when it comes to teacher education?

REFERENCES

Asante, M. K., Jr. (2008). *It's bigger than hip-hop: The rise of the post-hip-hop generation.* New York, NY: St. Martin's Press.

Combahee River Collective Statement. (1971) In B. Guy-Sheftall (Ed.), *Words of fire: An anthology of African-American feminist thought* (pp. 232–240). New York, NY: The New Press. Retrieved from circuitous.org/scraps/combahee.html

Garcia, A., & Dutro, E. (2018). Electing to heal: Trauma, healing, and politics in classrooms. *English Education, 50*(4), 375–383.

Garcia, A., Mirra, N., Morrell, E., Martinez, A., & Scorza, D. (2015). The council of youth research: Critical literacy and civic agency in the digital age. *Reading & Writing Quarterly, 31*(2), 151–167.

Greene, M. (1995). *Releasing the imagination: Essays on education, the arts, and social change.* San Francisco, CA: Jossey-Bass.

Johnson, E., & Vasudevan, L. (2012). Seeing and hearing students' lived and embodied critical literacy practices. *Theory into Practice, 51*(1), 34–41.

Jordan, J. (2007). Calling on all silent minorities. In *Directed by desire: The complete poems of June Jordan*, (p. 149). Port Townsend, WA: Copper Canyon Press.

Kinloch, V. (2018). Necessary disruptions: Examining justice, engagement, and humanizing approaches to teaching and teacher education. *TeachingWorks Working Papers*, 1–23. Retrieved from teachingworks.org/images/files/TeachingWorks_Kinloch.pdf

Love, B. (2019). *We want to do more than survive: Abolitionist teaching and the pursuit of educational freedom*. Boston, MA: Beacon Press.

Mirra, N., Coffey, J., & Englander, A. (2018). Warrior scholars and bridge builders: Civic dreaming in ELA classrooms. *Journal of Literacy Research, 50*(4), 423–445.

Mirra, N., & Garcia, A. (2017). Re-imagining civic participation: Youth interrogating and innovating in the multimodal public sphere. *Review of Research in Education, 41*, 136–158.

Rankine, C. (2015, June 22). The condition of Black life is one of mourning. *The New York Times Magazine*. Retrieved from nytimes.com/2015/06/22/magazine/the-condition-of-black-life-is-one-of-mourning.html

Rhoades, M. (2012). LGBTQ youth + video artivism: Arts-based critical civic praxis. *Studies in Art Education: a Journal of Issues and Research in Art Education, 53*(4), 317–329.

Torrez, E. (2018). Responsibility, reciprocity and respect: Storytelling as a means of university-community engagement. In M. Castañeda & J. Krupczynski (Eds.), *Civic engagement in diverse Latino communities: Learning from social justice partnerships in action* (pp. 143–158). New York, NY: Peter Lang.

Tuck, E., & Yang, K. W. (2016). What justice wants. *Journal of the Critical Ethnic Studies Association, 2*(2), 1.

Tuck, E., & Yang, K. W. (Eds.). (2018). *Toward what justice? Describing diverse dreams of justice in education.* New York, NY: Routledge.

Poetic Musings
Remembering Our Black Youth/Our Black Lives

Carlotta Penn, Valerie Kinloch, and Tanja Burkhard

"The Case of Masonique Saunders,"[1]
A 16-year-old Black teenage girl,
Present when her unarmed teenage boyfriend,
16-year-old Julius Tate Jr.,
Was shot dead by undercover police officers.
A witness to his murder, his death,
Charged with aggravated robbery and murder,
Although she did not kill him.
But Ohio Revised Code 2903.02
Allows Masonique Saunders to be charged,
Because this is the law, that if it is judged that
"They cause the death of another
as a proximate result of the offender's committing or attempting to commit
an offense of violence that is a felony of the first or second degree."

Her mother wants "to know what actually took place."
She said, "I don't know, really. It's hard and I'm emotional."
She doesn't "think that's right."
"They shouldn't be able to do that."[2]

We do not know Masonique Saunders,
We did not know Julius Tate Jr.,
And we did not know 13-year-old Tamir Rice,
A Black boy who was shot dead
While running away (unarmed) from police officers
Two years before and only a few streets from where Tate was killed.
In this same square mile,
A Black teenager hung himself from a tree just a few months ago.
All of these tragedies happened blocks away
From schools and community centers,
From churches and mosques.

There are dozens more Black youth
Who we do not know
But we know.

These are our people.
We are afraid for our Black children/our Black lives
Because we know how quickly their joys/our joys
Can be blown out of the space their heart should beat.

We know that we "dark people" (Love, 2019)
Are seen as disposable to many, but not to us.
Yet somehow, we remain dedicated to justice, freedom, and liberation.
Calling on our foremothers—
Kathryn Ferguson, Maria Stewart, Mary McLeod Bethune—
Black women who have been at the forefront
Of educational advancement in Black communities,
Demonstrating perseverance, resilience, and rigor
In the face of disenfranchisement, poverty, and violence.
From "Generations of Fugitive Literacy Teacher Education and Activism,"
And "Preparing Literacy Teachers in the Digital Age" to
"Students Developing Critical Language and Literacy Perspectives,"
"Rethinking Curriculum and Pedagogy in Schools"
To "Arlene's Actionist Work" and "Pardon this Disruption."

We will continue to write and fight
And push for liberating literacies and social justice.

NOTE

1. See 10tv.com/article/mother-masonique-saunders-says-daughter-told-her-julius-tate-did-not-have-gun-night-he-was
2. See Love, B. L. (2019). *We want to do more than survive: Abolitionist teaching and the pursuit of educational freedom.* Boston, MA: Beacon Press.

PART II OVERVIEW

Tanja Burkhard

Robert Kelly (2002) asserts that "[i]n the poetics of struggle and lived experience, in the utterances of ordinary folk, in the cultural products of social movements, in the reflections of activists, we discover the many different cognitive maps of the future, of the world not yet born" (p. 10). The section that follows not only brings together chapters that invite us to consider the ways Teachers and Students of Color co-construct and explore knowledges theoretically and in practice, but each chapter also beckons us to imagine this "world not yet born." In particular, each chapter differently invites us to reimagine how we engage in language and literacy learning and to examine our values connected to both. Collectively, the section highlights the implications of race, justice, and activism in literacy instruction.

For example, in Chapter 7, Thomas does this work by centering Black literature, history, and culture to take students in a multicultural classroom on a journey of discovery and knowledge of self. This chapter highlights the ways teacher activism, active discussions on race, and the exploration of work by racialized peoples can push forward a justice-based agenda for students of all backgrounds. In Chapter 8, Lyiscott demonstrates how after-school spaces created with the literacies of Students of Color in mind can function as catalysts for meaning-making in ways that further support students in developing, questioning, and understanding their own politics, as well as the politics of their community.

Relatedly, Chapter 9 by Saeedi and Richardson articulates the tensions and potentials of considering language- and literacy-based approaches to the concept of code-switching. The implications of this work extend far beyond classrooms, formal education, and even theoretical approaches, as it highlights the complex and often hidden forms anti-Black racism can take, even within discourses and approaches intended to counter it. This is important to note, given the need to focus on how students, teachers, and researchers can use literacy as a tool by which to combat anti-Blackness. In many ways, this latter point is highlighted in Watson, Deroo, and Skogsberg's Chapter 10, which illustrates the various ways in which young people create, enterprise, and innovate through language and literacy when given the freedom, opportunity, and space to do so. Finally, Chapter 11 by Ghiso, Campano, Player, Krishanwongso, and Gultom concludes this volume by compellingly highlighting the power of stories, lived experience, and identity construction for educators and students. Their work exemplifies how to approach solidarity and work across difference by treating the story of each person with respect, dignity, and care.

Taken together, the chapters in this second section all provide necessary roadmaps for literacy instruction that is rooted in a deep care for students and educators alike, or, in the words of Robert Kelly (2002), "the many different cognitive maps of the future" (p. 10).

REFERENCE

Kelley, R. D. G. (2002). *Freedom dreams: The Black radical imagination* (1st electronic ed.). Boston, MA: Beacon Press.

CHAPTER 7

One Love, One Heart

Donja Thomas

ONE LOVE

The lyrics to "One Love/People Get Ready," the reggae song written and re-corded by the great Bob Marley and the Wailers from their 1977 album, *Exodus* (Marley,1977), communicate the need to have universal brotherhood and global unity. Marley's overarching message that everyone in the world should stop fighting and become one is grounded in a sentiment of spiritual redemption for those whose faith is strong and whose deeds are righteous. Its universal power encouraged listeners across geographic, racial, and religious lines to rise above racism, stand apart from despair, and work to end cycles of pain and injustice. It is important to acknowledge that "One Love/People Get Ready" is a powerful song that is influenced by Black vernacular traditions of expression (spirituals, gospel, blues, and soul) and ways of being that high-light the struggles and hardships people of African descent continue to face. Additionally, the song is rooted in the foundational belief of Pan-Africanism and Black consciousness.[1] Although the ballad does not specify any particu-lar nationality or racial group in its declarations toward love, humanity, and unity, in its second stanza, Marley (1977) asks the question: "Is there a place for the hopeless sinner, who has hurt all mankind just to save his own?" From both a historical and educational perspective, this question acknowledges and cross-examines the centuries-long suppression of African cultures and Black excellence by Europeans in their conquest to accumulate power and wealth through the dehumanizing practices of chattel slavery and legalized racism. It also further emphasizes the prophetic redemption ordained upon those of African descent to reclaim their cultural connections in spite of their suffering in order to "come together and feel all right" (Marley, 1977).

Throughout this chapter, I draw inspiration from "One Love/People Get Ready" as I argue that a focus on Blackness and Black studies is an import-ant foundational component in educating young people to reclaim historical and cultural knowledge rooted in African ancestral heritage that has been left out of traditional education curricula. All Black people across the world share blood and history in their bond to the motherland of Africa. This legacy also carries with it the power to unite a people so long oppressed and to liberate new generations of people to break destructive cycles and create for themselves a better future. However, few educational spaces, in the presence of racist educational policies meant to standardize and minimize teaching and learning in indeterminable ways, are designed to value and make visible the cultural knowledge that contributes to the formation of racial consciousness and positive cultural identity constructions.

Thus, this chapter speaks to my own creation of an academic space where no "space" naturally existed. That is, there was not a space or a community of practice[2] (Kinloch, Nemeth, & Patterson, 2014; Lave & Wenger, 1991) within the school where I teach for students to deeply examine Black contributions to the world and their own interconnectedness to Black history, culture, and literature. I created such a space in my English literature classroom as a way to showcase how exposure to and attainment of critically conscious knowledge that is centered in Blackness encourages growth toward enlightenment in matters of identity, acceptance, achievement, and cultural collectivity. To demonstrate aspects of this work, I focus on four racially and socially diverse young ladies who participated in a qualitative action research study in my African American Voice course. Connected to this discussion is a description of how parallels among curricular development (why I created the course), instruction/praxis (how I collaborated with students as influenced by how and what I taught), and research (how theory and methodology impact teaching and learning) lend themselves to supporting student achievement, identity constructions, and critical consciousness development. Overall, this chapter highlights implications that emerge when students are supported by their teacher to form communities of practice within traditional educational contexts and encouraged to critique topics centered on race, class, and identity through examination of Black cultural and literary practices.

TOWARD THE BELOVED COMMUNITY

Communities of practice are formed by people who engage in a process of collective learning in a shared domain, or space, of human encounter (Wenger, 2000). These groups are comprised of people who share a passion for learning and/or doing something, and through their regular interactions, they learn how to do it better. They develop a shared repertoire of resources: experiences, stories, tools, ways of addressing problems, and so forth that help them help and learn from one another. As a Black woman educator, my identity and epistemologies are greatly influenced by my individual experiences, collective memories, ancestral knowledge attainment, critical literacy practices, and historical and cultural pride rooted in the power of "Blackness." I grew up in a close-knit community of practice that consisted of men and women who collectively and consistently shared their resources with one another to support Black autonomy and resist white hegemonic systems. I can relate to the importance of collective learning that emerged from a community of practice. I have been loved, protected, and enlightened by many in my community, including righteous men and wise women, and their love, support, and criticism have greatly influenced my decision to be an educator. More importantly, their love and support have created within me great pride in my community, our history, and the beauty that Blackness encompasses. The ongoing support of these men and women has helped create my passion to build curricula and provide spaces that encourage the formation of communities of practice inside my classroom centered on Black literary and cultural traditions.

Therefore, I believe that educational spaces that ignore cultural histories, perspectives, and experiences of Black people can contribute directly to a lack of knowledge of self. This leads to a generation of young people lacking the tools they need to be powerful community members and leaders committed to the reclamation of truth and reconciliation needed to bring to fruition the ideal existence of a loving and equalizing society that honors all of humanity. Through my positioning, I seek to make visible some of the ways students can question, analyze, and resist institutionalized racism through historical and investigative studies of Blackness.

In order for young people to both question and resist injustices, I believe spaces must be made available in schools and communities for young people, teachers, and researchers to explore race, power, and identity. In particular, reading Black literature, discussing historical and cultural perspectives, and critiquing popular theorizations of Blackness can help dispel miseducated learning practices and help young people discover the value of Black literature, history, and traditions—that Black people have contributed (and continue to contribute) an important intellectual knowledge base throughout the world. Additionally, teachers, teacher educators, and literacy researchers could benefit from utilizing culturally relevant practices (Kinloch, 2012; Ladson-Billings, 1995; Paris, 2012) in their pedagogical engagements with students as they address topics of racism, sexism, and power. Doing this work can help young people explore how they can contribute to addressing some of the many educational inequities and social inequalities that plague public schools and that have a devastating impact in our world.

Thus, the overall context of African American Voice (AA Voice) as a community of practice focuses on Black cultural, educational, literary, and intellectual ways of being and knowing. The creation of literacy spaces that support a critical examination of Black history, cultural contributions, and intellectual traditions (Hill, 2009; Kinloch, 2012; Nasir, 2012), and attend to the global dimensions of literacy instruction that fosters discourses of care (Delpit, 1995, 1996; Ladson-Billings, 1994, 1995; Paris, 2012; Woodson, 1990) is a portal through which liberation and transformation can occur. This was the case in my AA Voice course.

FINDING A VOICE

The collective will, fortitude, and spirit demonstrated by people of African descent in the face of racism, oppression, and injustice are the very factors that give me the strength to be an educator committed to teaching about Black historical and cultural perspectives. These factors have also given me the bravery to create an academic space (within a traditional schooling context) in which multiple voices of Black people are present and made known to young people so that they may be studied and appreciated. Undoubtedly, when I created and began to teach African American Voice, I found my own voice. In turn, I have been able to encourage and support the amplification of the voices of students by exposing them to Black studies.

In 2009, I created AA Voice as a core credit high school English course at "We Gon Be Alright," a suburban public high school in the U.S. Midwest. The high school population currently is around 2,300 students. Approximately 62% of the students in the district population are white, 22% are African American, 6% are multiracial, 3% are Asian, and nearly 6% are Hispanic/Latino. Around 170–200 students in the district attend English language learner classes, with approximately 26 different native languages spoken.

I see the course as a revolutionary academic adventure in which high school seniors explore aspects of the Black experience through song, language, literature, history, and film. The course supports students' inquiries into multiple aspects of Black literary and cultural experiences by utilizing novels, essays, letters, poems, plays, musical texts, lectures, documentaries, and other media resources. Students learn about the richness of Black studies, study how Black culture supports academic achievement, and consider the role of Black culture in American society and throughout the African diaspora. For example, they might read James Baldwin's (1962) "Letter to My Nephew" and Angela Davis's (1997) *Race and Criminalization* as they study how racism interacts with the concept of social justice in America. Baldwin's thoughts on his nephew's future in a country with a terrible history of racism brings a personal, powerful, and still relevant narrative to the harsh realities facing those who are Black in America 100 years after the emancipation of slavery, while Davis's piece provides insight into the proverbial systematic ways in which racism permeates throughout the political and social spheres of this country, leading to the creation of the prison–industrial complex as a form of modern-day slavery. They might also listen to Nina Simone's (1968) "Backlash Blues" and, among many others, Kendrick Lamar's (2012) "Sing About Me," bringing attention to how American Black vernacular traditions are oral histories used to document and creatively express the Black human experience. Including diverse texts in the course exposes students to a range of literature by and about African American scholars, writers, and intellectuals, all while helping to enrich the knowledge base of students who might not have otherwise studied this often-overlooked body of scholarship.

Additionally, students learn about a range of contributions by people of African descent and how these contributions have influenced and transformed America and the world. My goal is to provide students with a greater awareness of the Black experience as they investigate, research, and critique major issues directly related to Black literature, history, cultural perspectives, social issues, and experiences (such as cultural practices, "secret" communities of practice, white hegemony, discrimination, and oppression). With their increasing awareness, I witness how students begin to discover and utilize an array of literacy practices across school and community contexts. For example, after reading an exposé about the early-20th-century legacy of Black Wall Street in Tulsa, Oklahoma, students read the article "Black Artists Unite to Revive Black Wall Street's Legacy" (2019) from *The Root*, an online magazine. They made connections to how actions from the past can inform the present. They also connected the exposé and the article to lessons they learned from a lecture by John Henrik Clarke in which he stated, "History is a current event" (2012). In an effort to make larger textual connections across the readings, students elected to listen to an interview that aired on Power 105.1 (a radio station) featuring economist Dr. Boyce Watkins (2017), who discussed the importance of Black ownership. As I reflect on this experience, I can imagine how students could then watch an episode of Viceland's "Hustle" (2019) titled "What It Takes to Launch a Company" as they consider ways to create the type of reality they seek for themselves. My point is that in AA Voice, students have a shared repertoire of resources (experiences, stories, tools, texts, and ways of addressing problems) that help them work with, learn from, and build with one another.

Important to note is that AA Voice was born out of the ideology that it is inaccurate to teach American literature from only a white patriarchal dominant perspective. This perspective, whose gaze continues to define the direction of American literature in traditional U.S. high school classrooms, does not include the important contributions, perspectives, and voices of Black people as connected to "American" history and culture. Toni Morrison (1998), for example, asserts that this perspective would have us believing that "our [Black] lives have no meaning and no depth without the White gaze." This philosophy of Black exclusion in education has given me the courage to teach differently and to incorporate relevant lenses and diverse representations of Black literature and vernacular traditions into English curricula so that students are well rounded in their understanding of Black culture and so that they can be active learners, thinkers, participants, and doers in the world.

LET'S GET FREE

In "Black Studies: Bringing Back the Person," poet June Jordan (1981) states, "Body and Soul, Black America reveals the extreme questions of contemporary life, questions of freedom and identity: How can I be who I am?" (p. 46). Jordan poses an important question for young people to consider. The lack of knowledge about issues of "freedom and identity" that isolates many young people from one another stems from forms of miseducation that result from the ongoing exclusion of the Black voice as a significant resource in national and global discussions about social and educational progress. For Jordan, education, especially in the United States, parallels "the history of our Black lives," which have been largely "characterized by punishment of nonconformity, abridgement, withered enthusiasm, distortion, and self-denying censorship" (Jordan, 1981, p. 50). As a result, state-sanctioned forms of education have mostly benefited the lives and interests of white America and have been marked "by reverence for efficiency, cultivation of competence unattended by concern for aim, big white lies, and the mainly successful blackout of Black life" (Jordan, 1981, p. 50; see also Kinloch & Grebowicz, 2004). This is why the emergence of Black studies, as an academic area of interest for all people (Black and non-Black students), is an important part of the curriculum of schools and universities.

Within the AA Voice curriculum, there is an intentional focus on Black studies and Black historians, educators, philosophers, authors, artists, and civil and human rights advocates, whose systems of thought and broad conceptual frameworks of cultural representation, social justice, self-determination, and resistance are analyzed in a classroom community. For example, in regard to the topic of Black nationalism, the great influence of the scholar and activist Marcus Garvey and the role he played in garnering Pan-Africanist thought and ideals of economic independence among Black Americans as the founder of the United Negro Improvement Association would be an essential resource as students learn about and analyze Black power. The purpose of this curriculum is to challenge students to move closer toward a critical consciousness that, in many cases, has been kept dormant and "caged" by design through traditional schooling practices. In my experience as a student, teacher, and researcher, I find that traditional schooling practices in American schools do not educate students; instead, they indoctrinate students. Humans are social beings shaped by cultural context, and most educational curricula adopted by school systems today are void of diverse and equal cultural representation. Therefore, there are many truths replaced with lies in order to produce "good" Americans who learn and accept foundational principles that align with white supremacist power structures. The freedom referenced in the title of this section ("Let's Get Free") speaks to the concept of freeing into consciousness minds that have "cl[u]ng tenaciously to their thinly disguised philosophical idiom" (King & Swartz, 2016, p. iv). Some of my students are aware of the distortion of history, but admit to feeling helpless in knowing how and where to attain the knowledge they need to break free of this distortion. Others confess to believing the false narratives they have been told in order to affirm their lack of action and responsibility toward debunking this propaganda. For example, one year, as my students were engaged in unpacking the ways in which the U.S. government has systematically discriminated against Black Americans, one of my students spoke candidly to the class about how she now realized that her beliefs that Black people were innately lazy and were the cause of their own destructive condition were based on fallacies that she chose to believe in order to benefit from her white privilege. Those in both groups are given the option of freedom in AA Voice through student-led, co-constructed learning opportunities, writing assignments that allow student privacy and freedom of speech, and classroom discourse that honors every student's voice and perspective. As a community of practice that seeks knowledge and whose members fall into both categories, we find that miseducation, to some degree, has crippled all of us. There is an intentional approach on recovering historical content, one that entails "re-membering" or reconnecting knowledge of the past that has been silenced or distorted (King & Swartz, 2016). I believe it is necessary to work alongside students as we collectively seek healing and renewal, and as we work for freedom and move toward liberation.

In AA Voice, working for freedom and moving toward liberation requires that Black voices no longer remain silent/silenced, but are given a space to be studied, talked about, and represented. I tell my students that the best way to conquer a people is to divide them and the best way to divide them is to keep them ignorant of the love that binds them. By centering the study of Black culture in our classroom community—a community made up of diverse student identities—the importance of valuing humanity and talking explicitly about racism, identity, and opportunity becomes the focus that overrides the ignorance meant to divide us.

FOUR YOUNG GIRLS: LAUREN, SYDNEY, SHANNON, AND MYA

In response to readings and culminating discussions about such topics as Black studies, the Black arts movement, roots of racism as a social construction, the great African civilizations, the Moors, and the importance of knowing one's history, four young girls with fluid identities[3] partially shaped by their different racial, ethnic, socioeconomic backgrounds, and distinct interactions within and outside the various iterations of the African American Voice course, all demonstrate how their increasing knowledge attainment that centers Black culture transforms into the freeing of misconceptions that they once viewed as truths. Their experiences also demonstrate how centering Black studies in education can foster a culture of belonging and community that values the Black experience and a focus on diversity.

"ALLOW ME TO INTRODUCE MYSELF"

Lauren has attended "Lion's Den" schools her whole life and, although she is a biracial 17-year-old who has been adopted and raised by a Black family, she does not define herself solely by race or ethnicity, but by an identity that she has established beyond her family's influence. When Lauren and I conducted our first round of student–teacher interviews during the first quarter of the school year, I asked her to indicate how she identified herself. She said that she does not "like to identify myself by race. But I am biracial. And . . . that doesn't really matter to me." She continued: "Race and things like that don't really have, like, a meaning to me, in a sense. I mean, you are what you are, but at the same time it shouldn't depict how people think about you." Lauren's response made me curious about how she would respond to Black literature that specifically spoke to how one's Blackness did, indeed, impact how individuals continue to be treated and defined in the world, regardless of how they felt about themselves.

Lauren then shared, "I think that identity is how you feel about yourself. I don't think identity is defined by how or what other people think about you. I think that it's, um . . . you know who you are. And sometimes, you know, it takes a while to figure out . . . like, figure out who you are, yourself." This last statement was quite profound in that it spoke to the journey that she would be embarking on when it came to determining, or understanding, her own evolving identity, whether she recognized it or not. All the knowledge she would be exposed to and the experiences she would encounter during this school year, academically and personally, would, I hoped, inform how she came to (re)identify herself. I began to wonder: Would Lauren be consciously aware of what she allowed or did not allow to shape and contribute to her identity construction?

Raised by her mother, who is a single parent and an administrator in an inner-city school, Sydney, a 17-year-old African American girl, has a strong sense of who she wants to be, but she often lacks confidence in who she is at the present moment. Her father, a municipal court judge, also shows great support toward Sydney, but outside of her family life, she seems to be looking for positive confirmation and self-validation. Her experience at "We Gon' Be Alright" high school has been one of great highs but also unnerving lows. Considered a very good student during her junior year, Sydney shared during her first-round interview with me that she went through a phase where she really did not care about her grades: "I just made some bad decisions and started skipping school because I was just, like, why am I even here? And after I learned from that, before then, I had really good grades and like really good attendance, but I didn't know what I was doing it for." Then, she shared that she had a realization: "So, after that, I kinda had to reevaluate, like how I value education and why I want to go to school." This realization lent itself to understanding why Sydney chose to take AA Voice. She often found herself as the sole African American student in many of her classes at "We Gon' Be Alright" high school and was very interested in this Black literature course offering that centered her culture as its learning focus.

When I posed the question, "Who Am I?", which invited Sydney and other participants to openly reflect on their sense of identities, Sydney responded: "Just like a cake that you bake, I am a result of what was put into my upbringing." She went on to explain: "Some cakes turn out to be really soft, really sweet, or really heavy depending how much sugar you may have put into the batter as well as milk and flour. I was born an African American girl, but I have been raised or 'baked' to be who I am now."

Reflecting on Sydney's statement, I could not help but notice how she juxtaposed being an African American girl with being "baked" to be who she is now, as if the racial signification of African American was not a major part of the contents that went into her batter. I was curious to know if she saw her race as an essential or an additional ingredient, and I wondered: What exactly did she identify as the sugar in her makeup, how much sugar did she believe was added into who she was naturally, and did this make her soft, sweet, or heavy?

As I witnessed these young ladies learning and thinking deeply about Black excellence, Black resilience, and the ongoing and very real struggles of (and with) Blackness in this world, they encountered their own struggles. They grappled with internalizing concepts, ideas, and realities related to Blackness in direct relation to their own lived realities, epistemologies, and understandings of people, difference, struggle, and the world.

BLACK EXCELLENCE

Throughout her studies in AA Voice, Lauren felt a sense of renewal and she connected deeply with her Blackness because of the plethora of information she was receiving about the beauty and cultural importance of Black culture. In her written piece, "Black Studies," Lauren shares her thoughts on the importance of Black studies in education:

> Black studies is very important, especially in America, where it is commonly overlooked. Over time, African American students have had information held from them that is crucial to their lives. From the time a student begins school to the time they graduate, it is very rare that they learn about Black history and Black culture. All students learn about is what the textbooks teach. Most textbooks and curriculum plans do not teach the realities of what is going on now, simply because textbook information is not being constantly updated. As a result of this lack of education, ignorance has been brewing in America for many years. Relationships between Blacks and whites have been toxic. And also, disturbingly, the relationship between Blacks and Blacks have become toxic, too.

Throughout our class discussions and in her reflective writings, Lauren constantly reiterated her disappointment with the fact that she had not learned any of these insights about Black history and Black culture throughout her entire K–12 educational experience until now. This awakening of her critical consciousness that she believes every school-age youth should experience gave her a new sense of pride and allowed her to personally embrace the Black excellence that have been prevalent among those of African descent since the beginning of time. Lauren concludes her written reflection with these words:

> Black studies can teach every race the beauty of Blackness. Today's world is still very based on what someone looks like. By embracing all cultures and learning about Black people (the first people on Earth), it will begin to open everyone's eyes to see past color and judge people based off of their personality, integrity, and character.

To drive home a point she made in her student interview about the significance of including Black cultural perspectives in teaching and learning, Lauren references Chimamanda Adichie's (2009) "Danger of a Single Story." She writes, "Chimamanda Adichie's 'Danger of a Single Story' directly relates to why Black voices need to be included in classroom instruction because the school curriculum in my opinion hasn't changed in forever." She goes on to assert: "It's important for students to be taught different things to drive out ignorance and to open their minds to the truths about all kinds of things, not just learning about Shakespeare. Things that I have taken away from this class I can use later on in my life." Lauren finishes this point by taking a moment to consider what her last sentence means. Then she states, "This is life stuff. Yeah, life stuff! School curriculums need more life stuff."

It is here that it is important to make the observation that Lauren experiences African American Voice as a space where she can learn and become informed about concepts that have been routinely silenced in traditional classrooms that pertain to the world around her, and also where she can become encouraged to play an active role in using these concepts to shape the world. This involves breaking down the hierarchies embedded in the structure of "classroom"—between educators and students, among students themselves, and between "course material" and "the real world." In this moment, Lauren demonstrates the importance of students personal investment in their own learning process. Through her active analysis of her learning, she has become aware of the significance of "deep learning," self-assessment, and life application.

Sydney also finds tremendous value in learning about and connecting with knowledge about her own people. In her case, learning in AA Voice became an experience of belonging that acknowledged her cultural and individual identities. In her written piece, entitled "To Be Young, Gifted, and Black," Sydney reflects on her exposure to June Jordan's essay "Black Studies: Bringing Back the Person," and shares her thoughts on the importance of knowing one's history. She writes:

> Knowledge is power in most cases but especially when it comes to Black youth. Knowledge achieved through education about how the world works economically and socially, about science, math, and different cultures is an

advantage every young person should be trying to get. When young Blacks really know their history, their true history and not what is taught or not taught in most classrooms, and how their history relates to that of other races, it changes their identity and changes it for the better.

Sydney's words point to the reality that learning accurate knowledge can create a sense of belonging and reciprocity in a classroom community for those whose histories have been marginalized. It also emphasizes the role that a learning community plays in creating mutual appreciation and responsibility in understanding knowledge as grounded in a collective, communal experience in which everyone has something to contribute. She goes on to explain:

Since we have been studying Black literature and the contributions Black authors, musicians, activists, etc., have made, I have felt more comfortable in my decision to become a doctor of psychology, to plan to be comfortable financially and a lot of other goals I have that seemed "out of the norm." It shouldn't be deemed extraordinary for me to want these things for myself, but it is because I am a Black female. In June Jordan's written word, she makes several thoughtful points that I agree on some level with. For example; she talks about how our people undergo the "tyranny of ignorance" and how we can only overcome it with education and knowledge.

Finally, she ends her piece by making poignant points on why she believes AA Voice—as a classroom community of practice—succeeds in incorporating the lived experiences, perspectives, and identities of students while centering the study of Black culture. She writes:

The pieces of literature we have read have helped me realize the education students miss out on. We are not usually exposed to the truths of Black history, the contributions Blacks have made to our country, the mistreatment of different races in our country. On the other side, we also do not usually learn about the white and Black unity that brought about change right around the time of the Black Power Movement. I'm blessed to have taken this class and to have been exposed, in and outside of school, to the realities of society: the discrimination, the community, the struggles, and the achievements.

Through their written and oral reflective responses, both Lauren and Sydney have gained a level of confidence in their examinations of, and increasing interactions with, Black cultural ways of knowing that were not so prominent prior to their active participation as community members in AA Voice. By the end of their school year, they had become advocates for preserving the cultural capital and continuity that school knowledge has historically ignored and/or obstructed, which is also an experience of belonging. In this case, their experience of belonging connects to their experience with being active members in a learning community that is grounded in, and guided by, ethically informed practices (King & Swartz, 2016).

The perspectives of both Lauren and Sydney showcase how beneficial it is to incorporate cultural knowledges and platforms into spaces of learning introspection that advantage, or center, Black worldviews, philosophies, and cultural practices. Such practices are drawn from oral and written forms of Black literature, and are embedded in heritage and cultural knowledge that figure prominently in studies rooted in the Black experience. These cultural knowledges and platforms that are absent in traditional school curricula and experiences—not only for those of African descent, but also for other historically marginalized groups and for white groups—assist in correcting distorted, inaccurate representations of Blackness (such as history, intellectual and cultural practices, and so on). When teachers and students are given opportunities to draw upon their cultural memories, heritages, and intellectual legacies, they have the potential to bring goodness, harmony, and balance into educational spaces. In this way, they teach one another how to produce and sustain intellectual and cultural excellence, how to keep the past and the present connected, and how to facilitate community well-being and belonging.

"COMIN' FROM WHERE I'M FROM"

Shannon, a 17-year-old Caucasian girl, has had little interaction with Black people throughout her youth, and she was raised with the belief that white people are superior to all others. I am her first Black teacher and AA Voice is the first course she has taken inclusive of, let alone primarily centered on, Black perspectives. When I posed the question "Who Am I?" at the beginning of the school year, she responded: "I am skin and bones. Petals stretched over stems. Please don't pinch my leaves; don't poke my thorns."

As I reflected on her poetic sense of being, I pondered how much more her petals could stretch over the mountains of Black truths covered with white lies. Would they break? Or would they become stronger, thicker, strengthened, and enriched? Would her thorns become sharper in offense or defense? Or, could they become a tool for a greater purpose beyond herself and beyond the lessons of racial superiority that she had learned from her familial community? These questions and her participation in the AA Voice course were, initially, challenges and risks that we both agreed we were willing to take.

Raised by liberal parents and named after a Black female poet, Mya, a 17-year-old Caucasian girl, was grinning ear to ear as she entered AA Voice on the first day of class, as if she knew that this would be "the" experience to feed her internal hunger. When faced with the question "Who Am I?" she added: "I am the result of my memories and past experiences. I am the daughter of my father and my mother. I am friend, I am lover, I am stranger. I am student, and I am unconscious teacher. I am the captain of myself (right? Yeah, let's go with it, it sounds good)." As I read Mya's response, I began to think about her perception of self. I loved that she positioned herself as student and teacher. She had something to gain, but also something to offer. I hoped that I could play a role in transforming her unconsciousness into consciousness, her sleepwalking into alert awareness. Her reluctance to boldly and concretely proclaim her "captainship of self" was an indicator to me that she was in a transitional but vital state of becoming. There was still much Mya had to learn about building the ship she was planning to steer and the waters surrounding the ship that she would need to navigate. She needed to learn these lessons to successfully earn her captain stripes.

IT TAKES A VILLAGE

Although not of African descent, Shannon says that she saw herself as a valuable and contributing community member in AA Voice from the first day. This was the case because of the inclusive and loving environment, or classroom community, that we co-created, which included discussion of race and that moved beyond the limitations of racism in educational spaces. Always willing to share her opinions, she regularly engaged in classroom conversations. She was consistently introspective and open to gaining new insights about Black cultural and social ways of knowing in spite of the negative stereotypes she had been taught to associate with Black culture by her family members and by society. During her experience in AA Voice, Shannon began to better understand that members of all cultural groups have heritage knowledges (King & Swartz, 2016) and that members of all cultural groups can gain cultural knowledge of the histories and cultural legacies of other groups of people. Additionally, she came to understand the value of having as much cultural knowledge as possible by learning all she could within our classroom community.

In addition to Shannon, Mya had also become an active community participant in AA Voice, always speaking up when others hesitated to answer questions that she felt were important. Mya rarely missed class and she took pride in the respect she earned from her classmates for her dependability. She stood out as a classroom leader in our community and did not allow the color of her skin to intimidate her or make her feel like an outsider, especially because our community had already learned and accepted the fact that race is a social construction. Thus, Mya as well as Shannon wrote provocatively powerful pieces that expressed their sentiments on Black excellence and that highlighted insights they had gained in response to our classroom study of the Nile Valley civilization and the Moors.

According to Shannon:

The many people of African heritage in America have been told time and time again that they have no history worth remembering. The only information students receive is that Blacks were taken from African "tribes" during the time of the slave trade. However, when we dig for the truth among lies and propaganda, one will find a history not only worth remembering but vital. Recent history tells of the Black-created city Cordova. It was "the most wonderful city of the tenth century; the streets were well-paved, with raised sidewalks for pedestrians" (Lane-Poole, 1990). Lights illuminated the streets hundreds of years before there was a single street lamp in London. Long before that, ancient Egypt, ruled by Blacks, was a thriving country with lost technologies that perform greater than modern advances. While Egypt had complex social and economic culture, Europe was still in a divided tribal state, much like one often ignorantly thought of when thinking of ancient Africa.

Shannon goes on to write about how "the modern generation would benefit greatly from this knowledge [and] a greater respect and compassion is to be gained when we learn the origins of the culture we have today." She explains:

For example, when we acknowledge that "a brisk intellectual life flourished in all Islamic dominions" (Lane-Poole, 1990) we can learn Islamic culture brought with it many scientific advancements. Similar truths can be learned about all cultures. Analyzing the great things in other cultures would allow us to recognize what principles have been knows to improve society. When we appreciate rather than bury the histories of all cultures we can build a greater world.

For Mya, "While it is true that America has been known as a melting pot of many cultures and colors and referred to as a place where streets are lined with gold and opportunity, those statements neglect to recognize the evil lurking in the shadows and backs of minds: racism." She goes on to argue:

The twisted interactions between people with white and Black skin in the past are not limited to slavery, by any means, but Schomburg makes a critical point as he writes, "History must restore what slavery took away, for it is the social damage of slavery that the present generations must repair and offset." Instead, in the years since Schomburg composed the aforementioned thought, recent generations have taken a few steps forward in terms of race equality, but far more steps backwards.

Equally important is Shannon's statement, "According to Lane-Poole (1990), American law states that 'anybody with an African ancestry, however remote, is a Negro' (3). Thus, we all humans, sharing African as the original homeland of our species, are Negros." In conclusion, she asserts, "Therefore the accomplishments of the Spanish Moors are even more immediately important to everyone."

With these writing samples, it is important to note how both Shannon and Mya choose to express their views using assertive terms like *truth*, *lies*, *propaganda*, *evil*, and *racism* as they contemplate and engage with new knowledge and new awakenings. Doing so helps them grapple with, and better understand, how forms of miseducation continue to impact the state of being and social progress of their generation. Mya even takes it a step further by applying her learning in ways that directly confront possible misconceptions about her own genetic identity and cultural heritage in connection to Blackness.

Additionally, in their individual student interviews conducted at the end of the first semester, both Shannon and Mya shared important insights about why they think Black perspectives should be included in education and why they believe the AA Voice course offers a critical curriculum for all young people to experience. Shannon stated, "It's very important to get a well-rounded education. We've always known this. Um, but when we learn from only the white-centered history books, we are not getting a full education. We are not understanding the full history, um, that is behind us and that still impacts us today". She continued, "The way that I view the world and society has been vastly changed by this course. I can remember when I first thought about the Africans when they were taken and enslaved. The vision in my mind was of small tribes and people with very low technology. Just, um, very substandard." However, she decided to register for the AA Voice course and, according to Shannon, "I learn what the true history is, I learned that that was not the case and the societies of Africa are so advanced and there is such a strong culture there."

In her interview, Mya stated, "I think that being a white person, or a Brown person, or a Black person in this class, you learn the same. You know, everybody starts in the same place . . . well, not in the same place, but you know." Then, she stated, "Nobody knows what they don't know and through this we all learn together. And it's not in any way exclusive or you know, there is no shaming at all. It's one of the big parts of this class is the community feeling and without the diversity it's not really that same community feeling." Mya makes an honest observation of why she believes praxis rooted in the Black experience can foster a culture of belonging and community in classrooms for diverse students and teachers:

Without a community like this and a really open honest place where we can just discuss things and where no question is a dumb question and, you know, everybody has different levels of understanding of like current events and important historical events. Um, without having a community or place to talk about that, we are all isolated in our ignorance. So, we can't come together and share knowledge and become more knowledgeable and understand the different perspectives without this.

This statement by Mya drives home the point that classrooms can be communal spaces where teachers and students connect the study of Black culture to a larger purpose of realizing a communal vision of well-being and belonging that is congruent with all students' ancestral heritage.

On an intellectual level, these observations from both Shannon and Mya showcase great cognitive discernment and indicate that they are realizing that some important knowledge has been kept from them, thus motivating them to utilize this knowledge so as to no longer remain "isolated in their ignorance." However, they are still tentative about their positionings. For example, Mya slips into thinking, "We all start at the same place"; however, she quickly catches herself, understanding that in reality, we all do not start at the same place because of the oppressive racialized and systematic systems that exist and that have served as social barriers for centuries in this country. Although I am proud that she is making such conscious connections, I am still aware that she exists in a liminal space.

It must be stated that these young ladies are still in a state of becoming and there is evidence of that in the interviews. However, I acknowledge the effort they are giving and love them for their willingness to be open to learning new perspectives, especially about Blackness and Black histories, that push them to raise their critical consciousness. Through struggle comes progress, and these young ladies are working hard to know better and be better. The fact that these honest reflections and revelations in written and oral forms came from two white suburban high school students who had no real background or experience in learning Black perspectives before taking AA Voice is important to note. It lends itself to how experiences and theoretical practices centered on Black historical and cultural ways of knowing contribute greatly to cultivating students' and teachers' racial, social, and educational opportunities of community upliftment. It also showcases how curricular study and praxis rooted in the Black experience can foster a culture of belonging and community in classrooms for diverse students and teachers.

When students are encouraged to use heritage and cultural knowledge to collaboratively explore topics, and when teachers are a substantive part of this process, then students and teachers can begin to really experience the classroom as a place in which they belong. Structuring learning opportunities through praxis by centering the study of Black culture demonstrates how essential it is to focus on academic and cultural excellence with, for, and because of our students and their growing levels of critical consciousness.

TEACHING AND LEARNING FOR LIBERATION

In my approach to teaching and curriculum development and in regard to race and social relations, it is essential to teach young people to challenge dominant opinions on fundamental economic, educational, and sociopolitical issues. This lends itself to helping students gain a greater awareness of the conditions that exist in the world around them while also developing their own positions as action-oriented community members. These are strategies I use to cultivate students' critical consciousness, which, according to Freire (1970), is a sociopolitical educative tool that engages learners in questioning the nature of their historical and social situation. However, one cannot teach youth to be critically conscious if the teacher is not conscious first. As an educator, I demand from students, schools, the larger community, this country, and all of humanity what I demand of myself: critical forms of education, humanizing approaches to teaching and learning, and active collaborative engagements that are not grounded in racism, classism, sexism, and other forms of oppression.

Overall, this work addresses a major concern: that young people should learn to grapple with historical moments, cultural differences, and lived realities within academic settings in rigorous, culturally relevant ways while maintaining their integrity and dignity. I believe that this work adds to the scholarship on secondary cultural literary studies and critical literacy, highlighting pedagogical processes of sustaining Black cultural repertoires, traditions, practices, histories, and forms of knowledge. More specifically, this chapter highlights the benefits that emerge when students who are supported by their teacher to form "communities of practice" within traditional educational contexts are encouraged to critique topics in race, class, and identity through examination of Black cultural and literary practices. This research can provide needed insights for how teachers and researchers employ theories and practices that are culturally relevant and sustaining and that are rooted in the Black experience. Additionally, this research raises questions about how to establish learning spaces of introspection that encourage young people to construct expansive understandings about Black culture, and how to center Black Studies and Black people inside what is otherwise constructed as a traditional classroom space. It is my hope that more teachers and researchers will co-construct spaces with students in ways that support learning by exploring the various cultural perspectives, traditions, practices, and literary works of people of African descent.

ONE LOVE

"One Love/People Get Ready" is a call for unity. It represents a form of social and equitable unity that can, like the song implies, "prophetically manifest" if our young people are given authentic opportunities to engage in rich, meaningful learning experiences. Providing students with an education that empowers them to be fully human in both mind and body will, in turn, develop generations who embrace racial, social, and economic philosophies that can lead to a more just and humane society, like the one described by Bob Marley. One way to ensure that young people have rich and meaningful experiences is to have classrooms in which student learning encompasses diverse perspectives, epistemologies, and ways of being in the world. More specifically, classrooms that embrace curricula that dispel miseducated learning practices and help young people discover the truth about Black literature, history, traditions, and intellectual practices are the types of classrooms our students need.

In my teaching and research, I find that the majority of my students are not aware of the many literary, historical, and cultural contributions of Black people, specifically, and People of Color, generally. Their lack of knowledge impacts their perception of race, class, gender, and social patterns in society and allows them to accept misconstrued images and stereotypes that inform their understandings of self and other. In large part, this lack of knowledge stems from the lack of representation of Black forms of excellence in education (Clarke, 1993; Lane-Poole, 1990). Also, the lack of representation of Black perspectives in education speaks to the historical oppression that Black people have endured throughout American history (Woodson, 1990). This oppression cannot begin to subside until Black people are given the freedom and power to disseminate their truths (historical, literary, intellectual, cultural) authentically without the interference and internalization of white supremacist discourses.

Embracing Black cultural frameworks in public school classrooms can help teachers and students work toward equitable pedagogical practices and structures as well as cultivate a necessary critical lens in which to examine racialized social issues. To truly revolutionize current systems of education and promote social change and cultural advancement, I believe educators must be willing to implement transformative ideas, concepts, and understandings of Black culture within their teaching if we are to see true liberation and equality for all. One love.

REFLECTIVE QUESTIONS

1. How will we communicate with parents and administrators who might feel as if we are being political when we examine issues of race and racism in our teaching?

2. How can we reframe traditional pedagogical practices and research agendas to include the lived experiences, perspectives, and identities of students while centering cultural studies?

NOTES

1. Pan-Africanism focuses on the richness and complexities of Black political, cultural, and intellectual thought. On a fundamental level, it signifies the interconnectedness and unity of African peoples—on the continent of Africa and across the Black diaspora—their shared past and common history, and their intertwined destiny. Black consciousness reflects a deeply rooted commitment to rejecting the oppression and subordination of Black people (and their cultures, languages, and ways of being) to other people. In other words, Black consciousness recognizes that the beauty and brilliance of all Black people.

2. The concept of "community of practice" is part of a broader conceptual framework for thinking about learning in its social dimensions. According to Wenger (2000), the idea of communities of practice is a perspective that locates learning in relation to people and/in the world. A focus on the social aspect of learning in a community of practice emphasizes the person as a social participant, as a meaning-making entity for whom the social world is a resource for constituting (and reshaping) identity.

3. Fluid identities describes the idea that our identity is multifaceted, distinctly our own and constantly shifting. Identity is a function of where we come from: our parents' race, gender, age, socioeconomic status, and so on. Our identity is also shaped by the skills and interests we take time to develop. However, it is not just our past and our passions that define us. Our dreams and goals also must be taken into consideration, since these pull us into the future.

REFERENCES

Adichie, C. (2009, July). Chimamanda Adichie: The danger of a single story [Video file]. Retrieved from youtube.com/watch?v=D9Ihs241zeg

Baldwin, J. (1962). *Letter to my nephew*. Retrieved from progressive.org

Clarke, J. H. (1993). *African people in world history*. Baltimore, MD: Black Classic Press.

Clarke, J. H. (2012, August 12). A great and mighty walk [Video file]. Retrieved from youtube.com/watch?v=njdQzyQnHeg

Davis, A. (1997). *Race and criminalization*. Retrieved from macaulay.cuny.edu/

Delpit, L. (1995). *Other people's children: Cultural conflict in the classroom*. New York, NY: The New Press.

Delpit, L. (1996). The politics of teaching literate discourse. In W. Ayers & P. Ford (Eds.), *City kids, city teachers: Reports from the front row* (pp. 194–210). New York, NY: The New Press.

Freire, P. (1970). *Pedagogy of the oppressed*. New York, NY: Continuum International Publishing Group.

Hill, M. L. (2009). *Beats, rhymes, and classroom life: Hip-hop pedagogy and the politics of identity*. New York, NY: Teachers College Press.

Jordan, J. (1981). *Civil wars: Observations from the front lines of America*. Boston, MA: Beacon Press.

King, J., & Swartz, E. (2016). *The Afrocentric praxis of teaching for freedom*. New York, NY: Routledge.

Kinloch, V. (2012). *Crossing boundaries: Teaching and learning with urban youth.* New York, NY: Teachers College Press.

Kinloch, V., & Grebowicz, M. (2004). *Still seeking an attitude: Critical reflections on the work of June Jordan.* Lanham, MD: Lexington Books.

Kinloch, V., Nemeth, E., & Patterson, A. (2014). Reframing service-learning as learning and participation with urban youth. *Theory into Practice. 54(1),* 39–48.

Ladson-Billings, G. (1994). *The dreamkeepers: Successful teachers of African American children.* San Francisco, CA: Jossey-Bass Inc. Publishers.

Ladson-Billings, G. (1995). Toward a theory of culturally relevant pedagogy. *American Educational Research Journal, 32*(3), 465–491.

Lamar, K. (2012). Sing about me. On *Good kid, m.a.a.d. city.* Top Dawg.

Lane-Poole, S. (1990). *The story of the Moors in Spain.* Baltimore, MD: Black Classic Press.

Lave, J., & Wenger, E. (1991). *Situated learning: Legitimate peripheral participation.* New York, NY: Cambridge University Press.

Marley, B. (1977). One love/People get ready. (Recorded by Bob Marley and the Wailers). *Exodus.* Island Records.

Morrison, T. (1998, March). From an interview on *Charlie Rose. Public Broadcasting Service.* Retrieved from youtube.com/watch?v=F4vIGvKpT1c]

Nasir, N. (2012). *Racialized identities: Race and achievement among African American youth.* Palo Alto, CA: Stanford University Press.

Paris, D. (2012). Culturally sustaining pedagogy: A needed change in stance, terminology and practice. *Educational Researcher, 41*(3), 93–97.

Schomburg, A. (1925). The Negro digs up his past. *Survey graphic of Harlem.* Retrieved from www.politeonsociety.com/2012/09/16/the-negro-digs-up-his-past-commentary/

Simone, N. (1968). Backlash. (Recorded by Nina Simone). *The great show live in Paris.* Trip Records.

Viceland. (2019, February 11). What it takes to launch a company in NYC: Jammed Up.

Watkins, B. (2017, June 5). Dr. Boyce Watkins talks the importance of Black ownership, life insurance & the stock market [Video File]. Retrieved from youtube.com/watch?v=beRlvujKZRQ

Wenger, E. (2000). Communities of practice and learning systems. *Organization, 7*(2), 225–246.

Woodson, C. G. (1990). *The mis-education of the negro.* Trenton, NJ: Africa World Press.

CHAPTER 8

The Politics of Ratchetness
Exploring Race, Literacies, and Social Justice with Black Youth

Jamila Lyiscott

The Politics of Ratchetness

Wretched
Just wretched
Ratchet
Madd ratchet
Madd ratchet yo
You. With your pants sagging
Low
Like our hope in an American dream
You. With your loud ratchet self.
Neck twisting and turning like the Nile
Mouth smacking. Hands clapping.
With. Ev. ery. Word.
You with your skin so obscenely
And unapologetically Black
An onyx opulence
An ontological odyssey
Thick like the night
Black that blinds
Boogey man Black
You. With your skittles
And whatever is left of your spine
With your hands up
With your toy gun
You. With no arms.
Because they are cuffed behind your back.
And no arms.

Because the threat of you lived only in their minds.
You. With no breath.
Because it has been stolen from your lungs.
You. With your ghetto. violent. unruly. thuggish.
Ratchet self.
Wretched self.
Yo.

I love you.

It is the first day of the Cyphers for Justice program for a new cohort of youth. . . .

> *Jamila:* Y'all voluntarily signed up for a program called "Cyphers for Justice." Why? What brought you here?

Three hands shoot straight up into the air. . . .

> *Jamila:* Wait, before we continue, I need you to know that this a youth-led space. That means that the adults in the room do not have more power or authority than you and you do not need to raise your hands to speak. Let's have a genuine discussion, listening closely for when to enter the conversation and when to offer silence.

The new youth look slightly confused yet slightly intrigued. . . .

> *Youth participant 1:* I'm here because no one ever asks us what we think and I want to know how I can make a difference.
> *Jamila:* Nice! Well, what does that look like? What does justice mean?

The room falls silent. . . .

> *Jamila:* What's good with the crickets?
> *Youth participant 2:* No one ever asks us what we think about justice. . . . I guess it means to make the world better for everybody, equally.

The room is now filled with an energy that is almost palpable, but I cannot help but notice the quiet excitement coming from one Black girl in the corner of the room. . . .

Wanda (pseudonym) is the silent type. On her first day of Cyphers for Justice (CFJ)—an out-of-school program that apprentices New York City youth and educators as critical social researchers through youth participatory action research (YPAR), hip-hop, spoken word, and critical media literacy—she says nothing but her name. I watch her, along with the other Black and Brown students in the room as they eagerly feel out the space. She is afraid to be ratchet depending on context, but I will not learn that today on the first day of CFJ. I will learn it over the 2 years that I get to know her, as she blossoms into one of the youth leaders who present research all over the city. Today, she is committed to her silence. The other youth are committed to their questions: Youth-led? What does that mean? Cyphers? You mean like in hip-hop? We gonna rap? Nah, I'm not a rapper, miss. We can pick any social justice topic? Where you from, miss? CFJ is a space that pointedly sustains the inquiries, interests, and literacy practices of racially marginalized youth in the service of fostering youth-led research and activism. It turns out that, within such a space, Wanda will not be silent for long.

Wanda, age 16, is one of the many Black youth within this out-of-school space who have shown up to wrestle with the tensions of navigating their voices, identities, and power in a world where the average school day consists of relegating their perspectives to the margins in favor of rigid approaches to college and career readiness (Gaertner & McClarty, 2015); a world where schools often function as sites of Black suffering (Dumas, 2014), constructing Black students as delinquent, disengaged, and morally repugnant; and where adults rarely, if ever, engage them as valued contributors in conversations about their own schools and communities, much less national conversations about equity and justice. Today's hostile political landscape, where the poison of white supremacy has become increasingly overtly hateful in the form of racist symbols, hate speech, and oppressive legislation, marks a shift in the realities of all youth across America. But by nature of the history of anti-Blackness (Dumas, 2016), which shapes the very foundation of America, Black youth have long been deeply racialized politicized beings whose complex identities offer insight into their perspectives about the myriad injustices that mark their schools, communities, and lives. How, in these times, are literacy educators preparing to take up the charge that comes with the ever-more-politicized identities of these youth—young people who insist on being at the helm of social change in the wake of the 2018 March for Our Lives youth-led protest around gun violence and other sites of youth-led activism that have long existed across the nation? This moment presents us with new questions about the politics of literacy and how youth are working to read their world as they seek to inscribe themselves (write their world) into the landscape of history through their emerging activist identities.

Wanda and I first met in 2013 when she was 16 years old during her first visit to Cyphers for Justice. For months, Wanda was one of the most silent students in the program, but over time, she revealed herself to be a natural leader, open to opportunities to speak out against the social injustices that propelled her toward our community. Wanda spent her time in Cyphers for Justice refining her love for poetry as a craft and on her research, which focused on her concerns about body image in young women and girls. Throughout the program, Wanda kept a portfolio of her poetry, her findings, and her analysis for her YPAR research project, with the knowledge that she would have to pull it all together to present her work across various platforms throughout New York City. For the youth of Cyphers for Justice, the opportunity to share voice, art, findings, and calls to action with other youth and decisionmakers across the city is a crucial component of their action and activism in the program.

In this chapter, I explore how Wanda's relationship with race, language, and activism is often misread or not heard at all because it is shrouded in the politics of *ratchetness*, or what some might refer to as "ghetto" or "hood." Stemming from the word *wretched*, the first uses of the slang term *ratchet* signified a loud, uncouth, gaudy, socially unacceptable, poor Black woman. The word has since evolved to refer to any person who might engage in such behavior, but the picture of ratchetness finds its roots in the construction of the Black poor as ignorant, socially comical, crass, borderline coon-ish, and therefore, unworthy of being valued or heard in any true sense.

This chapter draws from a larger study of the Cyphers for Justice program that seeks to understand the capacity of multiliteracies (New London Group, 1996) to contribute to educational equity for youth by (1) challenging the ethos of traditional classroom environments, (2) shaping disciplinary knowledge, and (3) reimagining teaching and learning as centered on the literacies and perspectives of racially marginalized youth. The larger study that this chapter draws from focused on the ways that youth who self-identified as Black within Cyphers for Justice navigated their multiple literacies, racial identities, and critical consciousness in the quest to engage in research and activism. In this chapter, I first argue that Black students remain deeply engaged in linguistic and cultural practices that, though devalued within school spaces, offer rich insight into the complex ways they navigate their racial and political identities, and that exploring these practices, which are so often shrouded in fugitivity (Patel, 2016), can support literacy educators with better understandings of how Black youth are reading and writing themselves and their world. I then situate myself within the following: (1) the persistent disregard of Black literacies (Baker-Bell, 2009; Baldwin, 1979), which ensures that Black language and literacies continue to be marginalized practices in the United States; (2) sociocultural perspectives of language (Gee, 2004; Guerra, 1998; Street, 2012), which acknowledge the situated and enmeshed relationships between language and social context for Black people in America; and (3) culturally sustaining pedagogy (Paris & Alim, 2017), which discusses sustaining youth literacies, interests, and voices to facilitate youth activism. Through this positioning, I argue that the languages and cultural practices of Black students are forged in the context of systemic violence against Black lives and that they live in iterative relationship to that violence. Additionally, through continued participation in cultural and linguistic practices deemed unworthy by institutional spaces, Black students participate in a tradition of resistance that holds an inherent capacity for liberation. In these ways, then, it becomes important for literacy educators to work at sustaining these "marginal" literacies in order to truly engage in pedagogies of freedom.

THE FUGITIVITY OF BLACK LITERACIES

In antebellum America, to be a fugitive was to risk your life by breaking away from the physical confines of chattel slavery in hope of freedom. The enslaved Africans who dared to break the chains of ownership over their bodies had to engage in fugitive acts—that is, tactics of escape, resistance, and covertness—to subvert a system that refused to acknowledge them as more than chattel. To be a fugitive was to risk death to assert the fundamental value of your Black self within a system of white supremacy that sought to ignore and exploit your humanity. This chapter rests on the conviction that intellectual and rhetorical rigor exists robustly in the everyday linguistic and cultural repertoires of Black youth. Yet this rigor remains largely ignored or punished in traditional class-room environments (Baker-Bell, 2009; Kinloch, 2010; Kinloch, Burkhard, & Penn, 2017), forcing Black youth into fugitive acts of learning even beyond the classroom. To understand this, we must unsettle the assumption that true edu-cation occurs only in schools. I offer up the out-of-school context of this study as a site that critically supplements, disrupts, and often transcends the kinds of teaching and learning that we are limited to in traditional literacy instruction classrooms. Problematizing the notion that schooling is the primary place of learning, Patel (2016) writes,

> examples of the uncomfortable, risky, and core life practice of learning are every-where. They are particularly pungent and poignant within oppressive societies. Learning is, at its core, a fundamentally fugitive act, underscored with deeper fugi-tivity in societies where the dangerous, agentic act of learning is constricted with punishing precision. Learning as fugitivity exists as dialectic to the stratifying cul-tures of formal education that insist on contingent possibilities for well-being for some and unmitigated safety for others. (p. 397)

Despite decades of research and advocacy for the validity of Black En-glishes and their capacity to forge more pluralistic and equitable learning en-vironments (Baldwin, 1979; Ball & Lardner, 2005; Smitherman, 2000), their marginality persists within our ideological conceptions of intellectualism and academic rigor, and thus, in the pedagogies of schools. In this persistence, a parallel exists between the marginality of Black lives outside and inside class-rooms (Lyiscott, 2017).

Today, many Black youth navigate school spaces that relegate essential as-pects of their identities to secondary roles. In many situations, they are forced to adopt dominant linguistic and cultural practices thought to be more fitting for college readiness and access to power. That is, whether through code-switching (Auer, 2013; Baker-Bell, 2009) or other modes of suppressing "inappropriate" language within the space of school, Black youth spend ample amounts of time within contexts that require them to abandon the linguistic and cultural practices tethered to their homes, cultures, and communities. Young (2009) argues that the requirement to code-switch within school spaces is "steeped in a segregationist, racist logic that contradicts our best efforts and hopes for our students" (p. 51).

Such longstanding ideological commitments, rooted in a global paradigm of anti-Blackness, expose how thinly executed the work of *Brown v. Board of Education* truly was. The language of educational integration has long been euphemistic for how well all students can adhere to severely monolithic standards rooted in white supremacy rather than drawing from the rich cultural and linguistic repertoires of our world to reimagine what schooling might look like in light of a truly integrated society. However, in the face of a prevailing disregard for their languages and cultural identities within school, Black youth are not readily abandoning the community and linguistic practices that shape them; instead, they are existing in the tension of in-school and out-of-school environments in complex fugitive ways (Fisher, 2008; Penn, Kinloch, & Burkhard, 2016; Richardson & Ragland, 2016).

Black students' everyday uses of Black English; participation in community-based spaces; deep engagement in the consumption and production of memes, viral videos, and music on social media platforms; and avid participation in the production of popular culture, reveal a fugitivistic reading and writing of themselves into the world that is distinct from the literacies and ways of knowing that are privileged within classrooms. These linguistic and cultural practices are not at all static or neatly compartmentalized for in-school and out-of-school use. These identities are forged through an enmeshment of standard and nonstandard varieties of English, creolized within a history of slavery and survival, and today, layered with the digital and media practices that saturate the lives of any 21st-century student. At its root, the life of pedagogies and educational frameworks of social change such as culturally responsive pedagogy, culturally sustaining pedagogy, and the cultural modeling framework (Howard, 2012; Lee, Spencer, & Harpalani, 2003; Paris & Alim, 2017) all urge us to regard and sustain the cultural and linguistic repertoires of marginalized students as central to their wholeness and educational success.

Exploring the semiotics of language, culture, and literacies within the repertoires of the 21st-century Black students speaks to broader concerns about what it means to forge fugitive literacies, identities, and perspectives from the margins of our society. It begs pressing questions about (1) how Black youth navigate their racial and literate identities inside and outside of school, and (2) how their fugitive practices can be leveraged to enrich classroom environments.

SOCIOCULTURAL PERSPECTIVES OF LANGUAGE

Sociocultural theory frames literacy as a social practice (Gee, 1991), where language cannot be understood outside the social and cultural contexts within which it is produced. Rooted in genetic analysis and psychology, sociocultural theory asserts that cognitive functioning, genetic processes, and social functioning do not happen in isolation, but in relationship to the surroundings that mediate them (Vygotsky, 1978). Sociocultural theorists view language and literacy, when applied to the humanities, as social practices, so that linguistic expression in literature and society is always saturated with social meaning (Lave & Wenger, 1991; Rogoff, 1990). Emerging from these early theorizations of the inextricability of language and its contexts within which it is forged is the work of situated literacies, new literacy studies, and other theories that understand language as ideologically saturated, socially situated, and political (Gee, 2004; Guerra, 1998). In this way, literacy instruction must account for relationships among language, power, and identity (Barton, Hamilton, & Ivanič, 2000; Street, 2012). More recently, a field called "raciolinguistics" has emerged with the argument that language and race can and must be studied together (Alim, 2016). The central concern of raciolinguistics revolves around what it means to speak as a racialized subject in contemporary America. The field melds diverse methods of linguistic analysis for critical questions and answers about the relationship among language, race, and power across diverse ethnoracial contexts and societies.

For Black people in America, a long history of racial hatred and marginalization shapes the sociocultural realities that are tethered to language and identity. Echoing Du Bois's (1903) famous question aimed at the Black American consciousness—"how does it feel to be a problem"—is a history of explicit and coded language that continues to frame Black people, especially the Black poor, as lazy, subhuman, animalistic, superpredators, thugs, and *ratchet*. Existing fully in the history and context of these painful constructions about their communities and identities, the Black youth who come to work with Cyphers for Justice arrive as deeply racialized and politicized beings who are often ready to engage in addressing the sociopolitics of their own condition.

However, the 2018 March for Our Lives protest against gun violence, which was led by the survivors of the deadly Parkland, Florida, school shooting, exposed a double standard that has long been felt by Black youth across America wishing to engage in activism and advocacy. That is, though gun violence has been a decades-long public health crisis, impacting all poor Communities of Color in America, and though Black and Brown youth have long been advocating for changes in legislation and policies to better protect their communities, the collective emotionality, national attention, and momentous charge around gun violence did not capture the American imagination until predominantly white schools felt the immense tragedy of school shootings for themselves. This dynamic was known and felt by the youth activists of Cyphers for Justice, whose passion for equity and justice was often ignored. Through the lens of sociocultural perspectives of language, the opportunity to spend time with Wanda, to learn more about how she navigates her politicized racial and linguistic identities in a world where the voices of Black youth often fall on deaf ears, gave me unique insight into how underregarded spaces function as sites of fugitivity and pedagogical possibility (Kincheloe, Slattery, & Steinberg, 2000).

CULTURALLY SUSTAINING PEDAGOGY

Emerging from culturally relevant pedagogy and culturally responsive pedagogy, culturally sustaining pedagogy (CSP) invites educators to move away from the flat, one-dimensional inclusion of cultural difference that marks too many diversity efforts in our schools across the nation. Instead, CSP scholars argue that any education that seeks to move toward equity and justice must *sustain* pluralism in the classroom through the critical engagement of multiple languages, literacies, and heritage practices that exist in historically marginalized communities (Paris & Alim, 2017). CSP cautions us to move away from any static understandings of language, race, and culture, and to remain lovingly critical of the ways of knowing that we seek to sustain in teaching and learning (Paris & Alim, 2014). In this view, it is important to clarify that the literacies of Black youth are not static or bound to their racial identities in fixed and neat ways. CSP cautions critical educators against the impulse to essentialize any racial or cultural group with a one-to-one flat understanding of them, such as the assumption that only Black youth like hip-hop. Still, it is crucial that we recognize and acknowledge that, although there is no one way to be Black, Black youth hold shared histories that inform how they navigate their literate and racial identities. For literacy instruction, this pedagogical approach broadens the possibilities of what counts as knowledge and offers new understandings of how students might engage in language and literacy practices.

Within Cyphers for Justice (CFJ), this commitment to sustaining pluralism and criticality is largely realized through our commitments to engage multiple literacies (New London Group, 1996) and center youth participatory action research (Cammarota & Fine, 2008; McIntyre, 2000; Morrell, 2008). Through the use of hip-hop, spoken word, and critical media literacy, CFJ curricula invite youth critical social researchers to assert their diverse literacy practices as central to their qualitative inquiry and social action. In this way, youth use hip-hop, for example, to process their research questions, or critical media literacy skills to work through the theoretical framings of their studies. Within such a space, Wanda was well aware that her fugitive literacies could find refuge. For Wanda and other CFJ youth, opportunities to engage in YPAR through multiple literacies were connected to their evolving critical consciousness about the world around them.

With this framing in mind, I demonstrate how Wanda's freedom to engage in fugitive literacy acts within CFJ fostered a sense of refuge and agency, which powerfully shaped her voice, research, and activism in the program.

CYPHERS FOR JUSTICE:
A SPACE OF POSSIBILITY ROOTED IN PERSONAL NARRATIVE

I was born(e), raised, and schooled in an urban community where the languages and cultures of the people in my neighborhood were never welcomed into any of the classes I attended. As a first-generation Caribbean American Black woman, I navigate the linguistic contours of three Englishes (African American English, Creolized Caribbean English, and Standard American English). So, when as a 19-year-old, I sat on a college-prep panel before a cluster of Black and Brown high school seniors, I spoke in my most polished formal English. My decision to engage in "Standard" American English within this intellectual space was a silent and unconscious agreement I had been making for a very long time within institutional contexts where I knew implicitly that my other Englishes were not "appropriate." Having been unconsciously conditioned to engage in this code-switching, my decision felt natural until a woman in the room stopped me mid-sentence to congratulate me on being so "articulate." The word stung like an expletive. She meant this as a compliment, but I wondered to myself if she would have been less impressed with me if she heard me engaging in African American English with my friends in Brooklyn, New York. Would she have thought differently about my intellectual capacity or worth if she heard me speaking in Trinidadian creolizations of English with my family?

It was within the troubling answers to these questions that I realized how deeply interwoven my racial, cultural, and linguistic identities had been. This moment became the impetus for me to inquire into the intersections of language, race, and social justice as an analytic tool for understanding educational inequities. Consequently, my research seeks to understand systemic oppression within institutional spaces through the lens of Black literacies—that is, the living, breathing, and constantly evolving literacies of Black people across the African diaspora, having their roots in West African linguistic structure and having evolved throughout the violence of colonialism, imperialism, and slavery across the world. I understand that my racial and cultural identities have afforded me access to multiple literacies (African American English and Caribbean Creolized English) that are (1) situated and forged within the social contexts that raised me, (2) devalued and even punishable within schools, and (3) profoundly central to what truly makes me a complex articulate and intellectual being. Thus, it becomes important for me to seek spaces that nourish rather than attempt to obliterate the literacies of marginalized groups, including the Black participants involved in the out-of-school youth development program featured in this chapter. Cyphers for Justice is such a space. In centering critical social inquiry and culturally sustaining pedagogical approaches to emphasize the linguistic and heritage practices of racially marginalized communities, Cyphers for Justice offers rich opportunities for exploring and understanding unique pedagogical possibilities across the areas of race and social justice in literacy instruction.

At the time of the study, the program's curriculum was developed and executed collaboratively by one professor, one hip-hop–based education teaching artist, one graduate student of digital literacy in education, and by me, a Black female literacy researcher and practitioner. To engage participants in a critical analysis and production of multiple literacies closely connected to their racial and cultural identities, Black texts were centered throughout each session. These included musical lyrics from Lauryn Hill, Tupac Shakur, a bevy of underground hip-hop artists, and mainstream hip-hop music videos, and youth poetry from Brave New Voices. Participants were taught analysis and writing skills in hip-hop, spoken word, and digital literacies, and were encouraged to share their ideas in these forms as much as they saw fit in our discussions and in the assignments for the program.

During weeks 1–3, participants focused on the critical analysis of Black hip-hop lyrics and videos, and they produced hip-hop writings. During weeks 4–8, they began to learn qualitative research skills and examine critical perspectives of hip-hop and spoken word poetry performed by Black youth poets. Then, during weeks 9–15, they developed research projects and hip-hop or spoken word pieces that reflected their research in connection with a chosen social issue.

Committed to critical perspectives of YPAR as youth-led and action-oriented, facilitators offered tools for analysis, instruction on the qualitative research process, and skills for writing toward these goals. These served as a developing repertoire for youth in the program, who increasingly took ownership of the space as they (1) homed in on social issues of their choosing within texts; (2) brought in their own cultural artifacts for collective inquiry and analysis; (3) designed research projects deeply informed by the Black texts centered in the sessions; and (4) produced hip-hop, spoken word, and digital texts of their own.

Through this culturally sustaining approach, an explicit focus on Black texts invited us to unpack the deep sociopolitical realities that saturated the content and context of those texts. This was a crucial entry point for me to better understand how youth participants navigated language, race, and power throughout their everyday lives.

AWARENESS

On this particular evening when the youth and facilitators of Cyphers for Justice come together, the goal is to use a hip-hop cypher to begin drafting problem statements for the qualitative research process. It is within the cypher and within poetic moments that the once-silent Wanda first began to reveal a complex blend of self- and social awareness. The cypher is privileged within Cyphers for Justice because it readily centers the fugitive literacy practices (that is, literacy practices that are not valued in schools) found within hip-hop culture. The cypher finds its roots in West African culture. It is a circle of people who come together for extemporaneous expression of words and/or movement. In his work with young Black men, Kirkland (2013) writes:

> The cypha [is] the organic instrument of spirit and soul forged in a ring of bodies, hosting "the raw energy of the universe," was the young men's tool for freeing words that Nommo, the power of word, fettered to the long drift of imagination. For the young men, the cypha was a ceremonial ring for contesting silence. (p. 22)

We begin with one word, *injustice*, and from this word the ring of bodies in the room is expected to engage in an exchange of rhythmic dialogue, energy, and shared ideas about what it means to forge youth leadership and voice within the throes of #BlackLivesMatter, #NoDAPL, and a presidency marked by bigotry and oppressive politics. The language of hip-hop, a space that readily centers the linguistic practices and relevant interests of most of the youth in the room, challenges us all to engage in dialogue in new ways. Understanding the linguistic practices of these youth as socially situated, and regarding the cultural practices of hip-hop culture as powerful pedagogical tools, hip-hop pedagogy serves as a crucial culturally sustaining cornerstone of the program.

A sociocultural lens of how Wanda creates meaning within the cypher and during poetry writing exercises such as this one revealed a deep awareness of the myriad ways that she felt compelled to fit into racial, linguistic, and aesthetic images imposed by social standards of beauty and intelligence. Several weeks into the program, the once-quiet Wanda expressed the tension of wrestling against images imposed on her by society. Her contributions of poetry and rap were filled with reflections of the many ways that her racial and gender identities are sexualized and commodified within popular culture. For Wanda, the opportunity to create through hip-hop and poetry invited the complexity of her literate identity into the space in ways that allowed for playing with the identifications of self. Thus, her research topic evolved into an examination of body image, and by the end of the program, Wanda was using her poetry and her research to boldly assert a voice and awareness of self and world.

REFUGE

For Wanda, Cyphers for Justice became a place of refuge for her voice. She is a self-identified speaker of African American English. Aside from seeing Cyphers for Justice as a place that she could bring this part of herself to, unlike school, Wanda shared her distress about using Black forms of language in the "wrong places":

> *Jamila:* How do you think larger society influences young people's, Black young people's decision to speak whatever form of English they should speak at the moment?

Wanda: I think you, you kinda expect to hear a response if you speak a certain way. In public parts of society, if you considered loud, people look at you or, like, they give you a little glance or you kinda expect a ... You just decide, "Ohh, I'm gonna turn it down" or something ... like that ...

Jamila: So, has that happened to you?

Wanda: Yeah [laughs] yeah, so if I'm outside with my friends then imma be like loud. People be like, "Ohh, these ratchet kids."

Jamila: And how does it make you feel? How do you feel when that happens? Like, what are you thinking?

Wanda: Ummm ... I don't, I don't really pay it much mind, basically. Like, I guess it's just like an expected response....

Wanda demonstrates her knowledge that terms such as *ratchet* are racialized, and she connects this term to the way she negotiates her literate identity. Wanda is careful to use Black languages among friends and in spaces where she feels safe enough not to receive a "quick glance" of judgment, which translates in her mind to "these kids are so ghetto." Wanda expressed that being invited to use multiple forms of expression within the program made her feel safe and more connected. She also expressed that although she initially thought she felt indifferent about the label of *ratchet*, over time, she realized she feared the label and wanted to understand why. The sense of refuge that Wanda felt in the Cyphers for Justice program suggests that spaces that critically engage students within the crossroads of race, literacies, and activism can serve as sites of hope and possibility for Black youth who are too often silenced by the political construction of their identities as *ghetto* or *ratchet*.

AGENCY

Within her home, Wanda uses African American English playfully with her mother where she feels safe to do so. Outside of her home, there is a heightened awareness of how she will be perceived, and Wanda is careful to speak African American English only when she is among friends and people she knows. But in the face of a society that refuses to affirm the complex literate identities of Black youth, it is important to acknowledge that Wanda persists with her uses of African American English in spaces where she feels safe:

Jamila: So, do you speak African American English?

Wanda: Like, at home?

Jamila: Anywhere?

Wanda: Yeah, well, yeah.

Jamila: Like where?

Wanda: Yea, umm, I, uh, I probably . . . I probably do speak it at home. I feel like with my mom 'cause she kind of . . . [laughs]. She's like "Oh, that's hip" or whatever [laughs].

Jamila: That's cute.

Wanda: But when I'm like out with my friends, if we go somewhere where there's a bunch of people we know, we don't have to be, like, cordial. . . .

Jamila: Right.

Wanda: So, if we go somewhere, somewhere like Chinese food or the Chinese store or something.

Because Cyphers for Justice has positioned itself as a space of refuge for Wanda—that is, a space where she feels free to sustain and even develop the nuanced complexities of her literacies—the Cyphers for Justice community bore witness to Wanda's voice as it evolved in the program. Along with increased participation in the program over time, Wanda's emergence from her silence and into her poetic voice for advocacy and action throughout the program appeared to be an extension of the linguistic agency that she was already engaged in within other parts of her life.

In my time with Wanda, I learned more about Wanda's sense of agency in spaces beyond the program. Hanging out in the Chinese food store with her friends after school, for example, represented an informal opportunity to build community with friends. Within such a context, the ominous feeling of hyper-surveillance in school—a space where teachers might "catch" her sounding too ratchet—faded away, allowing her complex literate identity to exist fully. This sense of sustained refuge that she felt within Cyphers for Justice mirrored the safety of her home and spaces with her friends. It is this sense of sustained refuge that sets the stage for linguistic agency in Wanda—an emergence from the imagined pain of ridicule and judgment and into a young vocal activist who uses spoken word poetry and her own qualitative research findings to demand the kind of world she wants to live in.

THE POLITICS OF RATCHETNESS

In an increasingly multicultural, multilingual, globalized world, the Eurocentric practices that govern our institutions not only limit us, but become part and parcel with a history of violence and marginalization that exists for Black people throughout our society. However, through continued participation in cultural and linguistic practices deemed unworthy by institutional spaces, we open up possibilities for reimagining teaching and learning in powerful ways. The politics of ratchetness speaks to the tension of Black youth's continued engagement with their complex literacy practices in the face of an anti-Black society that frames their very existence as delinquent. Wanda is aware and agentive in the ways that she navigates race, literacies, and activism in her everyday life. Yet the way she navigates these interwoven dimensions is deeply connected to the sense of refuge or violence she feels across any given time and space. The small moment where Wanda shares her discomfort with being seen as ratchet, in fear of receiving quick, yet emotionally wounding glances from disapproving strangers, brings us to a larger sociopolitical conversation of how she is situated in our world.

Wanda's narrative challenges us to interrogate our conceptions of what is socially and linguistically palatable to the white gaze that marks the American consciousness. The loud, gaudy, ghetto, foul-mouthed, sagging pants, stereotypically ratchet depictions of Blackness, which fall outside of this gaze's approval, are perpetually ignored. Yet this is a complex component of the self that Wanda brings with her into her quest for activism and that Wanda sees as meaningfully woven into her racial identity as a young Black woman. For literacy instruction, which is faced with the young Wandas of the world who refuse to fit into an image that society defines, who refuse to relent in their quest for agency and activism, the call to responsibility is clear. The ratchetness must be welcomed into the classroom. The ratchetness must be sustained as a means for Black youth to author themselves into the world in ways that they cannot begin to do without psychological and emotional refuge.

Wanda's testimony about her experiences within and beyond the Cyphers for Justice program illustrates a young woman's journey navigating race and literacy for access, safety, power, and achievement against the backdrop of a society plagued with racial injustice. What does this mean for critical educators who wish to nourish our engagements with Black youth? For one thing, Wanda shows us that our ability to truly access the powerful voices of such youth is contingent on our willingness to confront our own complicity in sustaining any climate where their racial and literate identities are under constant policing and threat. When Spivak (1988) posed the question "Can the subaltern speak?" she admonished Western cultures for attempting to hear or portray the "other" in valid ways with the understanding that any perception of the other is necessarily filtered through the ideologies and institutions that inform Western cultures. Can Black youth speak? Yes. But their voices are shrouded in the politics of ratchetness.

Wanda also shows us that dismantling the politics of ratchetness means that while confronting our complicity in the policing of students' identities, we must actively create room for the linguistic agency and dexterity that students bring with them into any context. For example, most woke educators today are happy to affirm the racial and literate identities of their students with a message along the lines of "All of your languages are beautiful, but there is a time and place for everything." For Wanda to emerge from her silence in Cyphers for Justice, it was crucial for her to feel that the time and place for African American English, the time and place for spoken word, for hip-hop, and the time and place for ratchetness, was right there in the midst of the pedagogy, the curriculum, and the climate of a space that is committed to critically sustaining her whole self.

REFLECTIVE QUESTIONS

1. How is the construction of ratchetness racialized, and how does this impact the ways that Youth of Color navigate their racial and linguistic identities?
2. What pedagogical choices might support youth with navigating literacy for access, safety, power, and achievement against the backdrop of a society plagued with racial injustice?

REFERENCES

Alim, H. S. (2016). Introducing raciolinguistics. In H. S. Alim, J. R. Rickford, and A. F. Ball (Eds.), *Raciolinguistics: How language shapes our ideas about race* (pp. 1–30). New York, NY: Oxford University Press.

Auer, P. (Ed.). (2013). *Code-switching in conversation: Language, interaction and identity.* New York, NY: Routledge.

Baker-Bell, A. (2009). *Code-switching and African American vernacular English: Bridging the gap between disciplinary conversation and classroom practices.* Unpublished manuscript.

Baldwin, J. (1979, July 29). If Black English isn't a language, then tell me, what is? *New York Times.* Retrieved from archive.nytimes.com/www.nytimes.com/books/98/03/29/specials/baldwin-english.html

Ball, A. F., & Lardner, T. (2005). *African American literacies unleashed: Vernacular English and the composition classroom.* Carbondale, IL: Southern Illinois University Press.

Barton, D., Hamilton, M., & Ivanič, R. (Eds.). (2000). *Situated literacies: Reading and writing in context.* London, UK: Psychology Press.

Cammarota, J., & Fine, M. (2008). Youth participatory action research: A pedagogy for transformational resistance. In J. Cammarota & M. Fine (Eds.), *Revolutionizing education: Youth participatory action research in motion* (pp. 1–11). New York, NY: Routledge.

Du Bois, W. E. B. (1903). *The souls of Black folk.* Chicago, IL: A.C. McClurg & Co.

Dumas, M. J. (2014). "Losing an arm": Schooling as a site of Black suffering. *Race Ethnicity and Education, 17*(1), 1–29. doi: 10.1080/13613324.2013.850412

Dumas, M. J. (2016). Against the dark: Antiblackness in education policy and discourse. *Theory into Practice, 55*(1), 11–19. doi: 10.1080/00405841.2016.1116852

Fisher, M. T. (2008). *Black literate lives: Historical and contemporary perspectives.* New York, NY: Routledge.

Gaertner, M. N., & McClarty, K. L. (2015). Performance, perseverance, and the full picture of college readiness. *Educational Measurement: Issues and Practice, 34*(2), 20–33.

Gee, J. (1991). Socio-cultural approaches to literacy (literacies). *Annual Review of Applied Linguistics, 12*, 31–48.

Gee, J. (2004). *Situated language and learning.* London, England: Routledge. Retrieved from doi.org/10.4324/9780203594216

Guerra, J. C. (1998). *Close to home: Oral and literate practices in a Transnational Mexicano community.* New York, NY: Teachers College Press.

Howard, T. C. (2012). Culturally responsive pedagogy. *Encyclopedia of Diversity in Education, 1*, 549–552.

Kincheloe, J. L., Slattery, P., & Steinberg, S. R. (2000). *Contextualizing teaching: Introduction to education and educational foundations.* New York, NY: Longman.

Kinloch, V. (2010). *Harlem on our minds: Place, race, and the literacies of urban youth.* New York, NY: Teachers College Press.

Kinloch, V., Burkhard, T., & Penn, C. (2017). When school is not enough: Understanding the lives and literacies of black youth. *Research in the Teaching of English, 52*(1), 34–54.

Kirkland, D. E. (2013). *A search past silence: The literacy of young Black men.* New York, NY: Teachers College Press.

Lave, J., & Wenger, E. (1991). *Situated learning: Legitimate peripheral participation* (Vol. 521423740). Cambridge, UK: Cambridge University Press.

Lee, C. D., Spencer, M. B., & Harpalani, V. (2003). "Every shut eye ain't sleep": Studying how people live culturally. *Educational Researcher, 32*(5), 6–13.

Lyiscott, J. (2017). Racial identity and liberation literacies in the classroom. *English Journal, 106*(4), 47–53.

McIntyre, A. (2000). Constructing meaning about violence, school, and community: Participatory action research with urban youth. *The Urban Review, 32*, 123–154.

Morrell, E. (2008). Six summers of YPAR: Learning, action, and change in urban education. In J. Cammarota, & M. Fine (Eds.), *Revolutionizing education: Youth participatory action research in motion* (pp. 155–187). New York, NY: Routledge.

New London Group. (1996). A pedagogy of multiliteracies: Designing social futures. *Harvard Educational Review, 66*(1).

Paris, D., & Alim, H. S. (2014). What are we seeking to sustain through culturally sustaining pedagogy? A loving critique forward. *Harvard Educational Review, 84*(1).

Paris, D., & Alim, H. S. (Eds.). (2017). *Culturally sustaining pedagogies: Teaching and learning for justice in a changing world.* New York, NY: Teachers College Press.

Patel, L. (2016). Pedagogies of resistance and survivance: Learning as marronage. *Equity & Excellence in Education, 49*(4), 397–401. doi: 10.1080/10665684.2016.1227585.

Penn, C., Kinloch, V., & Burkhard, T. (2016). The languaging practices and counternarrative production of Black youth. *Educational policies and youth in the 21st century: Problems, potential, and progress* (pp. 23–38). Charlotte, NC: Information Age Publishing.

Richardson, E., & Ragland, A. (2018). #StayWoke: The language and literacies of the #BlackLivesMatter movement. *Community Literacy Journal, 12*(2), 27–56.

Rogoff, B. (1990). *Apprenticeship in thinking: Cognitive development in social context.* Oxford, UK: Oxford University Press.

Smitherman, G. (2000) *Talking that talk: Language, culture, and education in African America.* New York, NY: Routledge.

Spivak, G. C. (1988). *Can the subaltern speak?* Basingstoke, UK: Macmillan.

Street, B. (2012). New literacy studies. In M. Grenfell, D. Bloome, C. Hardy, K. Pahl, J. Rowsell, & B. V. Street (Eds.), *Language, ethnography, and education: Bridging new literacy studies and Bourdieu* (pp. 27–49). New York, NY: Routledge.

Vygotsky, L. (1978). Interaction between learning and development. *Readings on the Development of Children, 23*(3), 34–41.

Young, V. (2009). "Nah, we straight": An argument against code switching. *JAC, 29*(1/2), 49–76. Retrieved from jstor.org/stable/20866886

A Black Lives Matter and Critical Race Theory–Informed Critique of Code-Switching Pedagogy

Sina Saeedi and Elaine Richardson

As a pedagogical method used to teach Standardized English to Black students who speak African American Language (AAL), code-switching has been predominantly conceptualized by proponents of contrastive analysis as a way to find practical solutions to "linguistic problems" (Fisher & Lapp, 2013; Fogel & Ehri, 2006; Wheeler, 2010). In contrastive analysis instruction, teachers work with Black AAL speakers to differentiate the linguistic features of African American Language from those of Standardized English. For example, students may be presented charts that separate the two systems based on context to reduce or eliminate AAL in their academic writing and in their speech. Such solutions, which attempt to separate home language from academic and social language, (re)impose sanctioned structural barriers to equity, as measured by discourses that emphasize standardized testing, academic achievement, communication in mainstream social contexts, upward mobility, and employment. Although proponents of contrastive analysis show some willingness to recognize AAL or, as they often refer to it, "dialect," as a system of communication and meaning-making, they rarely view it as a cultural, linguistic, political, social, and independent system of language (Smitherman, 2004). Instead, they see AAL as "culturally different" from Standardized English, a view that reinforces a limited recognition of the language and a subordination of Black people. As Debose (2007) argues, education and socialization are the tools that perpetuate the values of a ruling through state power and control. In this chapter, we seek to disrupt this perpetuation.

More specifically, this chapter adds to the extant scholarship in language and literacy studies that is informed by the movement for Black lives and critical race studies. As scholars dedicated to social transformation, it is our goal to problematize the field's accommodation of anti-Black racism. To do so, we juxtapose code-switching concepts with current movements for social justice and Black Lives by discussing a threefold critique (political, social, and moral) of

147

the code-switching paradigm. This critique, we hope, demonstrates our commitment to eradicating all forms of anti-Blackness.

Many language scholars and practitioners have emphasized code-switching as a way to avoid pathologizing AAL. Their emphasis on code-switching, however, often reproduces pathologizing viewpoints, but in more implicit ways. For example, scholarship that seeks to distinguish between what is academic and what is not may avoid centering race in favor of the discourse of "situational appropriateness," with its focus on register and setting (Fisher & Lapp, 2013; Wheeler & Swords, 2004; Whitney, 2005). Although some scholars characterize Black students' language as a systematic and respected form of communication, a focus on teaching Standardized English for employment or social success, which establishes a dichotomy between home and school, can perpetuate inequity. Such contrastive approaches depoliticize social spaces (such as classrooms) and portray them as universally compatible. They emphasize *how* things are supposed to be in different spaces without engaging the question of *why* things are the way they are. This misplaced emphasis ignores how Standardized English is socially contextualized within white ways of being (ontologies) and white systems of meaning-making (epistemologies), especially in the United States. Requiring Black AAL speakers to code-switch bars AAL from formal and educational spaces in the name of "situational appropriateness;" it also imposes specific ways of being and meaning-making onto Black students. The obvious implication of the code-switching argument is that there are spaces in which being Black and thinking Black are not appropriate. This is an inherently anti-Black stance.

STANDARDIZING THE LANGUAGE OF BLACK STUDENTS

Attempts to standardize Black students' language work to erase race in order to position language as nonpolitical, objective, and colorblind, particularly with respect to educating all students, regardless of their race. Although seemingly well intentioned and for the good of Black students and their future lives, proponents of this approach to code-switching re-create a politics of place that keeps Black people out of white spaces by insisting that *they are not welcome into white spaces unless they have assimilated into Standardized English*. Historically, school has been normed on the values and cultures of middle-class white Americans, whose languages are seen as monoglossic and authoritarian, while the languages of People of Color are ethnically and racially marked, stigmatized, and excluded from professional contexts (Flores & Rosa, 2015). Under the insidious cloak of standardization, neutrality, and correctness, the white supremacist educational system established a line between formal and informal (or appropriate and inappropriate) discourses, especially for Black disenfranchised people with histories of fighting for freedom and justice.

Furthermore, though civil equality for Black people was the primary drive for legal cases such as *Plessy v. Ferguson* (1896) and *Brown v. Board of Education of Topeka, Kansas* (1954), equality in and out of schools still remains elusive for Black communities. For example, desegregation never required previously segregated white schools to change their pedagogies and/or ideas about the alleged inferiority of African American language and culture. On top of this reality, re-segregation unfolded for various social, economic, and legal reasons, and as Alim (2005) explains, 80% of Black and Latinx schools are in poverty while only 5% of white segregated schools are in poverty. As Smitherman (2006) asserts, a child's language tends to follow the racial pattern of segregated neighborhoods and communities "since communities in the U.S. have been separated and continue to exist along distinct racial lines" (p. 5). Considering this context, even legal recognition of Black Language as legitimate—as in the 1979 case *Martin Luther King Jr. Elementary School Children et al. v. the Ann Arbor School District Board*, and as is realized in contrastive analysis approaches—does little in terms of equity and justice for Black students' right to their language. This will remain the case unless schools follow a language policy that ensures full recognition and application of AAL (Smitherman, 2006). We would add, however, that all schools do have a language policy (some variant of situational appropriateness or placism), whether explicitly or implicitly stated, and that they actually do reiterate discriminatory practices against Black students' language, history, and culture.

CODE-SWITCHING PEDAGOGIES

Critical scholars have argued against code-switching pedagogies, which draw a line between "formal" and "informal" language use for Black students (Andrews, 2014; Baker-Bell, 2018; Orzulak, 2015). They emphasize that this line inevitably positions Black Language as inferior to Standardized English by reinforcing blatant racist-segregationist ideologies against Black lives and languages. Similar to Flores and Rosa (2015), these scholars argue that such approaches dehumanize Blackness and Black identity, and do not ensure that Black students will have access to the privileges of whiteness that might result from speaking Standardized English. Those who are racialized as Black experience the effects of racism regardless of the code they use in their speech and writing. Therefore, granting access to forms of whiteness is an effort to sustain and not to eradicate racialized capitalistic hierarchies. What needs to be disrupted, then, are whiteness and white privilege, and not simply one's lack of access to it. Having or being granted access to Standardized English results in assimilating Black students into a system that operates on white norms and interests, and in so doing, Black students become part of a system that reproduces their own oppression. The enactment of racialized capitalism, especially for Black people, exploits their Blackness while maintaining power dynamics and economic hierarchies that further harm them (Leong, 2013).

None of the studies that argue for code-switching pedagogies for Black students uses the term *inappropriate* to refer to Black Language (Fisher & Lapp, 2013; Fogel & Ehri, 2006; Wheeler & Swords, 2004). The studies do promote the idea that every language variety or dialect (as they reference it) is valid, rule-governed, and systematic, and must be valued inside classrooms. They also insist that every dialect is associated with one or more appropriate situations for use. However, from their perspective, Black students' "home" variety is still seen as inappropriate for school and other formal settings. The point that usually goes unnoticed in their argument is that appropriateness has to exist in relation to "inappropriateness." It cannot exist in isolation as an objective, universal state of affairs. If it could, there would not be any need to require a specific group of students who live in the same society to learn a new set of norms. Within white dominant spaces, such as the schooling system in the United States, Black people are constantly demoralized by the white gaze (Alim & Paris, 2017), and code-switching pedagogies only reinforce such a systemic gaze.

From a political perspective, the existence of a racial bias cannot be denied in such approaches regardless of whether advocates for such approaches have racist intentions or are well-intentioned educators and scholars. Culturalizing AAL is in line with dominant colorblind ideologies that deny the social and political existence of race altogether (see Bonilla-Silva, 2014; Delgado & Stefancic, 2000; Goldberg, 1993; Mills, 1999; and Omi & Winant, 2015; for detailed discussions about ideologies that mask and rationalize racism). Understanding race as a cultural category that individuals choose freely has worked as a green light for white liberals who readily seek to depoliticize race by shifting attention away from the white gaze and onto issues of self-identification and free choice (Omi & Winant, 2015).

As both López (2000) and Goldberg (1993) have argued, race is not a vague, abstract "formation" that is called upon and assigned to Bodies of Color. Rather, it has been constantly (re)created in social and political tensions throughout history, and continues to be created in relation to whiteness and by white social actors. It exists in a very real moment of racialization and identification of the "other." As a result, race is irreducibly political in and of itself and influences, creates, and cuts across other categories such as nation, ethnicity, culture, class, and even politics (Goldberg, 1993; Omi & Winant, 2015). From this perspective, promoting code-switching pedagogies in the name of "cultural respect" for other varieties is a political act of racialization and identification where Black students and their languages are identified, categorized, and essentialized as "inappropriate" in spaces controlled by white people through white value systems. There is a simultaneous inclusion and exclusion of Black students that happens at the heart of the code-switching methods: respecting Black individuals while relegating their languages to their "homes" in the most essentialist and dehumanizing ways. As a matter of fact, liberalism remains committed to its universality through reinventing and rationalizing the exclusion of particular races (Goldberg, 1993).

The question of the political can also be considered from the perspective of Black students' right to their language. Although the contrastive analysis approach respects this right, it is only a procedural right without any substantive results (Delgado & Stefancic, 2001). In the so-called postracial era, the dominant white perception is that Black students are treated equally in language education. This perception is only valid according to proponents of code-switching, who employ a raceless lens; otherwise, Black students are dehumanized even in this seemingly egalitarian process as well as in other school experiences, including racist and discriminatory punishment and suspension practices (Mock, Jeannoel, Gilmer, Fuller, & Stahly-Butts, n.d.). However, even if we imagine that Black students have full access to a procedural right to their language, they still might not be able to exercise this right within schools, let alone outside of schools. Although contrastive analysis promotes the slogan "All languages matter," this does not entitle Black students to use AAL in the white system because as soon as they utter a word in AAL, they will be racially and linguistically profiled through dominant (white) discourses of appropriateness. "What counts as appropriate" and "who gets to define it" are exactly the white ideological and racist privileges in the de facto white supremacist society (Mills, 1999) that supports Standardized English substantively for white students. On the other hand, there is neither an ideology nor any material, de facto collective power behind AAL.

Even in the few contexts where Black students have been given a modicum of prestige for being English speakers, they are still violated. According to research conducted by Sung (2018), a school's multiracial inclusiveness policy in language and literacy education miseducated Black students and (re)produced deleterious relations between them and their Asian American and Latinx counterparts. More specifically, Sung observed that the school ended up reinstitutionalizing anti-Black linguistic ideologies, although it stopped tracking based on bilingual education needs and started positioning Black students as "true English speakers." This change did not work the way it was supposed to because it avoided dealing with concerns that Black students had with the ideological and linguistic nature of whiteness.

Additionally, the line of appropriateness ignores some important social realities in U.S. society. There are several types of discriminatory practices that get enacted onto Black people, many of which are not illegal, and others, although illegal, cannot be easily detected and proven in court (Bonilla-Silva, 2014; López, 2000). Some examples include de facto segregation resulting from white flight, both in housing and schooling; Black people being offered worse conditions and higher prices when searching for a place to live; discriminatory tracking practices in schools; different forms of micro-aggression in public places, such as receiving poor service in restaurants; neutralizing Black electoral impact or minimizing the number of Black election districts through practices such as racial gerrymandering; placing Black people in jobs that do not offer much mobility (pigeonholing); and social control of Black people through police brutality, mass incarceration, or capital punishment. These forms of "new racism," as Bonilla-Silva (2014) points out, are mostly practices that are "subtle, institutional, and apparently nonracial" (p. 14) and that attempt to keep Black people in their place.

Black students who grow up under such conditions in the United States will have different understandings of life and of the environment around them than their white peers from middle- and upper-class families. As Smitherman (2004) has argued, although AAL may be seen as a variety of Standardized English, its use of English words produces meanings that are lexically and grammatically different from what she refers to as the language of wider communication (LWC). According to Smitherman (2004), this is because AAL is socially and sociopolitically constructed within the history and aggregated racialized experiences of African Americans:

> For AAL is not only language structure, it is also language use and discourse practices. It is not just the language of Black children and youth in the public schools, but also the language of the Black Church, of everyday folk, of seniors, of the working class, of preachers, of Nobel and Pulitzer Prize winners, of a long line of "race" women and men. (p. 194)

Regardless of purely linguistic arguments and claims that serve as the focus within code-switching pedagogies, Black students come from different systems of meaning-making that have close ties with their sociopolitical lives, humanities, and identities. Therefore, their use of language is meaningfully different from a white person's use of language. This is the case regardless of existing similarities in vocabulary or grammar between AAL and Standardized English. The imposition of Standardized English usage onto Black students is, in fact, an imposition of another social system of meaning-making that has its roots in white, middle-class, colorblind experiences.

BLACK LANGUAGES/LITERACIES/LIVES HAVE ALWAYS MATTERED

We argue that viewing language education from a Black Lives Matter (BLM) perspective disrupts the hegemony of Standardized English to advance a critical understanding of how AAL is contextualized (sociopolitically and morally) in the lives of Black people and why "Black languages matter." To advance such a critical understanding, it is necessary to work at erasing the lines between home and school, informal and formal contexts, and to look to the *longue durée* of Black Liberation to push for social transformation. This approach is in line with the works of several Black language and literacies scholars (Alim, 2016; Gilyard & Banks, 2018; Richardson & Ragland, 2018). In fact, the push for social transformation is not separate from Black ontologies, as neither of the two can be separated from Black linguistic practices. AAL not only contributes to the lives and struggles of Black people, but it is also formed through those very lives and struggles. This is why Smitherman (2006) encourages Black people to view their language and identities in liberating ways, offering up the concept of ausbau (from Fasold and Kloss) language—a language that has been developed by remolding and reshaping to fit the needs of its people. According to Smitherman (2006), the sociopolitical dimensions of AAL and its grounding in the struggles of Black people for liberation represents their collective effort to "bring about the declaration and acceptance of the U.S. Black speech as a language" (p. 18).

In this context, "Black Lives Matter" is the linguistic realization of race in its unapologetic affirmation of Blackness, Black humanity, and Black power. "Black Lives Matter" grounds Black people's shared history, identity, and continued struggle. Morgan's (2002) discussion of "African American English" and "first-time narratives" helps us understand the historical and political importance of AAL in this continued struggle. As she clarifies, the very fact that African American English exists shows that "something has been silenced" (p. 12), and that language counts as a collective memory of oppression for Black people on which they can draw for liberation. Such affirmation of Black people and Black humanity, as Richardson and Ragland (2018) discuss, disrupts the normalcy of racism because it rejects all systemic evils of a capitalist society, including patriarchy, cis-gendered heterosexuality, and classist criminalization.

The moral importance of "Black languages matter" or "Black Lives Matter" lies in the fact that the terms and what they represent do not separate bodies, lives, and languages from one another. Rather, they hold on to the histories and realities of Black lives and languages, and strengthen Black positionality and ontology in the face of hypocritical and colorblind, homogenizing claims of "All lives matter." These movements also defend Black humanity and resist its erasure in the name of liberal equality and egalitarianism in a society where race still matters. As Alim (2016) has shown us, race and language are inseparable, as each forms and is formed by the other. As a result, he argues for approaches that study race through language or vice versa. Thus, it must be clear why the notions that "All lives matter" or "All languages matter" are not able to achieve their raceless goals about universalizing lives and languages and keeping them separate from already-racialized bodies. Such a separation would not be problematic if it were the case for everyone, including white students. However, we observe that it results in reproducing a vicious cycle where—despite the claims of valuing Black languages and lives as equal and similar entities to white languages and lives—devaluation of Black lives and languages to a sub-human level and valuation of white ones continues to be the case. This is because too many well-intentioned scholars do not see the status quo as a state of dominance of the white race and values in which there is only one valid form of humanity (white humanity). The "All lives/languages matter" formulation gives the required ideological "egalitarian" green light to agents of education and law to constantly surveil, normalize, and essentialize the "nonconformity" and "raceless criminality" of Black lives as well as the "inappropriateness" of Black languages from a so-called objective perspective (Garza, 2014).

For Black people, "Black Lives Matter" means:

Centering and amplifying voices of those not only made most vulnerable but most unheard;

Creating space for [Black people] to finally be unapologetic about who we are and what we need to be actually free, not partially free;

Standing in our own truth;

Demanding police accountability;

Bringing healing . . . caring for communities and ourselves;

Fighting against this presidency and stopping its Jim Crow–era aggressions;

Working collaboratively to create sustainable rapid response networks to violence and ICE [U.S. Immigration and Customs Enforcement] raids;

Building Black political power (getting Black men and women elected and working with organizers committed to advancing human-centered agendas . . . leaders who earn leadership);

Pushing for food and clean water justice; and

Imagining and working for the world we want to live in, rather than beginning with the compromise position.

(adapted from Khan-Cullors & Bandele, 2017, pp. 249–251)

Khan-Cullors's understanding of "Black Lives Matter" emphasizes that Blackness is a political stance that resists depoliticization and culturalization of race. It emboldens race to emphasize that disparities are political and exist alongside racial lines and, therefore, are systemic. As a result, demands made by Black Lives Matter activists are systemic and institutional (not individual) because they are being made within an oppressive system that is predominantly white and that benefits white people at the exclusion of Black people.

Such a systemic call for justice also includes linguistic rights where Black people can use their language independently and unapologetically in a society that is not divided along lines of appropriateness/formality. Genuine respect for AAL is realized only when Black students have a systemic right to use it freely and unapologetically in society. Understanding that the project of standardization of language is not separate from police brutality, criminalization, and mass incarceration of Black people; de facto segregated neighborhoods and schools; disproportionate school suspension and punishment of Black students; and many other forms of oppression against Black folks is crucial for bringing about change. Any attempts to depoliticize standardization and to render AAL as an "individualized right" of Black students just to be "respected" is necessarily aligned with a white supremacist will that looks for the "appropriateness" of white society. An understanding that is premised upon "individual rights" does not take into consideration a conceptualization of racism based on what Bonilla-Silva (2014) calls "racial structure"—that is, "the totality of the social relations and practices that reinforce white privilege" (p. 19).

The intersection of Black Lives Matter and "Black languages matter" hinges upon race. It exposes how white linguistic privilege is maintained in the name of standardization by protecting the individual and collective linguistic rights of white students. In turn, this way of ensuring the protection of whiteness violates the individual and collective rights of Black students and their languages. Black Lives Matter also gives us the required background to understand the social importance of AAL and why it cannot be isolated and barred from "formal or informal" social spaces. Critical Race Theory (CRT) scholars emphasize the value of Black "counternarratives" that disrupt the validity of dominant white racial narratives that are aligned with dominant postracial ideologies (Delgado, 2000). Counternarratives from the lived experiences of Black people help negate the validity of white discourse. Important to note here is that AAL gets contextualized within such narratives, but the use or interpretation of AAL occurs within the context of Black people's counternarratives, not within the context of white people's master narratives. Although Black experiences and counternarratives are often interpreted in colorblind ways through the white gaze, counternarratives represent Black people's ability to "create their own bonds, represent cohesion, shared understandings, and meanings" (Delgado, 2000, p. 60).

CRT considers the seemingly neutral white reality and objectivity as being "socially constructed" instead of as an inevitable truth (see, for example, Bonilla-Silva, 2014; Goldberg, 1993; López, 2000; Mills, 1990; Omi & Winant, 2015). Accordingly, white social accounts of reality are subject to criticism and Black people can foster their "counterreality" through stories that circulate and get reinforced. This goal would not be possible unless AAL is contextualized within Black historical experience. A good example here might be the U.S. mainstream media calling Black Lives Matter a "violent" movement. The term *violent* is understood in very different ways by Black people in comparison to many white liberals. This is especially the case given that many white concerns about Black Lives Matter presumed that chaos and danger were at its heart and that "everyone," regardless of race, should be included in conversations about who gets to matter and why. Such an understanding clarifies more what "violence" means in a white middle-class, meaning-making system. In other words, violence represents white concerns about the status quo that benefits white people more than Black people, which maintains the idealistic claims of liberalism in the 21st century.

On the other hand, there are Black folks living in the same cities under the most dehumanizing conditions such as lack of access to good health care, empowering forms of education, linguistic and racial profiling, unemployment, micro- and macro-aggressions, and criminalization of Black bodies (Bandele, n.d.; Mock et al., n.d.; Tutashinda & Cyril, n.d.). Many white people do not have the tendency to view even police brutality against Black people as a form of violence because the conceptualization of "police" gets conflated with "law and order" that distracts the public mindset from Black lived realities. Violence is the everyday experience of many Black people in the United States, even within the most reductionist definitions of the term offered by white politicians. However, the systemic ideology around a concept promoted by mainstream media always takes precedence over independent thinking. Not only is violence not intertwined with white middle-class lives, but many white people do not like to even hear the voices of Black folks discussing violence. Before listening to what Black people are saying, a hegemonized understanding of "violence" undermines a more pluralist understanding of it, in sharp contrast to all pluralist claims of the white society.

"Black Lives Matter" discourse, in its original ideological orientation, is an affront to dominating discourses, and it demands restructuring of oppressive social systems. Black Lives Matter–informed pedagogies are moral, unapologetically Black, and accountable and recognizable to Black communities.

BLACK LIVES MATTER–INFLUENCED LANGUAGE AND LITERACIES PEDAGOGIES

Kynard's (2018) discussion of "race-radical literacies" underscores the imperative of centering Black languages, lives, and literacies as liberatory pedagogy. As she argues, one of the most important assumptions of such liberatory work is that the audience represents marginalized communities and not white people. Therefore, it requires a different definition of literacy, one in which powerful discourses and ways of being Black replace paradigms of white individualist concepts such as voice, agency, or identity; this includes those discourses that have historically changed institutions that did not always welcome Blackness. Centering Blackness demands that we learn our herstories, histories, and ourstories, and support intersectional consciousness and coalition across genders, sexualities, trans, nonbinary, Black middle and poor classes, diasporic Black, undocumented, disabled, formerly incarcerated, and felons—all Black identities. Our classroom is the world, where we examine and engage discourses, where all of our language repertoires and selves are welcomed as part of building the community of critical language and literacies world-makers. As Baker (2016) points out, the intersectional commitment of Black Lives Matter keeps the movement free from accusations of nationalism or provincial racism. Rather, the movement takes the lead to expose and combat the historical and racist foundations of U.S. normalized exclusion and violence.

Therefore, Black Lives Matter and "Black languages matter" are not separationist or essentializing movements that emphasize the inherent differences of Blackness; rather, they are a response to a white society that has essentialized and objectified Black people as criminal and inappropriate through reproducing white normativity as raceless (Garza, 2014). This call for race consciousness is actually a call for claiming an equal recognition of Black humanities and autonomies—which is, ironically, the very idealistic goal of the white democratic society but not its reality—that are constantly ignored by imposing the norms of whiteness onto their lives, languages, and all other aspects of Black existence. It is a call for stopping the demoralization of Black lives and languages by emphasizing that the root of the problem is the dominance of whiteness, racism, and essentialization.

Black Lives Matter–influenced pedagogy seeks to switch the codes of normalized exclusion and violence. Our pedagogies, policies, and institutions must be made to serve the needs of communities and families. Seeking to forward an empowered pedagogy for Black students more aligned with Black literacy and language traditions, Young (2014) has argued in favor of code-meshing, "which simply means blending, merging, meshing dialects" (p. 465), in schools to replace code-switching pedagogies. Young (2004) defines the approach as one that allows the mixing of AAL with the academic register, a technique that brings together literacy and Black culture without deviating from how Black students speak and write naturally in real life.

As scholars dedicated to social transformation, we value a code-meshing approach to language education as a movement that does not try to standardize the language of Black students and draws upon students' linguistic funds of knowledge. However, we also believe that a code-meshing approach requires a clearer social and sociopolitical edge to it to be aligned with the Black Lives Matter agenda. Accordingly, we suggest that a Black Lives Matter language pedagogy, first and foremost, must foreground ontological knowledges of Black people that also form their epistemology (how they view and read the world around them) and how AAL is contextualized within such ontologies and epistemologies. Therefore, if a comparison between Standardized English and AAL is to be made in language classrooms, it must be in light of such subjugated knowledges. Instead of drawing a line between formal and informal, the line itself should be the focus of the language classroom to clarify how the project of standardization has its roots in the racist history of the United States and how AAL, instead of being located on one side of the line, is (and has always been) resisting this line.

If educators are to preserve the language of Black students (and support their code-meshing), then they must not focus solely on the linguistic funds of knowledge that Black students bring with them into classrooms. Rather, they must be aware of how Black students' linguistic funds are sociopolitically contextualized and how their life experiences shape their linguistic system, and vice versa. It becomes necessary for students to first become aware of how their language is (and has always been) irreducibly political. Second, students must understand how any attempts toward standardization or formalization of language represent a political white supremacist attempt to erase histories, herstories, and ourstories of the Black struggle for liberation. Third, they need to know that any vocabulary or grammatical structure used to describe AAL is sociohistorically contextualized and has important political and moral implications, and that AAL is a resistant linguistic system: The Black Lives Matter–informed language classroom should teach students how the formation of language is political and how interpretation and use of it needs political awareness of that formation.

In her discussion of education for social reconstruction, critical race theorist Dixson (2018) extends statements and observations made by the Movement4BlackLives (a Black Lives Matter affiliate) that underscore the need for pedagogical contextualization within Black liberation movement history and for educators who are ideologically and professionally prepared to teach on behalf of the 99% (as opposed to the 1%). Dixson emphasizes the importance of holding accountable universities and school districts to train teachers in culturally relevant pedagogies so that they are prepared to work in urban settings. According to Dixson (2018),

> if we are calling for community control of schools, eradication of alternative teacher and administrator programs, and charter schools, we must also have a vision and plan for curriculum, student outcomes that align with that vision and curriculum and teachers (and the training of teachers) who can teach in ways that support and advance an [education] that is social reconstructionist. These are important to ensure that students not only understand the history of movements and organizing but can also draw on that history to organize and form movements that are coalitional and intersectional. (p. 243)

Well-prepared teachers with ideological clarity can help students build on Black language resistance traditions, not for appropriateness and survival, but for thriving, rhetorical dexterity, and solidarity. People live their languages and languages live their people, too. Language plays the role of mediator in race relations and negotiations. Ways of conceptualizing language (for instance, as monolingual, bidialectal, or bilinguals, or as "Standard English" and African American Language) are not neutral systems for neutral, raceless communication, because there is no such thing. Every communication in a racialized world is already political. Because our work is political, we cannot shortchange our students when it comes to focusing on AAL. As the 2016 CCCC "Statement on Ebonics" indicates, "Black Languages are crucial to Black identity. Black Language sayings, such as 'What goes around comes around,' are crucial to Black ways of being in the world. Black Languages, like Black lives, matter" (CCCC, para. 13).

Scholars must take our cue from students, activists, and community members who work to interrupt the normalization of state-sanctioned violence in all of its forms against Black people and push beyond the immoral pedagogies and policies that support them.

REFLECTIVE QUESTIONS

1. How do Black Lives Matter inside of language and literacy classrooms? How do we teach in ways that seek to understand the social importance of AAL?

2. How do we work with students to ensure that they are aware of the value of AAL? How do we ensure that we are also aware of the reality that lived experiences shape our linguistic systems?

REFERENCES

Alim, H. S. (2005). Critical language awareness in the United States: Revisiting issues and revising pedagogies in a resegregated society. *Educational Researcher*, *34*(7), 24–31.

Alim, H. S. (2016). Introducing raciolinguistics: Racing language and languaging race in hyperracial times. In H. S. Alim, J. R. Rickford, & A. F. Ball (Eds.), *Raciolinguistics: How language shapes our ideas about race* (pp. 1–30). New York, NY: Oxford University Press.

Alim, H. S., & Paris, D. (2017). What is culturally sustaining pedagogy and why does it matter? In D. Paris & H. S. Alim (Eds.), *Culturally sustaining pedagogies: Teaching and learning for justice in a changing world* (pp. 1–21). New York, NY: Teachers College Press.

Andrews, K. (2014). Toward a black radical independent education: Black radicalism, independence and the supplementary school movement. *The Journal of Negro Education*, *83*(1), 5–14.

Baker, H. (2016). The black bottom line: Reflections on Ferguson, black lives matter and white male violence in America. *American Literary History*, *28*(4), 845–853.

Baker-Bell, A. (2018). "I can switch my language, but I can't switch my skin." In E. Moore, A. Michael, & M. W. Penick-Parks (Eds.), *The guide for White women who teach Black boys* (pp. 97–107). Thousand Oaks, CA: Corwin Press.

Bandele, L. (n.d.). An end to the criminalization of black political activity including the immediate release of all political prisoners and an end to the repression of political parties. Retrieved from policy.m4bl.org/political-power/

Bonilla-Silva, E. (2014). *Racism without racists: Color-blind racism and the persistence of racial inequality in America* (4th ed.). Lanham, MD: Rowman & Littlefield Publishers, Inc.

CCCC Statement on Ebonics. (2016). Retrieved from cccc.ncte.org/cccc/resources/positions/ebonics

Debose, C. (2007). The Ebonics phenomenon: Language planning and the hegemony of standard English. In H. S. Alim & J. Baugh (Eds.), *Talkin Black talk: Language, education and social change* (pp. 30–42). New York, NY: Teachers College Press.

Delgado, R. (2000). Storytelling for oppositionists and others: A plea for narrative. In R. Delgado & J. Stefancic (Eds.), *Critical race theory: The cutting edge* (2nd ed., pp. 60–70). Philadelphia, PA: Temple University Press.

Delgado, R., & Stefancic, J. (2000). Images of the outsider in American law and culture: Can free expression remedy systemic social ills? In R. Delgado & J. Stefancic (Eds.), *Critical race theory: The cutting edge* (2nd ed., pp. 225–235). Philadelphia, PA: Temple University Press.

Dixson, A. (2018). What's going on?: A critical race theory perspective of Black lives matter and activism in education. *Urban Education, 53*(2), 231–247.

Fisher, D., & Lapp, D. (2013). Learning to talk like the test: Guiding speakers of African American Vernacular English. *Journal of Adolescent & Adult Literacy, 56*(8), 634–648.

Flores, N., & Rosa, J. (2015). Undoing appropriateness: Raciolinguistic ideologies and language diversity in education. *Harvard Educational Review, 85*(2), 149–171.

Fogel, H., & Ehri, L. C. (2006). Teaching African American English forms to standard American English-speaking teachers: Effects on acquisition, attitudes, and responses to student use. *Journal of Teacher Education, 57*(5), 464–480.

Garza, A. (2014). A herstory of the #BlackLivesMatter Movement. Retrieved from thefeministwire.com/2014/10/blacklivesmatter-2/

Gilyard, K., & Banks, A. (Eds.). (2018). *On African-American rhetoric*. New York, NY, & London, UK: Routledge.

Goldberg, D. T. (1993). *Racist culture: Philosophy and the politics of meaning*. Malden, MA: Blackwell Publishers.

Khan-Cullors, P., & Bandele, A. (2017). *When they call you a terrorist: A Black Lives Matter memoir*. New York, NY: St. Martin's Press.

Kynard, C. (2018). Stayin woke: Race-radical literacies in the makings of higher education. *College Composition and Communication, 69*(3), 519–529.

Leong, N. (2013). Racial capitalism. *Harvard Law Review, 126*(8), 2152–2226.

López, I. F. H. (2000). The social construction of race. In R. Delgado & J. Stefancic (Eds.), *Critical race theory: The cutting edge* (2nd ed., pp. 163–175). Philadelphia, PA: Temple University Press.

Mills, C. W. (1999). *The racial contract*. Ithaca, NY: Cornell University Press.

Mock, T., Jeannoel, R., Gilmer, R., Fuller, C., & Stahly-Butts, M. (n.d.). An immediate end to the criminalization and dehumanization of black youth across all areas of society including, but not limited to, our nation's justice and education systems, social service agencies, media, and pop culture. Retrieved from policy.m4bl.org/end-war-on-black-people/

Morgan, M. (2002). *Language, discourse and power in African American culture*. Cambridge, UK & New York, NY: Cambridge University Press.

Omi, M., & Winant, H. (2015). *Racial formation in the United States* (3rd ed.). New York, NY: Routledge.

Orzulak, M. J. M. (2015). Disinviting deficit ideologies: Beyond "that's standard," "that's racist," and "that's your mother tongue." *Research in the Teaching of English, 50*(2), 176–198.

Richardson, E., & Ragland, A. (2018). #StayWoke: The language and literacies of the #BlackLivesMatter movement. *Community Literacy Journal, 12*(2), 27–56.

Smitherman, G. (2004). Language and African Americans: Movin on up a lil higher. *Journal of English Linguistics, 32*(3), 186–196.

Smitherman, G. (2006). *Word from the mother: Language and African Americans*. New York, NY, & London, UK: Routledge.

Sung, K. K. (2018). Raciolinguistic ideology of antiblackness: Bilingual education, tracking, and the multiracial imaginary in urban schools. *International Journal of Qualitative Studies in Education, 31*(8), 667–683.

Tutashinda, C., & Cyril, M. (n.d.). An end to the mass surveillance of black communities, and the end to the use of technologies that criminalize and target our communities (including IMSI catchers, drones, body cameras, and predictive policing software). Retrieved from policy.m4bl.org/end-war-on-black-people/

Wheeler, R. (2010). Fostering linguistic habits of mind: Engaging teachers' knowledge and attitudes toward African American vernacular English. *Language and Linguistics Compass, 4*(10), 954–971.

Wheeler, R. S., & Swords, R. (2004). Codeswitching: Tools of language and culture transform the dialectally diverse classroom. *Language Arts, 81*(6), 470–480.

Whitney, J. (2005). Five easy pieces: Steps toward integrating AAVE into the classroom. *English Journal, 94*(5), 64–69.

Young, V. A. (2004). Your average nigga. *College Composition and Communication, 55*(4), 693–715.

Young, V. A. (2014). Straight black queer: Obama, code-switching, and the gender anxiety of African American men. *PMLA, 129*(3), 464–470.

CHAPTER 10

Multiliteracies Toward Justice in Literacy Teaching and Research

Vaughn W. M. Watson, Matthew R. Deroo, and Erik Skogsberg

Vaughn recalls that he planned to distribute the composition notebooks he found bundled together in the second-floor book closet with a strip of plastic strapping tape to 82 10th-graders across three English classes that he taught at Brooklyn Public. He prepared a lesson plan asking youth to complete daily writing in the notebooks, to "write a paragraph responding to the question, 'What role do characters' choices play in determining their future?'" (lesson plan, December, 2011). Vaughn encouraged youth to write a paragraph about their lived experiences or about the book they recently read. A third option was to write to the song Vaughn and youth listened to and discussed in class titled "Phantom," where emcee Mr. Lif opens with a three-word phrase, complicating meanings of what may be understood as credit or what is to be valued: "Check it out."

As youth settled into seats arranged two to a table, taking one composition notebook and passing to their neighbor, four students asked Vaughn if the beige notebooks were "ours to keep" (research memo, December, 2011). "Yeah," he responded, excited for them to take up the notebooks across an everyday practice of journal writing. One student, Sean, thumbing through the notebook and its wide-ruled pages, hurriedly closed the cover, pushed it to the edge of his desk, and declared to Vaughn, "I don't want that old book. I had it in elementary." Sean repositioned possibilities Vaughn had envisioned in distributing notebooks to youth, and asserted a prior expertise in using notebooks to write in this school-sanctioned way. In the next class, another student, Mariah, told Vaughn, "You should have given these to us sooner," while Jenelle called Vaughn over and shared in an excited near-whisper to him and Tiana, sitting to her right, "You know what this is like? This is like *Freedom Writers.*" The 2007 movie, produced by MTV Films and based on Erin Gruwell's reflections on her 4 years of teaching with youth writers, featured Hilary Swank as a white teacher of primarily Youth of Color at a Long Beach, California, high school.

Swank, in the movie, buys composition books for students to write journal entries about lived experiences, underscoring what Cammarota (2011) observed as "the white savior syndrome in which a white person guides people of color from the margins to the mainstream with his or her own initiative and benevolence" (p. 243). Vaughn did not intend to evoke a *Freedom Writers* moment. Throughout his 12 years as a teacher at Brooklyn Public, he had situated his curriculum and pedagogy as more than a singular writing intervention. Moreover, as a Black man teaching primarily Youth of Color, Vaughn purposefully designed curriculum and teaching activities to build with the lived experiences and literacy practices of Youth of Color. Yet he did not fully anticipate the ways youth would remake the covers of composition notebooks. Students evoked broader uses of bundled-together volumes than popularized narratives of Youth of Color as needing blank pages and scripted prompts of a writing curricula to render new meanings extending their already-present literacies and lived experiences.

In this chapter, we construct meanings of youth enacting *community-engaged multiliteracies*. This purposeful accounting attends to what may be left behind or less regarded as fragments or the edges of literacy practices bearing sanctioned value: graffiti writing drawn boldly across notebook covers and affixed to school walls, art making and songwriting as entrepreneurial activities, and using mobile technologies and social media to compose and publicly share compositions of poetry and art. We assert community-engaged multiliteracies as extending meanings of teaching, teacher education, and literacy research for Youth of Color and building upon their already-present literacy practices by envisioning "a purposeful situating of English teaching and learning as all around us" (Watson, 2018, p. 10). Young people did not engage community-engaged multiliteracies for credit in an academic class. Rather, youth in graffiti writing, entrepreneurial activities, and uses of social media and mobile technologies powerfully asserted differing literary and/or entrepreneurial meanings, different from school-based performances of literacy that center intervention and deficit. Community-engaged multiliteracies draw attention to curricular approaches and teaching activities (such as teacher-selected writing prompts or narrowed views of what counts as literacy) that often (dis)credit and (de)value the already-present literacies of Youth of Color, and in so doing, assert new meanings of what may count as learning and literacy activities toward racial and educational justice.

In situating the urgency of attending to community-engaged multiliteracies, we understand literacies as necessarily enacted within broader contexts of racialized experiences and racial identities (Baker-Bell, Butler, & Johnson, 2017). We further consider community-engaged multiliteracies in conversation with Cammarota (2011), who observed, "ignoring the social and economic inequalities of ongoing market-based residential segregation, labor exploitation, health disparities, racial profiling, and racially tracked schooling that influence the daily experiences of most people of color is the most guarded privilege in America" (p. 256).

At a time of demographic changes underscored in 74 large public school districts across the United States, in which 40% of youth are Latinx and 29% are African American (Council of the Great City Schools, 2019), community-engaged multiliteracies of graffiti writing, entrepreneurship, and using mobile technologies and social media pointedly build on and unfold the lived experiences of Youth of Color. Additionally, community-engaged multiliteracies emerge as situated within and across the social and historical contexts of youth's lived experiences (Perry, 2012). We thus assert building with the experiences and literacy practices of Youth of Color as an urgent stance taking in a current moment in which, 3 weeks after the 2016 U.S. presidential election, "eight in 10" students of 25,000 educators surveyed reported "heightened anxiety" on behalf of Muslims, immigrant, African American, and LGBTQ+ identifying youth with whom educators teach and learn (Southern Poverty Law Center, 2016, para. 7).

THEORIZING COMMUNITY-ENGAGED MULTILITERACIES AS ENACTING MEANINGS OF PRESENCE

Attending to community-engaged multiliteracies in teaching, teacher education, and literacy research involves asserting Youth of Color within literacy activities as current and future contributors across communities (Fisher, 2005; Kinloch, 2010; Kirkland & Jackson, 2009); this is a participatory process of civic action taking (Knight & Watson, 2014). Moreover, the rise of digital media platforms has ushered in a new era of civic engagement through participatory, networked communities, rendered present in the daily lives and literacy practices of youth through mobile technologies (Jenkins, Ito, & Boyd, 2015; Jenkins, Shresthova, Gamber-Thompson, Kligler-Vilenchik, & Zimmerman, 2016; Mihailidis, 2014).

Within this context, community-engaged multiliteracies, such as the use of the hashtag "#BlackLivesMatter," retweeted more than 9 million times in 2015 (@AlzValz, 2015), highlight a civic stance taking referenced by a *New York Times* (2015) columnist as the "vanguard of the quest for racial justice in this country" (para. 1). Such literacy practices underscored "a unifying message" as social movements toward racial justice in Ferguson, Missouri; Columbia, South Carolina; and Baltimore, Maryland (para. 4), and demonstrated how youth may "begin to historicize their lives and to see themselves and their futures as historical actors" (Gutierrez, 2008, p. 155). This situatedness repositions Youth of Color as undertaking literacy activities and engaging in civic action taking that Tatum and Muhammad (2012) theorized as "literary presence" (p. 206). By literary presence, the authors historicized writing, public speaking, and other educational practices of Black youth and adults in literary societies in the 1800s in the Northern United States, to prompt the rethinking of curricular interventions, standards, and account-ability mandates of literacy that involve African American youth (Hess, Wat-son, & Deroo, 2019).

We further extend the concept of literary presence to capture what Zhao (2012) observed as an "entrepreneurial mindset" (p. 5) among young people. This mindset attends to "creativity, curiosity, imagination, risk taking, and collaboration [...] the desire and potential to create and innovate, to dream and imagine, and to challenge and improve the status quo" (p. 9). Confronted with the delimiting contexts of composition notebooks and scripted curricula prompts, of reform-based initiatives, assessment, accountability, and evaluation that often define literacy instruction for students from varying ethnic, racial, gender, religious, and economic backgrounds, they demonstrate a literary pres-ence that should count as career readiness in a global economy (Robertson, 2008; Sleeter, 2008)—thus, the use of the phrase *entrepreneurial presence*.

Theorizing community-engaged multiliteracies as a literary and entrepre-neurial presence reframes neoliberal positionings of education that prioritize the production of workers for economic systems and favor competition as a key aim of schooling (Apple, 2006; Robertson, 2008). This situating *of* and *as* literacy evokes a different view from narratives of standardization, college pre-paredness, and career readiness across which education is "defined by what it can accomplish in the remote future, not in the present" (Tucker, 2011, p. 115). Attending to nuanced meanings of entrepreneurial presence recasts a "schooli-fied" and oppressive learning economy that has traditionally privileged white, middle-class youth, and positioned the literacy practices of Youth of Color as deficit (Paris & Alim, 2017). Extending what is meant by entrepreneurial pres-ence ascribes credit to community-engaged multiliteracies of Youth of Color that are, that were, and that will continue.

CONCEPTUALIZING COMMUNITY-ENGAGED MULTILITERACIES AS "AFFICHISTE"

We envisage the layering of creative and artistic community-engaged mul-tiliteracies of graffiti writing, entrepreneurship, and the use of social media and mobile technologies within and beyond contexts of classrooms and stan-dardized curricula as what Block (2013) observed as "curriculum as affichiste." Block critiqued curriculum as "traditionally conceived, and as practiced in the vast majority of schools [. . .] [as] the path we follow to the goal of knowledge" (p. 333). Block evoked the work of "affichiste" artists: The "poster artists" in 1940s and 1950s Paris, France, collaboratively composed collages by tearing away scraps and fragments of existing advertising posters pasted one atop the other on building walls.

As graffiti artists of the 1980s provoked new meanings from and across canvases of public life, Block (2013) noted, affichistes, in "drawing on and from the materials of their daily world, and working with them idiosyncratically, produced in the process a new relationship between art and the world, a new way of being in the world" (pp. 336–337). Situating affichiste as "a model of curriculum" (p. 338), Block noted that affichistes, in their art making, "disrupted the order and symmetry of conventional ways of knowing and being, and created a private path available only in a consumption not of their work but of an awareness and exercise of the process in which they themselves engaged and which the work itself displayed" (pp. 338–339). In conceptualizing community-engaged multiliteracies as affichiste, we understand Youth of Color asserting notions of presence, a layering and enacting of already-present literacy practices, within and beyond narratives of standardization or readiness.

ENVISIONING AND ENACTING
COMMUNITY-ENGAGED MULTILITERACIES

We examine community-engaged multiliteracies of graffiti writing, entrepreneurship, and the use of social media and mobile technologies across three research and teaching contexts: teaching and learning with youth at Brooklyn Public, a 6th- to 12th-grade public performing and visual arts high school; literacy and songwriting activities in the Verses Project, an after-school initiative in Detroit; and a study of transnational immigrant youth's critical media literacy practices in and beyond a high school in the U.S. Midwest.

Graffiti Art in Schooling Contexts

Ammar spent the first two-thirds of independent writing time decorating the cover of his composition notebook, drawing the word *REAL* in bold black letters, interconnecting the E and A (see Figure 10.1). Only then did he open the notebook and begin the assigned writing task. Ammar told Vaughn that he aspires to study art or design in college, and uses a computer-based art program at home to create "graphic visualizations" (interview, January 2012). Ammar continued, "Every day, I go home and turn off the TV and think about the world." In carrying art-making practices back into the school day, inscribing unanticipated meanings and possibilities of more just schooling onto a school text in graffiti cover art, Ammar asserted that, through art, "you have to create real motions, and real emotions. You have to be careful because you can change the future." In cover art, Ammar emphasizes a youth perspective independent of the scripted tagline of a *Freedom Writers* movie poster promoting "their story, their words" beneath the gaze of a white teacher.

Ammar was one of 12 students in Vaughn's 10th-grade English class to tag composition notebook covers with hand-drawn, stylized graffiti art, and he and four peers explicitly rewrote and extended names across covers (without teacher prompting). Brandon, for instance, wrote his nickname on a slant, so

Figure 10.1. Cover of Ammar's composition book.

Figure 10.2. Cover of Brandon's composition book.

Figure 10.3. Cover of Boyce's composition book.

that it appeared as a pathway between his first name and the slogan of Odd Future, a popular Los Angeles-based rap group (see Figure 10. 2). He drew a camera, tilted downward, as if photographing his name, shutter flashing. Brandon's graffiti art showed an awareness of popularized narratives. Similarly, Boyce wrote his full name across the cover of his composition notebook, extending imaginings of identities on musical time signatures and stereo speakers drawn to appear as if a skyscraper was the backdrop to Boyce's name. Boyce, writing in green, evoked notions of expanding possibilities for his city, which was further reflected in blossoming stereo speakers and musical notes above his name (Watson & Beymer, 2019) (see Figure 10.3).

Boyce's example, similar to the examples of Brandon and Ammar, underscores the value of attending to literacy practices on young people's terms. In this way, we understand Boyce as projecting identities toward a grander imagined space, his New York City neighborhood redrawn as a musical skyline, gestured to in the rocket propelled from beneath his name toward a cluster of planets sketched above. Boyce's graffiti art cover compels a consideration of how youth simultaneously situate themselves across civic imaginaries of neighborhoods as present and future lived experiences, and how we may understand social and geographic contexts of youth's communities as sites of learning beyond sanctioned, walled-off classrooms.

Ammar, Brandon, and Boyce did not call attention to their work during, or after, the composing process. Therefore, their art exemplified community-engaged multiliteracies undertaken outside of a teacher's pointed directions, albeit within the sanctioned space of a classroom. Their public graffiti making gestured to a broadened audience, asserting a literary presence both within a classroom and beyond the school community.

Graffiti Art in Community Contexts

Each day of the month in October 2013, Banksy, the self-selected pseudonym for the British graffiti artist whose identity is not publicly known, created a new artistic work across New York City (Alliance for the Arts, 2015). That first week in October, Vaughn and his students visited Banksy's website, where, by mid-morning, a photo was posted of Banksy's latest artwork. The class also read articles and opinion columns in *The New York Times* and *New York Daily News* debating the role of graffiti as art and watched *Exit Through the Gift Shop*, a documentary directed by Banksy. Vaughn asked students to respond in an argumentative essay to the prompt: "Do you consider Banksy's graffiti to be art? Explain why, or explain why not. (Or explain how the best answer is somewhere in between.)" (lesson plan, October 2013). Just as young people, using their composition notebook covers, had simultaneously reframed and extended the uses of their notebook covers and the meanings of the class assignment, Ana, a 10th-grade student at Brooklyn Public, asserted complex identities across her classroom and community.

During their lunch period a week after the Banksy unit, Ana shared with Vaughn and her classmate Jessica, "My whole family likes art," and "my cousin is good at graffiti art." Her sharing about lived experiences introduced a broader story of community-engaged multiliteracies, and of traveling from Brooklyn into Manhattan. She explained:

> I went to some sights, and saw a guy doing graffiti art. He was like, "If you see cops, look out for me." He was making [a picture of] himself, drawing something. I just sat. I was on my way to classes at FIT [the Fashion Institute of Technology]. I take Saturday classes there. He was like, "You want to learn?"

To Ana and Vaughn, Jessica noted, "That reminds me of Banksy; that's his name, right?"

Ana nodded in agreement, and continued, "When I was on the A train, I be underground, the electricity from the thing sparks up. […] I think I saw his [Banksy's] piece. I think that was him. It was like a [picture of a] couple, they were writing something [...]. That was cool."

Ana further reflected, extending possibilities of art as literacy practice across contexts: "I'm gonna make a selfie book [...]." Jessica asked, "Of you?"

> "No, a selfie book."
> "Of your friends? If it's selfies, it's you."
> "No, a selfie book."
> "A collage?" Jessica asked. "You putting a whole bunch of [pictures] together, right? A scrapbook."
> "No! A selfie book."

That spring, in a community-engaged multiliteracies practice that broadened meanings of the school-time assignment where youth were asked, "Do you consider Banksy's graffiti to be art?" Ana created her first graffiti artwork. It was a cutout of her profile, eyes shut, wearing her hair down and a hat bearing her pseudonym, "Unknown."

Ana explained that an hour after school ended, she affixed the cutout with clear adhesive tape just to the right of the exterior front doors of Brooklyn Public, the white paper cutout not far from the yellow-and-blue triangular design formally signaling the main entrance in school colors (see Figure 10.4). Ana taped another cutout to the stop sign at the corner just under the Brooklyn-Queens Expressway, and a third to the utility box, at the base of a light pole across the sidewalk from the playground yard rimmed with an iron fence where Ammar, Brandon, Boyce, Ana, Jessica, and their peers regularly gathered. Ana's graffiti cutout on the utility box on the light pole was most visible from the swing set in the playground where youth often awaited the city bus after school.

Figure 10.4. Ana's graffiti cutout, taped near the exterior front door of Brooklyn Public

By "selfie book," Ana was referring to the act of placing selfies in her neighborhood. Ana's tagging of her community with a selfie—a graffiti cutout of Unknown—demonstrated community-engaged multiliteracies as an emboldened exemplar of literary presence. Throughout the week, Ana's cutouts remained, taped to the school, the stop sign, and the utility box, undisturbed even by a graffiti-removal van from the New York City Economic Development Corporation.

Several weeks later, Ana, discussing her literacies practice with Jessica and Vaughn, shared:

> I did a whole bunch of graffiti at my building. I almost got arrested. The landlord guy was like, "Hey, what are you doing?" I was like, "Uh, I'm scraping the wall." He was like, "See, you better be lucky I know you. Now go upstairs and tell your mom." I was like, "Mom! I want to do graffiti."

Ana's literacy practices, which traveled across school and community contexts, complicate popularized narratives of school-bound texts or texts that may school us. Also, she complicates traditional notions of youth as writers by actively engaging in school, home, and community contexts with a literary presence.

Entrepreneurship in Community Contexts

In the final moments of open mic, Alex concluded the original song she performed in the Verses Project. A youth mentor in the literacy and songwriting initiative, Alex looked up from her acoustic guitar and smiled broadly as other youth applauded. Chante, a youth songwriter and rapper who, the following spring, guest taught a literacy and songwriting lesson to undergraduate preservice teachers on a university campus, said softly to Alex, "I like your song." Alex responded, "Thank you," and shared that Chante and the class of youth and teaching artists could buy the song for a dollar on Bandcamp, a social music-sharing website.

In this exchange, Alex asserted her literary and entrepreneurial presence by noting that the song she had written and performed was available for audience members to purchase. Moreover, she located her original music as globally accessible for digital download for the same one-dollar price as a chart-topping popular music single. This is important to note at a time when, in 2017, music streaming grew more than 12% from the prior year (Nielsen, 2018). A few weeks later, Alex held a CD release party, excitedly announcing her music career milestone on Facebook, where she also shared that she would give away a free copy of her CD to all attendees. In this community-engaged multiliteracies practice, songwriting activities emerge as creative practices that hold value beyond a singular classroom space. Additionally, Alex's efforts represent an entrepreneurial presence that resisted a traditional learning economy of credits for school-based literacies.

In Alex's evocation of entrepreneurial presence, we recall Gerald, the year after he was a student in Vaughn's 10th-grade English class at Brooklyn Public. Gerald was designing and selling iPhone cases, gray V-neck T-shirts, and sweatshirts with his "LazyMan Clothing" label to classmates and teachers (see Figure 10.5). The LazyMan clothing logo featured a Black adolescent youth wearing a fitted baseball cap bearing a music note and headphones. Seated at a school desk with a chin resting on arms crossed in front of him and eyes closed, he feigned sleep. The student in the logo also wore a sweatshirt adorned with elbow patches—a fashion choice that signified popularized narratives of academic contexts in secondary and/or university classrooms.

In his community-engaged multiliteracies practice of designing "Lazy-Man" products for sale, Gerald simultaneously asserted and rewrote a deficit notion of Black youth as not engaged. In this way, the LazyMan logo complicated meanings of what and who is understood as holding value, similar to the cover art of rapper Lauryn Hill's first solo CD, *The Miseducation of Lauryn Hill*. On the cover of the CD, Hill's profile, which is drawn into a wooden school desk, maintains a purposeful gaze that stares in the direction of a camera. A sharpened pencil rests in the groove at the top of the desk, awaiting more stories to be written. In fact, the title of her CD affirmingly calls back to and extends from the title of Carter G. Woodson's book *The Miseducation of the Negro*.

Figure 10.5 Gerald's iPhone case featuring the LazyMan logo

A year after graduating from Brooklyn Public, Gerald shared on Facebook that the LazyMan attire was available for retail purchase. His statement, "Everybody please go" and check it out (Facebook, June 2015), was his way of asserting an entrepreneurial presence as emboldened civic imaginary. Similarly, Suae, a teaching artist in the Verses Project, asserted possibilities by building with youth to see their creative and artistic multiliteracies practices as future entrepreneurial possibilities. Joining the literacy and songwriting initiative during its third semester, Suae brought forth an entrepreneurial focus. When introducing Suae to youth in the Verses Project, Will, a poet and teaching artist, positioned Suae as a "professional in the industry, you can go and see [her] webpage" (observation, August 2017). With the young people in the program, Suae shared experiences about her entrance into the music industry as an independent artist. She challenged them to cultivate an online presence and encouraged them to recognize that their work as independent artists might be building an artistic brand beyond mainstream positioning from corporations. For example, she encouraged young people to "Go through iTunes, but by genre not the main page, where artists are paid and promoted" (observation, October 2017). This recommendation drew students' attention to considering how corporate factors influencing music promotion and distribution and might affect their work as independent artists.

Later, Suae shared a YouTube video from an independent artist with more than 892,000 views and 10,000 likes. She noted that although students might not initially monetize their work through a paid YouTube channel, they could gain valuable exposure by posting their artistry on the platform. Throughout her interactions, Suae continually coached and mentored youth on how they might represent their songwriting and instrumentation to varied audiences of peers, family, and community members.

At the Open Mic Listening Party, where songwriters shared vocal and beat-making compositions to conclude the Verses Project's summer-camp session, Suae positioned youth beyond the singular role of student, as emerging talents in a broadened music industry. After one student group, Elementz, presented their song, Suae asked, "What have you gained from the program that's going to go with you as you continue your career?" (observation, August 2017). Band members noted the impact of "working with a big group, [through] disputes and disagreements, and being goal oriented." Suae then reminded students that "networking is very important" in the profession. Across these interactions, Suae positioned young people as being able to capitalize upon already-present community-engaged multiliteracies, a positioning that underscored nuanced meanings of entrepreneurship and that extended youth's literary and entrepreneurial presence.

Social Media in Community Contexts

Matt recalls Aura excitedly pulling out her cellphone and opening it up to her photography app. Aura, a Muslim-identifying transnational immigrant Youth of Color from Iraq who had moved to the United States 3 years prior, began sharing her multimodal social media practices after Matt expressed interest in them during 2 academic years in Aura's social studies class. Now, meeting with Matt in the high school library after classes had ended, Aura shared an image she created: an arid land indicated by interlocking brown cracks, with a faucet, positioned in the lower righthand corner and dripping water onto the parched ground. New life, appearing as a plant, sprang forth from the place where a pool of water had collected (see Figure 10.6).

Aura had recently created the picture for a special art class project where students at Aura's high school partnered with youth from a high school English class in Flint, Michigan. Students collaboratively composed multimodal representations collected into a book of poems that a community-based artist made freely available, with accompanying art that commemorated a public art installation at a regional museum. To bolster their collaboration, Aura and her partner used social media to communicate across distance as they finalized the content of their artistic creations.

The exhibition highlighted broader frustrations that Flint and surrounding communities experienced as they processed and dealt with unresolved issues stemming from the water crisis. In the exhibition space within the

Figure 10.6 Aura's drawing in response to the Flint, MI water crisis

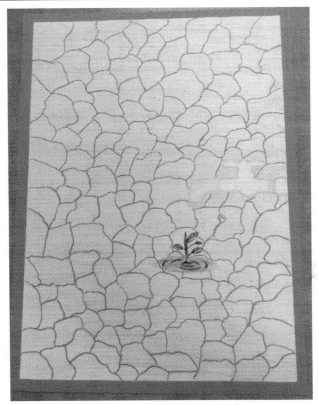

museum, visitors encountered a wall of copper pipes, and could turn on and off faucets connected to the pipes. Aura recounted, "I was proud because it took us a lot of time to do it, and my partner recorded her writing and if you open the faucet you can hear [her poem] from the pipe and if you close it you can't hear it anymore" (interview, May 2017).

In the Flint water crisis, which is rooted in unjust economic practices and racialized discrimination, Aura and her partner's multiliteracy composition contributed to the broader museum exhibition on inequality. In reflecting a civic stance taking as envisioning a more just future, Aura recounted, "We were upset that the governor did not do something about it" (interview, May 2017).

Aura was dismissive regarding the lack of U.S. government response. Given her transnational background and experiences under two systems of governance in Iraq and the United States, she anticipated a better and different response to the crisis, stating, "I mean, it's America" (interview, May 2017). In sharing their collaboration more broadly beyond the museum installation and the commemorative book, Aura and her partner posted their work on their social media accounts, further asserting their literary presence and raising awareness of their civic action.

"WHO ARE YOU?": QUESTIONS FOR EDUCATORS TOWARD JUSTICE-ORIENTED CIVIC IMAGINARIES

The Youth of Color we describe here, who enacted community-engaged multiliteracies, did not complete literacy activities for credit in an academic class. Rather, they expanded narrow meanings of school-sanctioned literacy in demonstrating literary presence. They also enacted an entrepreneurial presence in their creative and artistic practices. In this way, community-engaged multiliteracies emerged as markedly different from school-based performances of literacy that center intervention and deficit. Through their graffiti writing, entrepreneurial activities, and uses of social media and mobile technologies, young people powerfully extended their presence beyond traditional classroom spaces and across communities by asserting differing literary and/or entrepreneurial meanings and value. With this in mind, we draw on Tucker (2011), who compels us to focus on what may be understood as "in the present" (p. 115) in support of and not at the expense of a more fully realized and just future. That is, toward a fuller enactment of what Watson and Knight-Manuel (2017) discussed as a civic imaginary, we seek to recognize how young people's already-present community-engaged literacies reframe and reclaim the present, making a more just future possible. Paradoxically, we usher forth the understanding that, in the way of affichiste, an idealized future might only be fully realized by beginning to layer and construct such a world into existence through present civic action.

We believe that these notions of presence hold significant implications for our collective justice-oriented work as teachers, teacher educators, and literacy researchers. In light of this, we pose the following questions in conversation with our own work, toward deeper engagements with learning with, by, and for young people. We hope the questions and responses will open dialogue to serve as entry points for those committed to justice and to building on young people's already-present community-engaged multiliteracies:

How do/might I value youth's already-present community-engaged multiliteracies? In building on researchers' calls for assets-based approaches to youth's literacies (Kirkland, 2013; Paris & Alim, 2017), we assert a valuing of the already-present through community-engaged multiliteracies as providing enriched possibilities *in* and *as* justice-oriented work. Such work entails a deep(er) engagement with youth practices beyond classrooms and perhaps outside how educators, teacher educators, and researchers may readily enact teaching and learning. It is through our work, away from classrooms, that we have been drawn to the creative and artistic practices of youth, and have come to engage community-engaged multiliteracies with youth in new ways.

How do/might I co-facilitate dynamic learning spaces through which youth's already-present community-engaged multiliteracies and civic imaginaries guide learning? It takes vulnerability to open up classroom work outside classroom walls. However, as we sought to illustrate in this chapter, there is much to be gained by building out of the literacies and learning all around us. Skogsberg (2016) has called for a more dynamic curriculum design that opens space for youth literacies to exist alongside traditional classroom practices. We seek to co-design learning with youth that values their literacies and credits their literacies practices and their lives.

How do/might I credit youth's already-present community-engaged multiliteracies as what youth seek beyond our classroom? Often, classroom value is credited through sanctioned letter grades and transcripts, and we understand that this system is not going away soon. However, what if we afford, for example, more opportunities for youth to assert varied meanings of entrepreneurial presence? Learning takes on new forms and functions as it reflects young people's understandings of literacies practices in ways that they, themselves, seek. Rather than solely crediting youth work in ways that institutions value, how might we co-design opportunities with youth toward the credit that they seek and the learning economies that they value?

"Phantom," the song Vaughn asked 10th-graders to write across in considering their lived experiences, closes with a verse narrated as call and response between the emcee, Mr. Lif, and a chorus of singers named in the liner notes as "hard working U.S. citizens" (Mr. Lif, 2002). In the verse, Mr. Lif names the citizens' social identities and workplace narratives as he repeats a question to each: to a "single mother," an "office worker," a person "caught up in the system," a citizen "tryin to earn a living," one "depressed and uninspired," and a person "hard workin, broke, and tired." The emcee names each citizen, and asks, "Who are you?" Each time, the voice of a citizen individually responds, "I phantom."

The song's closing two lines further complicate narratives of inequity and education. Mr. Lif pointedly asks of those "seekin education" and yet "can't get ahead no matter what [they] do?"—"Who are you?" The citizens then answer as a chorus of voices, an affirmation of a (dis)crediting American education system rendered more somber in the repetition of their collective response: "I phantom."

Mr. Lif, performing "Phantom" live, reaches that final verse, and in prefacing the ending lyric implores the crowd, "People, I need you to respond" (YouTube, 2018). It is in between these questions—in and as a layering of responses—that teachers, teacher educators, and literacy researchers have an opportunity to teach and learn, through practice with youth, differently and toward justice.

REFLECTIVE QUESTIONS

1. How do you value youth's already-present community-engaged multiliteracies?

2. How do you co-facilitate dynamic learning spaces through which youth's already-present community-engaged multiliteracies and civic imaginaries guide learning?

3. In what ways do you credit youth's already-present community-engaged multiliteracies as what youth seek beyond our classrooms?

REFERENCES

Alliance for the Arts. (2015). BanksyNY: Better out than in. Retrieved from nyc-arts.org/collections/80384/banksy-better-out-than-in

Valasek, A. [@AlzValz]. (2015, December 6). This #YearOnTwitter. Retrieved from blog.twitter.com/official/en_us/a/2015/this-yearontwitter.html

Apple, M. W. (2006). Understanding and interrupting neoliberalism and neoconservatism in education. *Pedagogies, 1*(1), 21–26.

Baker-Bell, A., Butler, T., & Johnson, L. (2017). The pain and the wounds: A call for critical race English education in the wake of racial violence. *English Education, 49*(2), 116–129.

Block, A. (2013). In W. Pinar (Ed.), *Curriculum: Toward new identities* (2nd ed., pp. 325–342). New York, NY: Routledge.

Cammarota, J. (2011). Blindsided by the avatar: White saviors and allies out of Hollywood and in education. *Review of Education, Pedagogy, and Cultural Studies, 33*(3), 242–259.

Council of the Great City Schools. (2019). *Fact sheet.* Retrieved from cgcs.org/domain/24

Fisher, M. (2005). Literocracy: Liberating language and creating possibilities: An introduction. *English Education, 37*(2), 92–95.

Gutiérrez, K. (2008). Developing a sociocultural literacy in the third space. *Reading Research Quarterly, 43*(2), 148–164.

Hess, J., Watson, V. W. M., & Deroo, M. (2019). "Show some love": Youth and teaching artists enacting literary presence and musical presence in an after-school literacy-and-songwriting project. *Teachers College Record, 121*(6), 179.

Jenkins, H, Ito, M., & Boyd, D. (2015), *Participatory culture in a networked era: A conversation on youth, learning, commerce, and politics.* Hoboken, NJ: John Wiley & Sons.

Jenkins, H., Shresthova, S., Gamber-Thompson, L., Kligler-Vilenchik, N., & Zimmerman, A. (2016). *By any media necessary: The new youth activism.* New York, NY: NYU Press.

Kinloch, V. (2010). *Harlem on our minds: Place, race, and the literacies of urban youth.* New York, NY: Teachers College Press.

Kirkland, D. E. (2013). *A search past silence: The literacy of young Black men.* New York, NY: Teachers College Press.

Kirkland, D. E., & Jackson, A. (2009). "We real cool": Toward a theory of Black masculine literacies. *Reading Research Quarterly, 44*(3), 278–297.

Knight, M. G., & Watson, V. W. M. (2014). Toward participatory communal citizenship: Rendering visible the civic teaching, learning, and actions of African immigrant youth and young adults. *American Educational Research Journal, 51*(3), 539–566.

Mihailidis, P. (2014). *Media literacy and the emerging citizen: Youth engagement and participation in digital culture.* New York, NY: Peter Lang.

Mr. Lif. (2002). Phantom. *Emergency rations.* New York, NY: Definitive Jux.

Muhammad, G. E. (2012). Creating spaces for Black adolescent girls to "write it out!" *Journal of Adolescent & Adult Literacy, 56*(3), 203–211.

Nielsen. (2018). 2017 U.S. music year-end report. Retrieved from nielsen.com/us/en/insights/reports/2018/2017-music-us-year-end-report.html

Paris, D., & Alim, H. S. (2017). *Culturally sustaining pedagogies: Teaching and learning for justice in a changing world.* New York, NY: Teachers College Press.

Perry, K. H. (2012). What is literacy? A critical overview of sociocultural perspectives. *Journal of Language & Literacy Education, 8*(1), 50–71.

Robertson, S. (2008). Remaking the world: Neoliberalism and the transformation of education and teachers' labor. In M. Compton & L. Weiner (Eds.), *The global assault on teaching, teachers and their unions* (pp. 11–36). New York, NY: Palgrave Macmillan.

Skogsberg, E. (2016). Just tweets and hashtags: Justice-oriented youth literacies education. *Michigan Reading Journal. 49*(1), 54–56.

Sleeter, C. (2008). Equity, democracy, and neoliberal assaults on teacher education. *Teaching and Teacher Education, 24*(8), 1947–1957.

Southern Poverty Law Center. (2016). The Trump effect: The impact of the 2016 presidential election on our nation's schools. Retrieved from splcenter.org/20161128/trump-effect-impact-2016-presidential-election-our-nations-schools

Tatum, A., & Muhammad, G. E. (2012). African American males and literacy development in contexts that are characteristically urban. *Urban Education, 47*(2), 434–463.

Tucker, B. (2011). The dream deferred: How "college and career readiness" looks from below. *English Journal, 100*(3), 115–116.

Watson, V. W. M. (2018). Envisioning the already-present literacy and learning of youth. *English Journal, 107*(5), 10–11.

Watson, V. W. M., & Beymer, A. (2019). Praisesongs of place: Youth envisioning space and place in a literacy-and-songwriting initiative. *Research in the Teaching of English, 53*(4), 297–319.

Watson, V. W. M., & Knight-Manuel, M. G. (2017). Challenging popularized narratives of immigrant youth from West Africa: Examining social processes of navigating identities and engaging civically. *Review of Research in Education, 41*(1), 279–310.

YouTube. (2018, December 3). Mr. Lif—I Phantom. [Video file]. Retrieved from youtube.com/watch?v=P2zqsolUjkQ

Zhao, Y. (2012). *World class learners: Educating creative and entrepreneurial students.* Thousand Oaks, CA: Corwin Press.

CHAPTER 11

Braiding Stories Toward a Common Cause

Coalitional Inquiry as Activism

María Paula Ghiso, Gerald Campano, Grace Player,
Brenda Krishanwongso, and Frianna Gultom

On a Saturday afternoon in a local community center, youth from the Community Literacies Project intricately folded crepe paper into colorful flowers, creating individual artifacts that in the coming weeks would be put together to compose a collective message. The youth were part of an inquiry community of Indonesian and Latinx students who had been coming together every week, some over a span of years, to investigate educational access, equity, and identity. As part of this phase of their inquiry, the youth drew on collaging, printing, and culturally inflected crafting techniques as a form of critically engaging their worlds and how they might be transformed (Thomas, 2017). They viewed the work of contemporary and historical artists, including poetry from the Harlem Renaissance, Bengali folk arts, political photography from across the world, collage artists such as Kara Walker, and paper flower making born of Mexican traditions as inspirations for crafting their own representations of self and community, linking particular identities to broader legacies of social change.

In this chapter, we explore how storytelling and the arts can be vehicles to forge coalition across difference and toward a vision of educational equity and immigrant rights. We spotlight the youth arts project as one inquiry within the context of university research partnership with a multilingual, multiethnic Catholic parish and social justice community center in south Philadelphia (Campano, Ghiso, & Welch, 2016). Community members brought their cultural, linguistic, and transnational knowledge as a resource for our collective inquiries, and they also worked across boundaries to identify and take action on issues that impacted multiple cultural groups. Youth researched the social justice issues they were experiencing in our city, such as the impact of "Doomsday Budget Cuts" on city public schools and the role of immigration histories in educational access (Campano, Ngo, & Player, 2015). They also researched the potential of more equity-oriented curricular opportunities and coalitions for change (Campano et al., 2016; Player, Gill, & Campano, 2016). In the process, they unearthed micronarratives of identity and experience that unsettled both the xenophobic discourse on immigration in the public sphere as well as static notions of cultural identity that too often characterize multicultural education efforts.

The paper flowers project was inspired by a public art action in our city, directed by artist Michelle Angela Ortiz, in solidarity with the Shut Down Berks Coalition that seeks to close down a local family detention center where families with undocumented status, including infants, are being incarcerated, and which is currently operating in violation of its license ("Shut Down Berks," n.d.). As part of the campaign, Michelle taught individuals from all across the city to make paper flowers, which they inscribed with messages of freedom, and joined these with flowers made by Mexican mothers being held at Berks (Ortiz, n.d.). Together, the flowers were assembled into the word *Libertad* (*Freedom*), which was installed outside City Hall (see Figure 11.1). Michelle Ortiz's social action using the paper flowers mobilized cultural touchstones as a political act of solidarity on an issue impacting community members from a range of backgrounds in our research. Using this social action as a model for our own inquiries underscored how the personal is political (Anzaldúa, 1999; Collins, 2000; The Combahee River Collective, 2017), and shifted from valorizing an object as a token of inclusion to seeing cultural knowledge as a part of a larger movement for change.

Figure 11.1. Message of freedom from the arts project spearheaded by Michelle Angela Ortiz

We believe collaborative research using the arts is one avenue for linking schooling to the layered histories, experiences, and advocacy efforts of youth from immigrant backgrounds. As we discuss in the sections that follow, we draw on the concepts of "rhizomatic identities" (Glissant, 2010) and epistemic privilege (Mohanty, 1997; Moya, 2002) to challenge bounded and essentializing notions of culture that are characteristic of, on the one hand, deficit perspectives on the education of immigrant children and, on the other, of resource-based approaches that too narrowly demarcate cultural belonging. We interweave our particular stories of immigration from our various positionalities—three university-based researchers and two youth community-based researchers—in order to make visible buried subaltern and colonial legacies that impact education as well as to imagine conditions through which coalitional partnerships toward educational access and equity may blossom.

EDUCATION AND IMMIGRATION IN NEOLIBERAL TIMES

The education of immigrant students, long a subject of research, policy, and pedagogical attention, has taken on increased urgency in the current political moment. Beyond being a curricular issue, supporting the learning of students from immigrant backgrounds is tied to broader factors that are materially experienced by youth and families, including economic precarity, language access, race and racism, and xenophobia (Suárez-Orozco, Darbes, Dias, & Sutin, 2011). We are writing this chapter during an especially horrific period of anti-immigrant racist rhetoric and state-sanctioned violence. Though the *Plyer v. Doe* Supreme Court decision has guaranteed the right to an education regardless of immigration status, this "don't ask, don't tell" legislative solution (Mangual Figueroa, 2017) belies the contested nature of what such an education would/should entail and how we perceive its relationship to equity and access. Most schools are organized around assimilationist ideologies that view the cultures, languages, and literacies of immigrant students as an obstacle to be overcome on the pathway to academic success (Gutiérrez & Orellana, 2006). From this perspective, educational access entails instruction in academic skills students are identified as missing, such as "background knowledge" or "academic language;" these skills are treated as neutral indicators of achievement, and pedagogical practices aim to transmit such knowledge.

Attempts to fill the so-called gaps in students' knowledge, however, too often lead to subtractive schooling (Valenzuela, 1999), where children and youth have to leave their linguistic and cultural resources outside the classroom door. As Janks (2000) argues, "access without a theory of domination leads to the naturalisation of powerful discourses without an understanding of how these powerful forms came to be powerful" (p. 179). Literacy researchers have long made the case that attention to academic skills in teaching students from historically minoritized communities also requires situating those skills within contexts of power to underscore how social hierarchies come to define whose language and literacies are legitimated.

There is also a robust scholarly lineage that has documented educational contexts seeking to leverage the cultural and linguistic funds of knowledge of students (González, Moll, & Amanti, 2005). These may include specific repertoires born of their experiences of migration, including family literacy practices such as translation and cultural brokering (Martínez, 2010; Orellana, 2009), as well as "politicized funds of knowledge" (Gallo & Link, 2015) that encompass awareness of the complexities of documentation status and advocacy efforts toward change. Yet, there remains a disconnect between what we know about the dynamism of immigrant students' funds of knowledge and attempts to organize schooling to value these contributions. Ladson-Billings (2014) notes that in discussions of culturally relevant pedagogy, "the fluidity and variety within cultural groups has regularly been lost" and "few have taken up the sociopolitical dimensions of the work" (p. 77). Despite the efforts of many individual educators, changing school cultures to attend to the insights of immigrant populations is often reduced to a more easily packaged multiculturalism that can essentialize cultures, treat them as overly static, and detach them from the social and political factors that shape schooling (Ghiso & Campano, 2013).

Although ostensibly quite different, these two approaches share a focus on the individual student and thus on a system of meritocracy underlying educational success. Whether overcoming the obstacle of one's language and culture or leveraging these for access into the codes of power, the emphasis is on individual achievement rather than on systems that produce and sustain inequality (Vasudevan & Campano, 2009). Widening the lens, however, reveals shared struggles regarding how neoliberal policies and ideologies have reshaped education. The "sharp retrenchment of the public sphere" and "champion[ing] the privatization of social goods" (Lipman, 2011, p. 6) that are characteristic of neoliberalism have further compounded the already-precarious circumstances impacting the schooling experiences of immigrant youth. The members of the Community Literacies inquiry group had in common that they were navigating an educational landscape that focused on productivity and accountability, which has exacerbated pressures for individual performance around white English dominant norms (Menken, 2008), and a public school system that had been charterized (Suárez-Orozco et al., 2011). There seems to be an ever-yawning gap between the world of policy and the on-the-ground, lived realities of immigrant youth.

RHIZOMATIC IDENTITIES AND EPISTEMIC PRIVILEGE: LINKING THE INDIVIDUAL AND THE COLLECTIVE IN PROJECTS FOR CHANGE

How, then, do we honor the knowledge derived from transnational migration without flattening or essentializing identities, or reducing them to romanticized inner properties (Mohanty, 2018)? How can exploration of our entwined histories inform collective work toward educational equity across the boundaries of race, class, culture, language, and institutional roles? To address these complexities, we ground our work in theories regarding the "epistemic privilege" of nondominant communities (Campano, 2007; Mohanty, 1997; Moya, 2002) and Édouard Glissant's (2010) concept of "rhizomatic identities" (for a longer discussion on Glissant and literacy studies, see Campano et al., in press). Glissant was an anti-essentialist who critiqued cultural purism. He believed that one's identity was always created "in relation" with others and perpetually in the act of becoming. Glissant was in dialogue with Deleuze and Guattari and his use of the metaphor of the rhizome was a way of critiquing dominant understandings of identity as adherence to a "single root, of racial or linguistic purity" (Hiepko, 2011, p. 256), often tied to exclusionary assimilationist, national, and racist ideologies. He strove to acknowledge and even celebrate the multiple, ever-evolving intertwined root systems that shape subjectivity. Conceiving identity as dynamic does not, however, imply a type of unfettered, neoliberal self-invention, unconstrained by history and the material world. Glissant, unlike many of his European colleagues, also retained the idea of "identity," signaling the centrality he placed on the realities of history and the ongoing legacies of colonialism and genocide that differentiate group experience.

Postpositivist realist theories of identity (Mohanty, 1997, 2018; Moya, 2002) argue that members of minoritized social groups have an epistemic privilege or advantage in understanding social hierarchies and inequality. From this perspective, identities are not descriptive claims or essential properties of bounded groups, but "claims about a system of social relations and about the world in which the relations among groups are shaped and defined" (Mohanty, 2018). Through reflexive inquiry, members of minoritized groups are more likely to arrive at objective understandings of the world we share, creating the conditions for collective efforts. As Mohanty (2018) contends, "in order to enrich and deepen our notion of genuine universalism, we need fine-grained accounts of the socially-produced vulnerabilities of actual human agents, going beyond our conceptions of disembodied, idealized, and ahistorical persons." Taking action to address educational inequity necessitates that we take seriously the perspectives of those most impacted by neoliberal educational policies and the segregation and underfunding of schooling.

STORIES AS SHARED KNOWLEDGE PRODUCTION

The youth inquiry into educational access involved learning from others, including artists and activists, while simultaneously viewing our own stories, identities, and experiences as a source of knowledge necessary for equity-oriented and coalitional work. In the tradition of practitioner research methodologies, we created a community of inquiry among the youth, graduate students, and faculty: a space to "theorize and construct [our] work and to connect it to larger social, cultural, and political issues" (Cochran-Smith &

Lytle, 1999, p. 250) and thus "conjoin [our] efforts to construct knowledge" (p. 273). Together, we investigated issues of educational equity and access, and how they were manifested locally. We realized that as the students documented their experiences in the educational system, it was important for those of us in the university to share our own narratives as well. We documented the work of the inquiry group through qualitative data sources such as fieldnotes, photographs, and artifacts.

Our practices in the community of inquiry draw from intellectual traditions that value the knowledge of historically minoritized communities as a way to make visible—and challenge—racism, xenophobia, and the myth of meritocracy in schools, and the erosion of public education more generally. In particular, we were inspired by Latinx testimonios (Latina Feminist Group, 2001), counternarratives in critical race theory (Kinloch, Burkhard, & Penn, 2017; Ladson-Billings & Tate, 1995; Milner & Howard, 2013), and the idea of writing and theorizing from buried experiences in Asian American studies (Ichioka, 1974; Lee, 2014). What began to come out in the storytelling was the way in which people's identities and histories were not insular, but in fact, connected and at times overlapped in ways that helped foster coalition.

In the sections that follow, each of us shares one of our own narratives as a specific "fine-grained account" (Mohanty, 2018) that expands representations of immigrant identities and points to the possibilities of "identities as relation." These narratives germinated in the inquiry group, and took shape through the shared writing process for this publication. We believe that together, and as part of an inquiry community, these narratives can contribute to a more universal understanding of social inequities in education and how the system might be transformed for the better.

The following vignettes are of the rhizomatic and migratory histories that have shaped our own personal, familial, and educational experiences. Four of us have Asian heritage, and María Paula is an Argentinian who was raised in Queens, New York. As university researchers, we each received assimilationist educations in our early years of schooling. Relatedly, the youth authors are navigating a severely underresourced city school district that often relies on standardized forms of instruction and assessment. We all could be read, or might even read ourselves, through assimilationist lenses, such as "model minority" stereotypes. But we believe the intentional mining of our own rhizomatic histories and experiences through storying is one way to (re)claim epistemic resources and subordinated forms of knowledge that enable us to work toward "a common cause" (Hames-García, 2011, p. xv).

Educator Stories and Self-Reflexivity

It is common for educators who are looking to honor the experiences of immigrant students to invite them to share their narratives. Though we value this type of curricular opening, we wanted instead to begin with the stories of educators because we believe self-reflexivity to be the first step in fostering coalitions. We offer our three stories uninterrupted—Grace reflecting on performing identities and the shortcomings of a multicultural activity in her own schooling, Gerald tracing the buried and covered histories of the names in his family, and María Paula exploring the complexities of trying to mobilize her multilingual and immigrant background in the curriculum—before bringing them together to consider how educators may lay the foundation for learning from others by first learning from themselves.

Grace: What is not seen. For just one day, I was invited to bring an ethnic self to the classroom, wrapped in the white silk of my child-sized kimono, passed to my sister and then to me from my older cousins in Brazil, bought by their father on one of his journeys back to his home country of Japan. My hair, an abundant mass of silken flyaways, some hybrid of my mother's heavy black hair and my father's fluffy light curls, was pinned into a messy bun and pierced with a tasseled kanzashi. I stood in front of my mostly white classmates for that one day, to perform an ethnic identity, to please their exotifying eyes. There, in front of my class, I performed a Japanese identity, one that was easy to understand, one that matched, closely enough, story book images of "Asian"-ness, a pretty little girl with almond eyes and dark hair, adorned in silk.

For just one day, an invitation was made to "celebrate" my culture. And, because it was just for one day, my teachers' and classmates' idea of "Asian"-ness, a neat East Asian conception of an entire continent, was reified. Although I stood there with pride, feeling so special, so pretty, so unique in front of my classmates, in front of my teachers, a great deal of my transnational identity, my mother's family, their immigrant journey across the globe, was concealed by this performance of a simple, digestible Japanese identity (Figure 11.2).

What of the nearly 2-month sea journey that my grandparents and eldest aunt and uncle made, my mother in the womb, in a boat from Japan to Brazil? What of the impending violence of World War II they narrowly escaped? What of the dirt floors of my mother's childhood home in rural Brazil? What of the racial slurs she faced as a child attending a small country school in her parents' new country? What of her migration to the United States? What of the ways her accent was mocked, the lack of patience given to her as she learned to communicate in a third tongue? What of her white husband, who didn't allow her to speak Portuguese with her daughters? What of the dozens of cousins I never learned to speak with because my mother's language was not good enough for my father's home? What about all these stories, these pieces of me, that were hidden by this sole performance of an ethnic self, this one day of cultural celebration that invited a Japanese me into the classroom?

Sitting now among my own students, I bear witness to their own complex identities. I testify to my own. The invitation I extend is not one of false celebration extended for just one day, but to a critical praxis of exploring, sharing, storying, understanding, questioning, evolving, relating, differing, connecting,

Figure 11.2. Performing identity

claiming, and, indeed, celebrating identities. When I sit with my students for this *critical* celebration of identities that is in the fabric of our curriculum, of our learning culture, we see one another, we see our strengths, we see our pain, we see the ways our identities, in all their complexities, are foundational to our political strength as minoritized people. Our ethnic identities are not merely performances for a white gaze, but rather, a source of power that can be harnessed toward change.

Gerald: Names and rhizomatic legacies. One way to trace my own rhizomatic identity is through some of my family names, including those that have been covered or repressed. My surname is Campano, which many assume is Italian but is in actuality a legacy of European colonization of the Philippines. I go by Gerald, and that is indeed my middle name. But my birth certificate reads Hans Gerald. Throughout my life, Hans has flickered in and out of visibility. My faculty webpage reads *H. Gerald*. My undergraduate degree reads *Gerald H.*, suggesting my own efforts to squeeze Hans almost into nonexistence.

My mother is an immigrant from Germany and my father is a New Yorker, with ancestral roots in Mindanao, on his father's side, and southern Italy, from his mother. It was my father who originally wanted me to have a German first name and my mother who soon afterward petitioned that I go by Gerald because it did not have the stigma of being too German. My mother's last name is Braunleder. Her two earliest memories were of World War II: rushing to bomb shelters, and the despair of her own mother whose husband, my grandfather, disappeared in Stalingrad. He had four brothers, three of whom also died in the war. My own mother's grandfather died in World War I, and she grew up in a village largely without men. It was also a village that would have trouble confronting its own complicity in the Holocaust. I often heard stories of the war but not of the Holocaust.

One of my father's earliest memories is moving from apartment to apartment of different Filipino families throughout New York City. One later memory that continues to haunt him is that of one of his brothers, Dennis, was lost to the streets.

My paternal grandfather was from a subaltern community within the Philippines. His full name is Faustino Yamba Campano, and I am told from relatives that Yamba, from his maternal lineage, is most likely a Lumad name, designating indigenous roots to the precolonial people of northern Mindanao who had not converted to Islam.

My grandfather migrated, as an orphan and young teenager, from Mindanao to California via Hawaii in the 1920s, during the period of American colonization and a decade or so after an imperial war that killed hundreds of thousands of Filipinos—this genocide was omitted from my school textbooks. His passage was on a U.S. Navy ship working as an assistant to the officers, where sailors called him "Friday," after the native servant character in Defoe's *Robinson Crusoe*. He himself initially adopted the name Friday but changed it to Freddy, which was less demeaning than Friday and more intelligible than Faustino to many white American ears. In California, his generation of Filipinos could not own land, were subject to antimiscegenation laws, and were targets of violence fueled by racism and xenophobia. They also organized to protest exploitation and agitate for their rights.

After laboring in several migratory contexts, my grandfather eventually found his way to New York City, working on an oil tanker that passed through the Panama Canal. He eloped with my grandmother and they raised seven children in Queens—my father, also named Freddy, was the eldest (Figure

Figure 11.3. Gerald's grandparents in New York City

11.3). It was during the Depression, and my grandparents had to do what they needed to do in order to survive, including working multiple jobs. My grandfather also took great joy and pride in being a musician and a member of the musicians' union.

I am still just learning about and processing many of my grandmother's experiences and stories that I didn't know despite having been close to her my whole life. Both her parents immigrated from Italy, and she also has some roots in North Africa and West Asia. Her surname was Valente, and she spoke what she called "Hillbilly Italian" as a child at home. In November of 2018, my grandmother celebrated her 100th birthday in Queens, which has now become the homeland for future generations.

I do not speak any of my grandparents' first languages and am the product of largely an assimilationist early education. *Hans, Yamba, Faustino, Dennis,* and *Valente* are just a few examples of the covered, repressed, and fading names that represent a range of histories in my own family: histories of colonizers and colonized, oppressors and oppressed; genocide and war; mobility, trauma, and disappearance; as well as resistance, survival, remaking, and joy. They reflect the experiences of people who have lived their lives and sometimes survived under conditions that could never be considered ideologically or culturally pure. In a nation that has orchestrated a mythos of exceptionalism on the ravages of historical amnesia and genocide, I, like many others, believe it is imperative for educators to confront the truths of history if there is ever to be collective healing and reconciliation.

I also believe that understanding the multiplicity within the self is the first step toward cultivating a genuine love for and sense of interdependence with others as we try to work in solidarity together for a better future.

María Paula: Teacher and student solidarity. I pull out several pictures of the neighborhood, show them to the 1st-graders gathered in front of me on the carpet. I show a picture of my elementary school, "my English school," and tell them how the teacher didn't think I was smart because I didn't speak English. "*No era justo,*" Brian chimes in. It was unjust because, he says, "*Todos son inteligentes en algo*"—we are all smart at something. You don't know English well but you know Spanish, he reassures me. Natalia raises her hand. "*Tenías una amiga?*" Did you have a friend? No, I tell her, because the other children couldn't understand me. I felt very alone. "And then what happened?" she pressed. "Did you make a friend? Did your mom take you to a school like ours, where you could speak both languages?"

I share my pictures of my Saturday Argentinean school, how my sister and I would dress up in uniforms to walk across the street to the school, my dad documenting it all from the top-floor bedroom with his camera. I tell the 1st-graders about speaking Spanish, tell them about feeling smart, tell them about my successes. "I know that place!" Brian interjects. "That's where my mom takes English classes." Andi looks at the neighborhood buildings and tells me, "*Yo voy por ahí*"—I go by there. Because I am teaching and researching in the neighborhood where I myself grew up, the resonances in our shared references bubble up.

I ask the 1st-graders to look through their photos, pick the places that are important to them, and think about who they are there, how they feel, what they know, how others see them. I overhear children talking: "I'm going to write about Señora Maria, when she was little." In the community map, they paste my childhood picture next to the image of the local playground, tell me it's because we're playing there together (see Figure 11.4).

My interest in the systemic causes of educational inequity stems from my own childhood experiences as a Latina immigrant in New York City public schools. In my English-only classroom, I was placed in remedial instruction because of my "limited language proficiency," while in the Argentinean school I attended on weekends I qualified for advanced placement. These differential "readings" of my abilities, to which I was sensitized early on, suggest that academic success is not just a function of individual aptitude—a tenet of

Figure 11.4. Attending Argentinean school as a child (top) and immigrant children utilizing that image in their own arts inquiry (bottom)

dominant meritocratic ideologies—but is more about creating learning environments where a range of intellectual and cultural identities might flourish. I tried to use my own experiences as an entry point to make visible, with young children, how language and power operate in school as well as the importance of their community knowledge.

In engaging with my story, it is evident that the children were listening to my teaching point, but they were also listening to something I hadn't known I was communicating. They listened to the difficulties I experienced. Through their empathetic responses and ethos of interdependence (Ghiso, 2016), the children helped imagine and bring into being a curriculum that was more attuned to my language and culture than my own schooling had been. As educators and school leaders, we can learn from immigrant children so that we can connect their worlds to academic requirements and support them in navigating the literacies of schooling. We can also learn from their care for one another—and for us—about how to transform schools to honor everyone's well-being and to have a more robust conception of community knowledge in the curriculum.

Student Stories: Arts and Activism

As adult university-based educators, we (María Paula, Gerald, and Grace) mine our past experiences in order to unlearn aspects of our own miseducation (Anzaldúa, 1999) and reclaim buried parts of our histories to imagine future possibilities, including working with newer generations. Brenda and Frianna, both of whom have been collaborative youth researchers on the project for 5 years, employ poetry and narrative to probe the present and a more just future.

Brenda shares a poem about the (mis)communication between her mother and herself—the foreign language she refers to in her title is not Indonesian or English (the home language and native language divide that is the commonly invoked trope of immigrant youth), but the mathematical language of her mother, who was an engineer in her home country yet has not been able to practice her profession in the United States. Frianna describes her participation in the March for Our Lives protest that brought together youth from across the city and the nation in March of 2018 to address gun violence in schools.

Brenda: "The undermining of our voices"

Foreign Language

I pick up the pencil
She picked up the pen
The algebraic equation already begins to formulate the sweat upon my
    forehead
what is this foreign language
The silent drips of Shakespeare begin to rain on the textbook she can't
    understand
what is this foreign language
Give every man thy ear but few thy voice
Her tongue seems to slack when it comes to that line why do the words
    twist and rhyme?
Give every man thy ear but very few thy voice
The line resonates so loudly in my head, giving power to the words
Power she will not understand
Sin, cos, tan

I begin to slack when my mind twists and devours the formula whole
Why has the alphabet created a monster, not the words I love?
She looks at my paper and I look at hers, look it's a language I understand.
Let me help you.
I could write you a poem and you could solve all the problems.
Mother, mother tongue
Our sin was never the understanding of the language but the undermining
    of our voices
The cos was always our pride and our culture
We stand now, tangent from all that was once our own
She picked up the pencil
I pick up the pen

Frianna: "Everyone was unified as one." It was March 14, days after the mass shooting in Parkland, Florida, when 17 young people lost their lives. Along with my Philadelphia high school classmates, I was following the lead of the youth activists from Parkland like Emma González, the young woman who has been so instrumental in this movement for gun safety, as I walked out of school in an act of protest. At 10:00, everyone exited the building. We stood outside our school in silence, waiting 17 minutes for the 17 lives that were lost. I felt touched to see how many students cared about ending gun violence and by the actions of the students directly involved in shootings that went on this year, who really tried to advocate for change. The energy among the students was lively and they were screaming. Many of us were not ready to end the protest there. We marched to city hall and protested there against the influence of the NRA.

As we marched down Broad Street, my peers were talking to one another about school, what the shootings were about, and their opinions on the issue, buzzing with energy. The sound of cars honking to show their support added to the excitement. People were chanting and singing Meek Mill's "Dream and Nightmares." Everyone was unified as one, marching for something they believed in. People videotaping us walking as well as cheering us made me feel like I was a part of a larger voice that really mattered. This walkout showed that the youth do care about their education and what happens around them. It showed that our narratives need more attention, that the district, the state, and the country need to actually listen to our desires and not disregard them.

Teachers and other adults thought the walkout was incredible, and my principal was so proud of us, that we did something that we believed in. Believing that we did have a voice and our opinions do matter. That our lives aren't something to be messed with. That we deserve to be understood as individuals because we are different and have specific needs and desires.

The youth in Philadelphia took action to organize the walkout, and it became clear that they had opinions, desires, and hopes for their future. If schools were built on students' desires rather than adults', they would have a different atmosphere. Students' passion for school would be different; they would enjoy school more and be more motivated and involved. Maybe then, with youth voices at the center of schooling, educational conditions would change. Maybe then, we would find ways to build together the safe environment we crave. Maybe then, we could stop the bullying we see every day. Maybe then, we could create educational equity whether we go to a public, private, or neighborhood school. Maybe then, we could finally center what the students care about. Maybe then, we will actually get funding to do the things we love to do, whether it is sports, clubs, school trips, prom, the things you experience in high school, and the things we all deserve, like school counselors, nurses, clean and safe schools. Maybe then, adults could see that the youth are the future and that they should be more attentive to what youth need to succeed. Maybe then, schools would be places where students could thrive.

Learning from Youth Stories

Brenda and Frianna's words invite us to expand our conceptions of educational equity as energized by artistic traditions of cultural critique and past and present social movements. In her poem, Brenda describes how her ways of knowing are both interwoven with and separate from her mother's. References to her mother's mathematical abilities shift the positioning of immigrant parents to that of knowledge producers and evoke the material consequences of migration that existed prior to and that persist after one's "arrival." The mathematical language is also a pathway for educational access that Brenda feels responsibility to pursue in order to fulfill her mother's dreams for her, to prove her sacrifices worthwhile. Yet Brenda is pulled by her own creative and artistic interests. The poem traces the ways mother and daughter are making efforts to understand each other, to pick up the other's mode of language, to create hybrid modes of communication. Through her words, Brenda creatively remixes her mother's language—*sine, cosine, tangent*—appealing to the universalism of mathematics to transcend the denial of her family's voice, and to craft hybrid identities that can communicate across difference, across generations.

Frianna's account of her school protests underscores the epistemic value of social identities as a movement for change. As Mohanty (2018) argues, "human knowledge is not simply the result of individual contemplation; molded as it is by historical and social forces, knowledge is often the product of activism, of social engagement, and deliberately partisan inquiry (p. 423)" Frianna is certainly an Indonesian immigrant, but she is also a young Woman of Color in the Philadelphia school system who has both overlapping and different experiences from those of many of her peers. Nonetheless, the young people are able to cooperate across boundaries to advocate for a more universal vision of educational justice. Brenda and Frianna, alongside their peers and their families, shared their insights at the American Educational Research Association (AERA) conference as part of a symposium on participatory methodologies.

Met with an overwhelming number of attendees and unable to fit within the room we had been assigned, we moved our presentation to the hallway, and Frianna closed the session by reading aloud her narrative of the march. Through the promise of collaborative research, individual accounts have the potential for much broader impact.

UNITED TOWARD A COMMON CAUSE: BEING IN RELATION

As students, former teachers, and educational researchers, we remain deeply invested in the promise of schooling. Nonetheless, we have found within our community-based partnership an invaluable context to explore educational equity because many schools continue to homogenize difference through policies such as standardization, high-stakes testing, and ethnocentric curricula. Over the course of our research, we have been reminded that the path to partnerships that have a more universal resonance is through the day-to-day work of building relationships across differences. These relationships have epistemic significance as we transform our interpretations and understandings of our own experiences in light of what we learn from one another and together through collaborative inquiry. Over the years, for example, María Paula, Gerald, and Grace have been inspired by youth such as Brenda and Frianna, as well as other members of the south Philadelphia immigrant communities, to continue to read our own familial stories through Feminist of Color and (post)colonial lenses, highlighting aspects of our own identities that do not fit neatly into assimilationist tropes. As María Paula's vignette demonstrates, we also continue to learn from students, even younger children, about alternative forms of sociality, ways of being in community that privilege interdependence and that exist within and against dominant neoliberal educational structures.

We have also learned that although the education system can be assimilationist, individuals should never be characterized as definitively "assimilated"—for example, as conforming to some reactionary idea of what it means to be an "American"—and that our identities are never fully exhausted by dominant ideologies. Identities, following Glissant (2010), are always potentially transforming "in relation" with others, and perhaps what is more important than the outward symbols of culture, such as clothes or a name, are the values and commitments we live by and develop alongside others. Brenda teaches us that one vehicle for transformation is the arts, such as poetry, where new forms of expression and meaning-making are created that defy static notions of culture, language, and identity. Frianna reminds us of the role that activism may play in creating coalitions across differences, in the process transforming one's understanding of oneself through a collective vision of educational justice. The five singular vignettes we share are just a small glimpse into the constellation of stories and experiences the constitute the expanding universe of our collaborative research.

CONCLUSION

Working in solidarity is not a given. It's an achievement, the product of humanizing relationships that honor the specificity of each person's history, story, and interests. What is often hidden behind declarations of unity are the unique stories that individuals weave together, stories that call into question fixed notions of identity. In the paper flowers project, while the identifiably "Mexican" character of the paper flowers would seem to align with some of the group members more directly, the youth were not only learning about one another's roots, but also about buried histories of oppression and resistance that underlie cultural representations. For example, the flowers reflect indigenous traditions of paper-like decorations that were well established before the introduction of paper by Spanish colonialism as well as influences from the Philippines that reflect global flows and colonial ties (Hutchins, Greenfield, Epstein, Sanders, & Galindo, 2013).

That busy afternoon, one of many in their time as part of the community-based research team, the youth folded, crimped, and glued paper into puffy flowers, which accumulated into vibrant floral piles. Some of them wrote tiny messages hidden within the paper petals of their hopes. Some of them cut precise squares to fold into origami butterflies. As the students worked, we discussed what sort of message we wanted to create with our collective art project. We gazed upon Michelle Angela Ortiz's message of "Libertad." Frianna said, "Unity." This word captured much of what was happening at the community center and in our research, and the youth immediately were on board. They

Figure 11.5. Students' selected message for the flowers project

ripped strips of colorful paper and glued them on each letter, forming a word that exuded the vibrancy of the group. With hot-glue guns, they arranged the flowers and butterflies around the word *UNITY*, braiding their creations into an artistic representation of their individual and communal aspirations.

REFLECTIVE QUESTIONS

1. What are the multiple stories that inform your identities and experiences? What buried histories or legacies of oppression and resistance do they speak to? How do your stories resonate (or not) with the norms of schooling?

2. How can stories inspire change and action? How can you re-story dominant narratives? You might examine, for example, the use of stories in activist movements, or how you can take up activist teaching through making space for student stories in the classroom.

REFERENCES

Anzaldúa, G. (1999). *Borderlands/la frontera: The new mestiza* (2nd ed.). San Francisco, CA: Aunt Lute Books.

Campano, G. (2007). *Immigrant students and literacy: Reading, writing, and remembering.* New York, NY: Teachers College Press.

Campano, G., Ghiso, M. P., Rusoja, A., Player, G., & Schwab, E. (2016). "Education without boundaries": Literacy pedagogies and human rights. *Language Arts, 94*(1), 43–53.

Campano, G., Ghiso, M. P., & Welch, B. (2016). *Partnering with immigrant communities: Action through literacy.* New York, NY: Teachers College Press.

Campano, G., Ngo, L., & Player, G. (2015). Researching from buried experiences: Collaborative inquiry with Asian American youth. *LEARNing Landscapes, 8*(2), 77–94.

Cochran-Smith, M., & Lytle, S. (1999). Relationships of knowledge and practice: Teacher learning in communities. *Review of Research in Education, 24,* 249–305.

Collins, P. H. (2000). *Black feminist thought: Knowledge, consciousness, and the politics of empowerment.* New York, NY: Routledge.

The Combahee River Collective. (2017). The Combahee River Collective Statement. In K. Y. Taylor (Ed.), *How we get free: Black feminism and the Combahee River Collective* (pp. 15–27). Chicago, IL: Haymarket Books.

Gallo, S., & Link, H. (2015). "Diles la verdad": Deportation policies, politicized funds of knowledge, and schooling in middle childhood. *Harvard Educational Review, 85*(3), 357–382.

Ghiso, M. P. (2016). The Laundromat as the transnational local: Young children's literacies of interdependence. *Teachers College Record, 118*(1), 1–46.

Ghiso, M. P., & Campano, G. (2013). Coloniality and education: Negotiating discourses of immigration in school and communities through border thinking. *Equity and Excellence in Education, 46*(2), 252–269.

Glissant, E. (2010). *Poetics of relation* (Trans. B. Wing). Ann Arbor, MI: University of Michigan Press.

González, N., Moll, L. C., & Amanti, C. (2005). *Funds of knowledge: Theorizing practices in households, communities, and classrooms.* Mahwah, NJ: Lawrence Erlbaum.

Gutiérrez, K. D., & Orellana, M. F. (2006). The "problem" of English Learners: Constructing genres of difference. *Research in the Teaching of English, 40*(4), 502–507.

Hames-García, M. (2011). *Identity complex: Making the case for multiplicity.* Minneapolis, MN: University of Minnesota Press.

Hiepko, A. S. (2011). Europe and the Antilles: An interview with Édouard Glissant. (Trans. J. Everret). In F. Lionnet & S. Shih (Eds.), *The creolization of theory* (pp. 255–261). Durham, NC: Duke University Press.

Hutchins, D. J., Greenfield, M. D., Epstein J. L., Sanders, M. G., & Galindo, C. L. (2013). *Multicultural partnerships: Involve all families.* New York, NY: Routledge.

Ichioka, Y. (Ed.). (1974). *A buried past: An annotated bibliography of the Japanese research project collection.* Oakland, CA: University of California Press.

Janks, H. (2000). Domination, access, diversity, and design: A synthesis for critical literacy education. *Educational Review, 52*(2), 175–186.

Kinloch, V., Burkhard, T., & Penn, C. (2017). When school is not enough: Understanding the lives and literacies of Black youth. *Research in the Teaching of English, 52*(1), 34–54.

Ladson-Billings, G. (2014). Culturally relevant pedagogy 2.0: a.k.a. the remix. *Harvard Educational Review, 84*(1), 74–84.

Ladson-Billings, G., & Tate, W. (1995). Toward a critical race theory of education. *Teachers College Record, 97*(1), 47–68.

Latina Feminist Group (2001). *Telling to live: Latina feminist testimonios.* Durham, NC: Duke University Press.

Lipman, P. (2011). *The new political economy of urban education: Neoliberalism, race, and the right to the city.* New York, NY: Routledge.

Lee, S. S-H. (2014). *A new history of Asian America.* New York, NY: Routledge.

Mangual Figueroa, A. (2017). Speech or silence: Undocumented students' decisions to disclose or disguise their citizenship status in school. *American Educational Research Journal, 54*(3), 485–523.

Martínez, R. A. (2010). Spanglish as literacy tool: Toward an understanding of the potential role of Spanish-English code switching in the development of academic literacy. *Research in the Teaching of English, 45*(2), 124–149.

Menken, K. (2008). *English learners left behind: Standardized testing as language policy.* Clevedon, UK: Multilingual Matters.

Milner, H. R., & Howard, T. C. (2013). Counter-narrative as method: Race, policy, and research for teacher education. *Race, Ethnicity, and Education, 16*(4), 586–561.

Mohanty, S. P. (1997). *Literary history and the claims of history: Postmodernism, objectivity, multicultural politics.* Ithaca, NY: Cornell University Press.

Mohanty, S. P. (2018). Social justice and culture: On identity, intersectionality, and epistemic privilege. In G. Craig (Ed.)., *Handbook on global social justice* (pp. 418–427). Cheltenham, UK: Edward Elgar.

Moya, P. (2002). *Learning from experience: Minority identities, multicultural struggles.* Berkeley, CA: University of California Press.

Orellana, M. F. (2009). *Translating childhoods: Immigrant youth, language, and culture.* New Brunswick, NJ: Rutgers University Press.

Ortiz, M. A. (n.d.). Familias separadas: Ongoing work on stories of deportation and detension. Retrieved from michelleangela.com/work/2015/october/familias-separadas

Player, G. D., Gill, V. S., & Campano, G. (2016). "Beyond the barriers: Listening to immigrant youth to transform higher education. *LEARNing Landscapes, 10*(1), 215–234.

"Shut Down Berks." (n.d.). Retrieved from vamosjuntos.org/Shut-Down-Berks

Súarez-Orozco, M., Darbes, T., Dias, S. I., & Sutin, M. (2011). Migrations and schooling. *Annual Reviews of Anthropology, 40*(1), 311–328.

Thomas, D. A. (2017). *Navigating transnational borderlands through critical media-making.* Doctoral dissertation. Teachers College, Columbia University. Retrieved from ProQuest, 10285512

Valenzuela, A. (1999). *Subtractive schooling: US-Mexican youth and the politics of caring.* Albany, NY: SUNY Press.

Vasudevan, L., & Campano, G. (2009). The social production of risk and the promise of adolescent literacies. *Review of Research in Education, 33*(1), 310–353.

Poetic Musings
Where Do We Go from Here?

Tanja Burkhard, Carlotta Penn, and Valerie Kinloch

In the face of never-ending injustice, violence, and pain:
Where do we go from here?
In light of our Black genius, creativity, and joy:
Where do we go from here, Donja Thomas?
What does it mean for us to
Get free with "One Love, One Heart?"

For our Black and Brown youth/Our Black and Brown communities,
Where do we go from here, Jamila Lyiscott?
How do we protect and love, unconditionally,
Our Black and Brown lives when
The threat of you lived only in their minds
Because of "The Politics of Ratchetness?"

For every time we advocate for our lives because #BlackLivesMatter,
For every time we resist the dangers of *the white gaze,*
We boldly commit to "Storying, Identity, and Counternarrative Production"
For Black and Brown lives (be)for(e) us
Who sacrificed so that we would read and lead, write and imagine a new world.
For Carlotta, Tanja, and Valerie/for us all, Black and Brown people.

There is no other choice
But to work on "Behalf of African American Language (AAL)–Speaking Communities,"
But to enact "A Black Lives Matter and Critical Race Theory–Informed Critique of Code-Switching Pedagogy in the Classroom and in the World."
For Sina and Dr. E, we must transform language and literacy studies for Black people
As we *interrupt the normalization of state-sanctioned violence* against Black people.

This is where we go from here.

And we lovingly "Check it out" by paying attention to
"Youth Layering Already-Present Community-Engaged Multiliteracies
Toward Justice in Literacy Teaching and Research."
We grapple with how Vaughn and Matthew learn from young people
To construct meanings of youth enactments of *community-engaged
multiliteracies.*
From graffiti writing and art making, to songwriting and entrepreneurial
activities,
They value the literacy activism of Black and Brown youth.

Because "Braiding Stories Toward a Common Cause"
Can lead us toward "Coalitional Inquiry as Activism,"
Across difference/toward a vision of educational equity and immigrant rights,
We stand with María Paula, Gerald, Grace, Brenda, and Frianna
Knowing that where we go and how we get there
Moves us toward equity-centered, justice-purposed literacy opportunities.

And this is where we go from here,
In solidarity with students: Lauren, Wanda, Arlene, Cody, Ammar.
Shoulder to shoulder with educators: Ms. L, Donja, Johnny, Jennell.
To social media and to protests in the streets,
In our classrooms and in our homes, as we #SayHerName and
#KnowJusticeKnowPeace,
Because your life and my life and our lives require no less.

Because of activism and justice in literacy instruction
And until *victory is won.*

Not a Conclusion

Keeping Focused on Race, Justice, and Activism in Literacy Instruction

Valerie Kinloch

There is really no appropriate way to end or to reach a conclusion for a book titled *Race, Justice, and Activism in Literacy Instruction,* especially when there are still injustices, oppressions, and sanctioned occasions of violence that define our everyday existences. Since beginning this project, Black lives and the lives of many other People of Color in this nation continue to be under constant attack by "white supremacist capitalist patriarchy" (hooks, 2001, p. 72). This is a painful reality when one considers that "the very basic idea of mattering," as Love (2019) tells us, "is sometimes hard to conceptualize when your country finds you disposable" (p. 2). How, then, do we remain committed to educational equity and social equality when many of the very people governing our nation sanctioned the separation of children from their families? How do we not forget about the contamination of drinking water in many of our Communities of Color? How do we not erase from our memories the lives of Tanisha Anderson, Sandra Bland, Miriam Carey, Antwon Rose, and, among so many others, the Black teenagers in bathing suits in McKinney, Texas, who were victimized at gunpoint by a white police officer? How do we continue to agitate and advocate for the types of schools, classrooms, communities, and futures that our children deserve, that we deserve, that our ancestors deserved? How do we sustain our focus on race, justice, and activism in literacy instruction? *How do we?*

This very question of *how do we* necessarily implies that we must also contemplate the questions: How do we recover and heal from the trauma of racism? Or, are recovery and healing for Black People and other People of Color not possible, given the historical and current-day conditions, encounters, and persistent realities of racism and white supremacy? Relatedly, this question, *how do we,* is both haunting and liberating. On the one hand, it haunts our every step when we come to fully understand that lives—of our children, our students, our families, our neighbors, and our very own—are not safe and protected within a society so obsessed with "the white gaze," because many people believe that Black "lives have no meaning and no depth without" it (Morrison, 1998). On the other hand, this question is liberating because it indicates a level of strength and hope that something is better, that something is always worth fighting for and valuing. In fact, it reminds me that something different is needed and that the work of a committed liberation agenda needs to direct our paths toward equity, equality, and justice. And yet, we still ask: *How do we?*

The chapters in this book help guide us down a path where we can think about this liberation agenda through the lens of literacy instruction. This lens requires that we always ask ourselves the question: Why do we teach? When we ask this question of why, we must also consider additional questions, including: Who are we teaching? How are we teaching? For what purposes are we teaching? Do we see literacy teaching as a *Project in Humanization* (Kinloch, 2018; Kinloch & San Pedro, 2014)? How do we understand literacy teaching as an always-present occasion of learning rooted in transformation? In fact, are we really teaching through, with, and because of love? If so, then how do we sustain this practice and nurture it within others? If not, then how do we learn to do so now? And, if our teaching is not deeply rooted in a discourse of love for the very children and young adults with whom we teach, then how do we refuse the tendency to take up space by acknowledging the dangers of our very presence in the learning spaces of our children and young adults? In other words, how do we get out of the way and how do we not continue to waste our children's time so that the work of liberation through literacy instruction can thrive? How do we keep focused on race, justice, and activism? *How do we?*

REFERENCES

hooks, b. (2001). *Salvation: Black people and love*. New York, NY: HarperCollins.

Kinloch, V. (2018). Necessary disruptions: Examining justice, engagement, and humanizing approaches to teaching and teacher education. *Teaching Works*. Retrieved from teachingworks.org/images/files/TeachingWorks_Kinloch.pdf

Kinloch, V., & San Pedro, T. (2014). The space between listening and storying: Foundations for projects in humanization. In D. Paris & M. Winn (Eds.), *Humanizing research: Decolonizing qualitative inquiry with youth and communities* (pp. 21–42). Thousand Oaks, CA: Sage.

Love, B. L. (2019). *We want to do more than survive: Abolitionist teaching and the pursuit of educational freedom*. Boston, MA: Beacon Press.

Morrison, T. (1998, March). From an interview on *Charlie Rose*. *Public Broadcasting Service*. Retrieved from youtube.com/watch?v=F4vIGvKpT1c]

About the Editors and the Contributors

Valerie Kinloch is the Renée and Richard Goldman Dean of the School of Education and Professor at the University of Pittsburgh. Her scholarship examines the literacies and community engagements of youth and adults inside and outside schools. She has authored various publications, including *Harlem On Our Minds: Place, Race, and the Literacies of Urban Youth* and *Crossing Boundaries: Teaching and Learning with Urban Youth*. Born and raised in Charleston, South Carolina, Valerie completed her K–12 education in public schools there. She received her undergraduate degree from Johnson C. Smith University and her graduate degrees from Wayne State University.

Tanja Burkhard is a postdoctoral researcher in the University of Pittsburgh's School of Education. Holding a doctorate degree in teaching and learning and a master's degree in applied linguistics, her research interests focus on race, immigration, language, and postcolonial theories. As a former ESL and EFL instructor, Tanja particularly centers qualitative methodologies to explore the educational experiences, identities, and languages of Students of Color inside and outside of formal educational settings.

Carlotta Penn is director of community partnerships for the Office of Equity, Diversity, and Global Engagement in The Ohio State University's College of Education and Human Ecology. She began her education career teaching English language courses to adult immigrant, refugee, and international students. Carlotta's research interests are in Black women in education, literacy and language instruction, and teacher education. She holds a master's degree in comparative studies and a doctorate in multicultural and equity studies in education.

Arlene Alvarado, education writer, California

BernNadette T. Best-Green, associate instructor, University of California Davis

Maneka D. Brooks, assistant professor, Texas State University

Tanja Burkhard, postdoctoral research fellow, University of Pittsburgh

Tamara Butler, assistant professor, Michigan State University
Gerald Campano, professor, University of Pennsylvania
Limarys Caraballo, associate professor, Queens College
Matthew R. Deroo, assistant professor, University of Miami
María Paula Ghiso, associate professor, Teachers College, Columbia University
Frianna Gultom, educator, St. Thomas Aquinas
Valerie Kinloch, Renée and Richard Goldman Dean, University of Pittsburgh
Brenda Krishanwongso, educator, St. Thomas Aquinas
Lindsey Lichtenberger, Queens College
Jamila Lyiscott, assistant professor, University of Massachusetts, Amherst
Danny C. Martinez, associate professor, University of California Davis
Johnny Merry, educator, Columbus City Schools
Ijeoma E. Ononuju, assistant professor, Northern Arizona University
Leigh Patel, associate dean and professor, University of Pittsburgh
Carlotta Penn, director of community programs, Ohio State University
Jenell Igeleke Penn, educator and doctoral candidate, Ohio State University
Grace Player, assistant professor, University of Connecticut
Detra Price-Dennis, associate professor, Teachers College, Columbia University
Elaine Richardson, professor, Ohio State University
Sina Saeedi, doctoral student, Ohio State University
Yolanda Sealey-Ruiz, associate professor, Teachers College, Columbia University
Eric Skogsberg, senior learning designer, Michigan State University
Donja Thomas, educator and curriculum developer, Gahanna Jefferson School District
Vaughn W. M. Watson, assistant professor, Michigan State University

Index